PRAI

"Oracle's remarkable
magical practitioner drawn to Hellenism, ancient Greece, and the mysteries of these Old Gods. Providing an excellent balance of academia and hands-on spiritual work, *Strix Craft* is a prolific offering [that] presents a glimpse into the mystical currents of the ancient world. Hail Hekate!"

—Raven Digitalis, author of *Esoteric Empathy*
and *Planetary Spells & Rituals*

"*Strix Craft* is an intriguing approach to modern witchcraft inspired by ancient Greek lore … Highly practical, the author covers magical tools, herbal lore, mythology, devotional rituals, and a large number of spells for love, healing, protection, and more, all informed with an ancient Greek aesthetic. *Strix Craft* effectively takes hold of what limited knowledge we have about ancient practices and works it into a complete and useful system."

—Patrick Dunn, author of *The Orphic Hymns:
A New Translation for the Occult Practitioner*

STRIX
CRAFT

© Tabitha D. Whidby TabCat Productions, LLC

ABOUT THE AUTHOR

Oracle Hekataios is a modern-day seer, iatromantis, Strix, and initiated Wiccan. A high priest (Minos) in the Minoan Brotherhood, he is also an elder in the Alexandrian Tradition of Wicca. Oracle has experience in other traditions and orders as well. A former licensed and ordained Christian minister, Oracle is currently an ordained minister in the Church of All Worlds, one of the first Neopagan and most influential churches in the modern world.

He is a practicing priest of the goddess Hekate since 2009, as well as a devotee of the god Dionysus. The founder and current Hierophant of the Ophic Strix Tradition—a Greek witchcraft tradition—he founded the Temple of Hekate: Ordo Sacra Strix in 2012. Oracle Hekataios is passionate about thealogy (goddess spirituality), philosophy, history, archaeology, and anthropology. He lives in Florida, where he lectures about various metaphysical topics, and seeks to help in interfaith work.

— ORACLE HEKATAIOS —

STRIX CRAFT

ANCIENT GREEK MAGIC FOR THE
MODERN WITCH

LLEWELLYN PUBLICATIONS
Woodbury, Minnesota

FIRST EDITION
First Printing, 2020

Cover art and part page art by Faryn Hughes
Cover design by Shannon McKuhen
Editing by Holly Vanderhaar
Interior sigil art by the Llewellyn Art Department

Llewellyn Publications is a registered trademark of Llewellyn Worldwide Ltd.

Library of Congress Cataloging-in-Publication Data
Names: Hekataios, Oracle, author.
Title: Strix craft : ancient Greek magic for the modern witch / Oracle
    Hekataios.
Description: First edition. | Woodbury, Minnesota : Llewellyn Publications,
    [2020] | Includes bibliographical references.
Identifiers: LCCN 2020027608 (print) | LCCN 2020027609 (ebook) | ISBN
    9780738763279 (paperback) | ISBN 9780738763361 (ebook)
Subjects: LCSH: Witchcraft—Greece. | Magic—Greece. | Strix—Mythology.
Classification: LCC BF1584.G8 H45 2020 (print) | LCC BF1584.G8 (ebook) |
    DDC 133.4/3—dc23
LC record available at https://lccn.loc.gov/2020027608
LC ebook record available at https://lccn.loc.gov/2020027609

Llewellyn Worldwide Ltd. does not participate in, endorse, or have any authority or responsibility concerning private business transactions between our authors and the public.
    All mail addressed to the author is forwarded but the publisher cannot, unless specifically instructed by the author, give out an address or phone number.
    Any internet references contained in this work are current at publication time, but the publisher cannot guarantee that a specific location will continue to be maintained. Please refer to the publisher's website for links to authors' websites and other sources.

Llewellyn Publications
A Division of Llewellyn Worldwide Ltd.
2143 Wooddale Drive
Woodbury, MN 55125-2989
www.llewellyn.com

Printed in the United States of America

Disclaimer/Trigger Warning

This book contains discussion of blood magic and sex magic. It also teaches how to use bodily fluids (including blood, semen, and urine) in its rites. It is important to know your STD status, especially if you are sharing fluids with another. When drawing blood, diabetic needles or sterile lancets are the only tools you should use, and you should do this from a finger only. Specific oils with certain herbs that are poisonous are also mentioned. Proper substitutions will be given.

CONTENTS

FOREWORD

It is said that we don't choose the deities we serve, but rather the deities choose us.

A life of service and devotion to a deity is richly rewarding in a way that those who limit themselves to a secular existence could never fully grasp. There is a sense of being connected to something far greater than yourself, an understanding of a much greater picture that transcends the physical, and accelerated spiritual growth. Truly there is no growth without pain, so the path has its thorns. It's not a path for everyone, but for those who choose it, there are blessings on a daily basis.

Those who feel that such a path might be for them would understandably have many questions. How do they know that they have been chosen? How do they go about building a relationship with the deity who has chosen them? How will their lives change? Obviously, each case will have its differences, but it would be useful to study the experiences of one who was chosen.

The man known as Oracle Hekataios accepted the call to live a life of service and devotion to the goddess Hekate. His experiences will be of interest to those interested in a path of service and devotion to the deities, as well as those seeking to intensify their own workings specifically with Hekate.

Oracle was raised Roman Catholic; however, his mother practiced Santeria and his father was immersed in New Age Theosophy, so he grew up surrounded by occult books. He was eight years old when Hekate first made herself known to him. His cozy world fell apart at the age of thirteen when his mother converted to the Pentecostal Holiness Church, which was a "deliverance ministry" that taught that all the ills of humanity were a result of the actions of demons. Church members aspired to perfection in God's eyes and minimized interaction with the world outside of their church. Because the pastor at that time said that demons lived in books not of God, most of his father's books were consigned to the flames. Oracle, however, liberated some of the books, keeping them hidden for years.

Oracle became a licensed and ordained minister, eventually becoming an assistant to a pastor as well as part of community outreach programs. He had his own fifteen-minute radio show. He began intensive studies that included analyzing the Bible in Hebrew, Aramaic, and Greek. His studies made him realize that he had been neglecting the Divine Feminine. He immersed himself in Canaanite, Greek, and Egyptian religious practices to better understand the religious climate of the times.

Oracle recalls an incident where the pastor at his church affirmed, "The sheep is a dumb animal, and it takes the shepherd to reach out and guide them." The pastor was referring to himself as the shepherd of course. This condescending attitude did not sit well with Oracle.

Oracle also remembers one preacher saying, "Don't worry if it don't make sense. Make faith not sense!" Anti-intellectualism is very prevalent within Christianity, but for those with a thirst for knowledge, it falls flat.

Not surprisingly, Oracle found himself splitting away from his church and attended a local Unitarian Universalist Samhain party, which introduced him to Neopaganism and compelled him to become an initiate in two Druid orders. To further round out his spiritual development, Oracle was initiated into two other traditions of witchcraft: the Minoan Brotherhood and the Alexandrian Tradition of Wicca.

During all this, Hekate called out to him again, leading him to learn from the family of the late Dr. Leo Martello's Sicilian-Continental Craft (a form of stregheria). While studying this, Oracle decided to formally dedicate himself to Hekate and renounce his Christian past. Eventually, he vowed to be her priest and maintain her shrine. He had powerful, evocative dream-visions for days after his vow.

Later that year, Hekate inspired and led him to practice a magical invocation in which she bestowed on him his function of being her oracle to the community. That same night, she blessed him with his magical name, "Oracle." This invocation was the first of many ritual possessions by Hekate on nights of the dark moon.

Hekate revealed to Oracle the title of Strix and the ancient magical workings of these spiritual ancestors. A new mythos was born, and he founded the Temple of Hekate: Ordo Sacra Strix. During his trance workings, he discovered through subsequent research that the magical practices and religious outlines his temple practiced matched up with what the ancients described. The Temple of Hekate is the first temple of the Ophic Strix Tradition, and it continues with the teachings and initiations of Hekate.

By way of historical background, it should be noted that from the fifth century BCE, Hekate became associated with magic and witchcraft, lunar lore, creatures of the night, dog sacrifices, and illuminated cakes (sacrificial cakes with lit miniature torches), as well as doorways and crossroads. She was portrayed as a virgin carrying torches and accompanied by dogs. She was known as the goddess of the crossroads, which were actually meeting places of three pathways. Her triple-form character arose from the practice of hanging three masks at crossroads. Hekate was aspected to the dark of the moon and was often invoked by Thessalian witches. She has been portrayed differently at different times, but this association is the most relevant and is amplified in great detail by Oracle in this book.

The path of the Strix, which is the path Oracle has been called to walk, involves the practice of magic. For most Neopagans, this is not an issue. However, many Hellenic reconstructionists who strive to re-create the religious practices of the ancient Greeks have the misconception that magic should be avoided and don't realize that it was very widely practiced. Oracle eloquently explains the role of different forms of magic to his path:

"Greek magics are a gift, a bounty, instruments of gratitude: something bestowed upon us with favor (*charis*). Greek magic is about a calling from the Divine to seek out our place in the world and provide cultus to the deity and service to humanity."

Oracle states that he has been practicing Strix Craft for almost a decade and a half. His devotion is made obvious by how much work he has put into this book, blending ancient and modern wisdom. The book is well-researched and self-contained. Importantly, the book is practical. In a private communication, Oracle stated that his attitude was, "Make your own magic system. If it works, use it."

This book is invaluable for those who wish to work with a proven system. I envisage this book providing inspiration to those called by deities to create their own Book of Shadows.

To me, Oracle is a man whose friendship I have valued over the years. He's been both a sounding board for spiritual concepts and someone I could turn to in times of crisis for comfort and advice. In early 2020, he lost his father and I lost my mother. We coordinated a joint working, calling on Hermes in his role as a psychopomp. In my case, my altar had a statue and candle to Hermes, along with candles to the Virgin Mary and the Archangel Michael, to accommodate my mother's devout Roman Catholic beliefs. We prayed for the safe passage of our parents into the afterlives of their choice. Comforting words from friends and family are very helpful in times of bereavement, but nothing comes close to a sense of knowing that you have done everything possible to facilitate passage into the next phase of existence for the dearly departed.

Tony Mierzwicki
Huntington Beach, 2020

INTRODUCTION

I was trained in several esoteric traditions, and I love each one of them. At their heart, the Divine exists and we are a part of them. Yet, it didn't always begin this way. I wasn't always an occultist or a witch. Yet despite that, the gods and spirits still called my way. My journey has been one of winding crossroads, a veritable labyrinth in which I have been guided by the goddess Hekate. My journey toward Strix Craft began when the goddess Hekate called me at the age of eight.

When I was eight years old, I saw the 1963 film *Jason and the Argonauts*—a beautiful film with special effects by Ray Harryhausen, I was immediately captivated by the Greek gods and the mythology of the film. But perhaps the most impactful scene was when Jason appears in the Temple of Hekate, and there Medea dances away in the sanctuary beneath a statue of the Titan-goddess. Later Medea's prayers and devotion to Hekate show when she is trying to make a decision as to whether to assist Jason or betray her people.

The movie was of course purely entertainment. However, something happened to me that night. I had a dream-vision of a beautiful woman showing a specific symbol and a labyrinth lit by torches. I woke up, and wrote the symbol down. As young as I was, I kept copious notes about so many things. I enjoyed journaling, and writing became a passion of mine.

It was this beginning that set me on the path of Greek magic: namely, that of being a Strix. All of the depictions in ancient literature are of women. However, men may also be Strix. I should know. I'm one of them.

As a Strix, I have been a part of my local community for some time. I have lectured at churches, teaching others about Greek polytheism, traditional initiatory Wicca, and Druidry. I have been a part of organizing main events for a local CUUPS chapter of the Unitarian Universalist church,[1] and I founded my own Strix Temple—the Temple of Hekate: Ordo Sacra Strix. The goddess Hekate, I have found, encourages work to be torchbearers for our communities. She is not a goddess of the shadows, although shadow work is a major part of her blessing. Shadow work is when we are to face our deepest and darkest aspect of ourselves in order to bring harmony to ourselves physically, mentally, emotionally, and spiritually.

Strix Craft is not for the faint of heart, but rather a path that calls us to shine the light on ourselves so that we may in turn fan the flame of renewal to our brothers and sisters in the Art Magical. I have found this to be true in my own journey, and the goddess Hekate will change your life, transforming you from the inside out. I find this even more important in clergy work, as I am an ordained minister under the Church of All Worlds, one of the first Neopagan church organizations in the world.[2]

---

1. CUUPS is the Covenant of Unitarian Universalist Pagans. CUUPS is usually an open circle of practitioners from various paths—both new and experienced. For more information, see https://www.cuups.org/.

2. Visit http://www.caw.org for more information.

The Strix (Latin, Strigae) was an owl that hunted for blood in the night. Like so many other groups that were feared, Strix were said to go after infant flesh and blood. However, this isn't the case. An example of an ancient depiction of a Strix is Pamphilë. Pamphilë was a Thessalian witch who anointed herself with a magical ointment while she stood naked and chanted. Pamphilë was then transformed into an owl and flew off into the night.[3] Strix were maligned in literature due to their feared powers of witchcraft and shapeshifting, flying by night using a witches' ointment.[4]

I have been practicing Strix Craft for almost a decade and a half. In that time, I have been initiated and trained in several esoteric traditions, including Druidry, stregheria (more specifically Sicilian-Continental Craft), the Minoan Brotherhood, and the Alexandrian Tradition of Wicca. Needless to say, the Strix Craft I practice has been one of adventurous studies in the workings of ancient Greek magic, and the ways it applies to the here and now. Along this road, the goddess Hekate has walked with me through the winding labyrinth and revealed much, and subsequent studies confirm many of the revelations she first brought to my attention. These revelations—which at first were merely that, without substantial evidence to support them—are called Unverified Personal Gnosis (UPG). Gnosis is a Greek word that means "knowledge," a type that is an innate "knowing." When revelations from deities seem to have been confirmed by evidence from literature and practices, these are VPG (Verified Personal Gnosis). I'll give examples of where Strix Craft is mentioned in literature.

In Book VI of the Fasti, the Roman writer Ovid describes a Strix as a bloodthirsty screech-owl, so-named because of the

---

3. Apuleius.

4. Hatsis, 70–74.

screeching they do in the middle of the night.[5] Strix were terrifying creatures, like the stregha and witches of later periods. All sorts of fantastical stories could be imagined about them, because they had magic that only they knew how to wield. Like Pamphilë, many were also quick to strike down a man if he advanced without welcome. This was a threat to the "natural order" of how things were run by the patriarchy of the time. As a result of this tale, I teach natural empowerment in Strix Craft, helping others to regain their personal power and sexual power, which is a frightening aspect in our current society.

In the Middle Ages, women described as Strix were hunted down by mobs because of their rendezvous with the devil, even though official belief in them (as justification for killing women) was outlawed by the Law of the Saxons in 785 CE.[6] Strix women were accused of leaving their bodies and having a rendezvous with the devil. As an aside, ancient Greek depictions of horned gods like Pan and other ithyphallic figures such as Priapus, the Herm (an image of bearded Hermes with a body and erect penis), and the satyrs were most likely the inspiration of the horned devil in some medieval depictions and literature.

Another example comes from 1523, in a published dialogue titled *Strix sive de ludificatione daemonum* (The Witch, or On the Deception of Demons).[7] The author, one Gianfrancesco Pico (or Giovanni Francesco Pico della Mirandola), was a Renaissance occultist whose dialogue affirms the existence of demonic activity in magic and sex, which is the purview of witchcraft. That an occultist would be afraid of witches is something I find amusing.

---

5. Littlewood.

6. Hatsis, 73–74.

7. Schmitt, 288.

I must keep in mind that the Christian Hermeticists of the Italian Renaissance would be very aghast—most likely—at how public a face witchcraft is given in the Western world today.

Due to their association with sorcery in ancient times and throughout the Middle Ages, it is no wonder then that in ancient times female Strix were connected with Hekate in Thessaly. In Thessaly, Hekate was known as Brimo—that is, the "Angry One," "Terrifying One," or "She with Rage." It is her aspect of fury, but one need only remember that an exciter to frenzy wasn't simply born out of pure wrath and was terrible to look at. I believe, based on my experiences with Brimo, that she was an aspect of justice and fate, and was the Averter of Evil. Like Kali-Ma, who looked terrifying to scare demons, Hekate-Brimo's power was a manifestation of the underworld and was a chasm of chaos that had to be bridged by those who knew how.

Hekate-Brimo was one who was worshiped in awe and reverence, because she is great. Brimo was later tied to the Orphic mysteries,[8] a mystery tradition founded by the legendary hero Orpheus (who traveled with Jason and the Argonauts). Orpheus was a Thracian bard whose powers included calming animals and moving even the gods with his music. The Orphic mysteries are believed to have possible origins in the region known as Magna Graecia ("Greater Greece"), although the cult was found as far as Ukraine.[9] Magna Graecia is an area spanning Southern Italy and Sicily, where more Greek temples and settlements were found than in Greece itself.

This book in your hands is a labor of love. I consider it an offering to my goddess, and to the communities of which I am a part.

---

8. Bremmer, 35–48.

9. Zhmud.

Ancient Greek magic was concerned with the affairs of the daily lives of our ancestors. Like us, our spiritual and physical ancestors were concerned with love, fertility, sex, hate, vengeance, money, and success in everything they put their hands to. They were concerned with the affairs of the afterlife and making their lineage proud. They were conservative and upheld the traditions of their forebears. However, there were also the lunar outcasts, the Strix, who dedicated themselves wholeheartedly to the path of Hekate and the underworld deities away from the state-sanctioned religious rituals of the city-states.[10]

As a Strix, I write to make ancient Greek magic applicable to modern understanding. The path of the Strix is an Ancient One, yet modern Hellenic witches are now returning to the cries of their blood and bone, to the ways of Hekate. If you are called by Hekate, then you too are a Strix. The Terrifying One calls her own, and from the ancient mountains to the wide sea she scours the landscape for her children who are hidden.

This book in your hands is not just about Strix Craft in general, but also about modern Greek magic—that is, magical methods designed to be used by the modern witch. I discuss everything from healing to hexing, from helping the living to communing with the dead. This is a book to use, not just read. It is in effect much like a grimoire.

Each tradition of witchcraft will have its own philosophies, and the ways of modern Greek magic have their own virtues. Yes, it is dangerous, but it is also an inherent part of who we are as human beings. Strix Craft is dangerous because we are handling primal forces of the underworld, and using ourselves in our own self-introspections to make magic happen. Magic, it is believed by

---

10. Clark.

many in this path, is a gift: the gift of fire that was our first magic. It is from the lens of the ancient Greeks that I teach these methods.

Tony Mierzwicki, a noted Neopagan scholar, practicing Hellenic polytheist, and Graeco-Egyptian magician, does point out that whatever our views of magic as a gift, in modern Hellenic Reconstruction circles, the practice of magic is generally frowned upon. He explains that these beliefs may stem from the disdain shown by academics when it comes to magical practices. Such disdain, however, is sorely misplaced. As Mierzwicki explains, nearly everyone in ancient Greece practiced and believed in magic.[11] In this book, I try to differentiate between magical practitioners, as there seemed to be no consensus in the ancient world as to how to actually define magic in and of itself.

Ancient Greeks had their own festival calendars, and the calendars varied from region to region, *polis* to *polis*. There was no single uniform calendar, as Greek city-states were independent regions and had different local landscapes, myths, and spirits. If you're interested in the Athenian calendar, the festivals are outlined in Tony Mierzwicki's book *Hellenismos: Practicing Greek Polytheism Today*.

In this book, I would like to differentiate the way I will be using the words "Strix" and "Strix Craft." Strix refers to Greek witches and is meant to be used in the singular and plural, depending on the context. For example, as a singular noun I will write, "A Strix practices magic." As a plural noun I will write, "The Strix practice magic." I will also use this as an adjective. Where this is used, the term "strix" will be lowercase. For example, I will write, "This is strix magic." The actual practice itself will be termed "Strix Craft." I will work to make these distinctions as clear as possible. Where it

---

11. Mierzwicki, 149–150.

is unclear, I apologize ahead of time and make those errors solely my responsibility.

You will note as you read this work that I have included a chapter on eight festivals. To Neopagans and modern witches, there is a sacred calendar known as the Wheel of the Year. Developed by Ross Nichols (a Druid) and Gerald Gardner (a witch who is credited with founding Wicca), the Wheel of the Year is a standard festival calendar for many today. Ancient cultures, however, were not so fixed. The Wheel of the Year is very much modern; however, the seasonal calendar works. With this in mind, I will be putting in comparative festivals related to the myths and themes of modern Strix Craft.

For modern Strix Craft, we have adapted the Wheel of the Year to fit in with the deities and their particular attributes unique to the practices and lore provided in this book. Their stories and symbols that are unique to us fit in well with this model, and so we gladly celebrate them in this fashion. I include them in this book on magic for those desiring to get to know the deities of modern Strix Craft better. I always say that the more we get to know deity, the better our magic will be; it is my experience that there is a direct correlation between the Strix and their connection with the god(s) they are choosing to work with for their magic. Worship before work, always.

In this book I will use Latin spellings for the deities and other individuals (e.g., Socrates, Circe). Greek spellings can be difficult with all of the nuances, diphthongs, and brackets. To be sure, this means that many of the spellings are Latin-derived ("Apollo" as opposed to "Apollon"). Some of the spellings may be derived from the Greek, however (e.g., Hekate, Asklepios, etc.). I want this book to be read as seamlessly as possible. I believe brackets and diphthongs will only cause confusion, and certain spellings are more common and well known than others.

This book is divided into four sections, with a total of fourteen chapters and a conclusion that summarizes and brings it all together. The chapters begin with Section 1, which has three chapters. In Chapter 1, "What Is Greek Magic?" I dive into the various magical practitioners and attempt the task of defining this word magic and its relationship with ancient Greece. Chapter 2 takes us into the witches' country: Thessaly. We explore the Thessalian caricatures of the Strix, and also how Thessaly was perceived by other city-states in literature. Chapter 3 is a chapter on ethics, something very important in any magical path as we work with primal forces of the underworld, especially hexing and love magic. This helps you, the reader and Strix, to get started on this path.

Section 2 has four chapters, beginning with Chapter 4 where we cover the tools of modern Strix Craft. Chapter 5 dives into an in-depth chapter on herbs, as they were important to the practice of the Strix both ancient and modern. Chapter 6 introduces you to the various deities and spirits of our modern practice. Some of their stories are also told. In Chapter 7 we look at altars and shrines.

Section 3 is divided into four chapters, beginning with Chapter 8, which covers healing magic. This chapter introduces the actual practices and methods of magic. Chapter 9 focuses on love and erotic magics. In Chapter 10, we focus on binding and hexing. In Chapter 11, we explore communing with the dead. In Chapter 12, we end the section with seasonal rituals. Following this chapter is a conclusion for the entire book.

As you walk this path, remember to meditate, write down questions, and work the altars and shrines mentioned. Be sure to always do the work with reverence toward the gods and spirits. Allow yourself to feel the ancient path, and listen to the songs and stories of our ancestors through your blood and your bone. Be well.

Eirene kai Hugieia!

(Peace and Health!)

Oracle Hekataios

SECTION 1
BACKGROUND

CHAPTER 1

WHAT IS GREEK MAGIC?

I n this chapter, we focus on just what Greek magic is and what it entails. Ancient Greek magic is a conglomerate of various practices and practitioners. In fact, it is more descriptive of what one is performing at any given moment. Sometimes the lines are blurred, as a Strix may practice more than one category.

Magic in ancient Greece was varied. It is safe to say that an entire unified system of belief and practice did not exist. In fact, I would venture to say that rather than ancient Greek magic, there were ancient Greek *magics*: different branches in which various groups or individuals practiced what they learned and were taught. Magic, I have found, has separate categories, often describing the kind of action one would take. Let us now dive into this wonderful subject!

MAGICAL PRACTICES IN ANCIENT GREECE

The word magic comes from the Latin *magice*, which itself is rooted in the Greek *magike*.[12] This word, which describes the whole rather

12. Weekley, 122.

than the sum of the parts, only appears in the fifth century BCE, but we know from the archaeological record that magical practices existed among the Greek tribes prior to this time.[13] Ancient Greek magical disciplines consisted of the following:

Magicians (*magoi*)

Purifiers (*kathartai*)

Herbalists and poisoners (*pharmakeia*)

Witches (*Strix*)

Seers and diviners (*manteis*)

Necromancy (*nekromanteia*)

Shamans / physician-seers (*iatromanteia*)

Summoners of spirits (*goēs*)

Miracle workers (*thaumaturgy*)

Enlightenment seekers (*theurgy*)

I should note, however, that while these categories seem to be neatly filed, the reality is that some practitioners may encompass more than one category. That's because Greek magics are descriptive of what you are practicing at any given moment. While specialists in each category did exist, others blurred the boundaries of what they could do.

For example, government sponsored oracles were in the manteis category, while summoners of spirits (goēs) might be purifiers, shamans, and necromancers all in one! But each practice, no matter what it was, took time and effort to master. Oftentimes

---

13. The Greeks were tribes prior to confederations of city-states, called *poleis* (sing. *polis*). These tribes in turn were divided into clans or *demes*. The major Greek tribes during the Classical period were the Ionians, the Dorians, the Achaeans, the Aeolians, the Threspotians, and the Molossians.

an apprenticeship between a master and a student was arranged. Other times it was a calling by the gods and spirits over an individual, in which case they might act alone. Still others joined roaming bands of like-minded people, connecting with them for the same purpose or calling. It was a kind of informal troupe, one might say. Examples of these troupes include thiasoi and kathartai. The former were roving bands of the followers of the god Dionysus, and the latter were mostly ascetic priests who made vows to the goddess Cybele, the Phrygian Great Mother (also known as Rhea). In Chapter 6 we will look over some of the deities and spirits of ancient Greek magics.

But this doesn't seem to answer our question, does it? Despite these labels, what exactly was ancient Greek magic, and how did it work?

MAGIC AS A GIFT AND CALLING

Magic was viewed by some as the providence of the gods—Aphrodite and her golden girdle, or Hermes and his good medicine, which he offered to Odysseus when the latter was about to meet the witch goddess Circe. The Pre-Socratics [14] believed that magic, divinity, and nature were one and the same. In fact, the writer Aelian (Claudius Aelianus [175 BCE–235 CE], a philosopher and Roman teacher of rhetoric who admired both Greeks and the Greek language) states, "This being so, one might say that even nature, though she does not boil anyone down nor apply drugs, like a Medea or a Circe, is also a sorceress." [15]

---

14. A school of philosophy that believed that the cosmos was created and functioned on its own terms, rather than theocentric (focused on the gods). They gave a more rational view and redefined the gods away from the epic traditions of Homer and Hesiod.

15. Aelianus, 2–14.

The Greek word for sorceress is *phármakis,* and in its literal sense Aelian was combining the realm of the Divine with that of magic (in this case herbs). What we have as magic is actually an alliance born from the Divine. Could magic, then, be a gift to humans from the gods?

It seems so. The categories listed above grant us a snapshot of how the different callings worked, as well as the functions and attributes of the various magic users in the ancient Greek world. Using divine aid, the various magic users were able to use that connection and make things happen. Oracles were blessed by various deities (e.g., Apollo, Gaia, Zeus, Dionysus) so that the wishes of that deity would be conveyed to the individual(s) seeking aid. Necromancers borrowed the aid of their nocturnal conjurings and spirits. Iatromanteia—physician-seers—called upon the power of the god Apollo in their working. In short, alliances with the Divine were the key to making things happen. It wasn't a matter of personal will, but rather a matter of keeping your deities and spirits happy so that they could always be of aid to you. I call this "devotional magic," wherein creating a shrine and administering cultus (that is, cementing a formal bond with a deity and/or spirit with regular devotions, offerings, and prayers) supports your own internal personal power. You have someone to help you, like a big brother or big sister (or both).

There is a famous story regarding the Titan Prometheus and Zeus, king of the gods. According to one account, Prometheus, the Titan of forethought and crafty counsel, created human beings. Zeus would have them dwell in ignorance, but Prometheus had his own plans, and with crafty wiles he secretly stole fire from Olympus. He brought it down in a fennel stalk, and humanity learned the art of fire. I believe that this tale takes us back to the times when we first discovered fire. Fire was our first magic! Think of it: the imagination to make it happen, the search for and gathering of the proper wood and ingredients, the offerings of kindle to fuel the power so that we might benefit from its action—magic! But fire is a gift that we have harnessed—for good or for ill—that manifests today in light bulbs, engines, missiles, guns, and other technologies honing heat and friction. But the tale itself brings forward an intriguing thought: Was fire (magic) forbidden by the gods but gifted to humanity? If so, we must treat it as a gift.

So, what is Greek magic (or rather, what are Greek magics)? Greek magics are a gift, a bounty, instruments of gratitude: something bestowed upon us with favor (*charis*). Greek magic is about a calling from the Divine to seek out our place in the world and provide cultus to the deity and service to humanity. It is always important to remember the gods when deciding to use a facet of their magic. Ancient Greek tales abound with stories of people who forget the gods and receive their retribution somehow: bad luck, no romantic favor, job loss, curse rebounds, etc. You don't want that. You want their favor, their energy behind yours. We want to cultivate a relationship with the gods and spirits around us. We want to be able to have an alliance that links us with the spirit world, the source of the power of a Strix.

But alliances with spirits aren't simple, especially in Hellenic philosophy. The gods (*Theoi*) are called "the Deathless Ones," or *Athanatoi Theoi*. Death cannot touch the gods. They are immortal, everlasting, and independent of human belief systems. They exist. The whys and hows of their existence are a hotly debated topic in many witchcraft and Greek Reconstructionist[16] circles. But make

---

16. Greek Reconstructionism is an approach that seeks to base modern religious practices on historically genuine cultural and religious practices.

no mistake: in my belief system they are as real as you and I. They are powerful forces of nature, even beyond it.

MIASMA

But what exactly is the boundary line between the gods and mortals? Where do we end and they start? What exactly makes us different?

There is a concept in Hellenism that addresses these questions. It's something called miasma (me-ahz-mah). Miasma is a spiritual principle in Hellenism that says basically that gods are immortal, humans are not. Therefore, to gain access to an immortal, we mortals must ritually prepare ourselves in a way that temporarily says, "This is your space, so I as a mortal will follow your rules. Your house, your rules." What are some examples of these rules? Well for one thing, birth was construed as miasma. Sex was construed as miasma. Being around the funeral or the dead. Being a midwife at a birth. Someone who killed another human being incurred miasma. Miasma surrounded mortals. It's an inevitable part of our life cycle. It's not "sin" or "pollution," but a type of energy that makes mortals, well, mortal.

Miasma is a very simple concept to understand: it is a ritual born of cleanliness.[17] Water is a highly valued resource, and so cleanliness was and is often important to separate the "sacred" from the "impure." It is an act that shifts the individual's mindset from one state to another. For example, *khernips* (that is, washing of hands) is a sacred act performed before a ritual. Wearing clean clothing and creating a proper space is done so that the favor of the gods and spirits might be drawn down. The water that makes up khernips doesn't need special ingredients; instead it may just

---

17. Burkert, 75–84.

need to be drawn from a particular source (e.g., springs, rivers). Like Roman Catholic churches, many ancient Greek temples had a fountain at the entrance so people might wash themselves before entering the sacred space. Priests skilled in purification methods (kathartai) would be able to divine what was happening, and listen to the oracles on how best to heal a person inflicted by madness, or to remove plague in a city.

Miasma has a lot to do with various Greek magics. Ritual purifications helped the people alter their consciousness. It prepared them physically, emotionally, and mentally to enter sacred space and commune with the gods and spirits around them. Because Greek magics rely on holy alliances with the deities and spirits, it is inevitable that cleansing be a part of the routine prior to approaching sacred space. I routinely wash my hands and my face. I then use the water to anoint my forehead, lips, and chest. Finally, I ritually dispose of the water and commence with what I am about to do.

When we ally ourselves with the gods or spirits, we have to remember the hospitality that we entertain when we worship the gods and spirits. Hospitality (xenia) is a major Hellenic virtue, and to entertain the gods was known as theoxenia. Xenia (z-nee-uh) was the concept of "guest-friendship," and was sacred to Zeus, as shown by his epithet of "Xenios." It arose in many circumstances whereby a host could and often would welcome a complete stranger (who might be a merchant, a traveler, a philosopher, etc.). Strangers were under the protection of the gods, and stories survive even still in which the gods would walk among the people as total strangers. Failure to practice xenia led to punishments by the gods. For example, in the Iliad, the Trojan War begins when the young prince, Paris of Troy, violates xenia and kidnaps Helen. As a result of this, while other deities take sides for their respective city-states, Zeus vows to destroy Troy for harboring a transgressor of hospitality.[18] That was his main concern.

SUMMARY

Strix are connected to the Theoi by their alliance. We want to ensure that we have good standing with those whom we venerate. The Strix know how to weave proper ritual etiquette, and this is paramount. Why? Because the Strix constantly find themselves surrounded by miasma. Not just by being mortal, but because we work with techniques that will purposefully incur it, such as working with the ancestral dead. We'll look at techniques and the importance of working with the dead in Chapter 11.

In order to better understand the Strix, let us now travel to the witches' country: that of Thessaly.

---

18. Aeschylus, *Agamemnon*.

CHAPTER 2

THE WITCHES' COUNTRY

Among the mountains of Greece and amid the ruins of the ancient war between the Titans and the gods, lies Thessaly. Thessaly was once considered the home of witches, a place at the end of the known world.[19] A mythic landscape born of legend and frightful imaginings, Thessaly was an all-encompassing home to figures of renown. Achilles, Jason, Chiron, Pamphilë, and Erichtho are just a few of names known in both ancient Greek and Roman literature as hailing from Thessaly.

The land known as Thessaly has settlements going back to the late Paleolithic period, and one of the most famous sites is the cave at Sesklo. Among the most notable achievements of ancient Thessaly was its dedication to the god Apollo, in whose name the Panhellenic Pythian Games were held (a competition like the Olympics, but which included the musical arts). The winners received laurel wreaths from the Thessalian temple to Apollo in Tempe.

Thessaly is considered by many ancient writers to be the haven of Hellenic witchcraft: Roman writers Lucan and Lucius, along with the Greek writers Plato, Homer, and Pindar, wrote about

19. Luck, *Arcana Mundi*, 6.

various magical practitioners from Thessaly. Thessaly was also known by the name Aeolia, since it was home to the Aeolian tribes described in the writings of Homer.[20] In Neolithic times, grain and barley were harvested in a settlement known as Sesklo. Statues of pregnant women, and even a gorgon mask, were found there, suggesting an ancient fertility cult had arisen in the area.[21]

Thessaly is bordered on the north by Mount Olympus and on the south by Mount Othrys. Both areas were, respectively, domains of the gods and the Titans in the final battle between them, according to Hesiod.[22] In such an impressive mythic landscape, I can only imagine the amount of magic and fear the legends of Thessaly would bring.

It has been hypothesized that the magical traditions of Babylon, Assyria, and Persia probably passed to Italy and Rome via Thessaly.[23] The region's mythologies are steeped in tales of witches and centaurs; it was also the homeland of semi-divine beings such as Chiron, Jason, and Asklepios. Chiron is the famous wise tutor of heroes such as Achilles and Jason. He passed on some of his healing secrets to Asklepios, the son of Apollo. The location of Thessaly was also sacred to Artemis; she would conduct her sacred hunts in the wild forests there. Several cults to Artemis arose in Thessaly, where she was variously known as Akraia, Phosphoros, and Throsia.[24]

The witches of Thessaly are often described as living on the edge of civilization—out of bounds, like hedge witches of sorts. The

---

20. Adrados, 79.

21. Gimbutas, 24–26.

22. Hesiod, *Theogony*, line 500.

23. Luck, *Witchcraft and Magic in Europe*, 93–156.

24. Kravaritou.

healing traditions of Chiron and Asklepios attest that these ancient shamanic practices were common throughout this forbidden region. Thessaly was a natural boundary between the more sophisticated southern Hellenes (such as the polis Athens) and the "less civilized" Balkan tribes and some Greek tribes in the north. Of course, they were civilized, just not in the way that Athens preferred.

ATHENS AND THESSALY

The polis that was Athens in the fifth century BCE was viewed by many Athenians as a sophisticated, urban center of progress. To this day, many in the academic field share the same view, looking to the culture and politics of Athens as the starting point for modern Western civilization.

By the time of the fifth century BCE, Athens was in full swing as a superpower. Athenians began to centralize themselves, looking to other people outside of their league as "barbarians." This dyad split Thessaly from Athens in the consciousness of the Athenians, who viewed the mythic figures of Thessaly as something foreign and untamable. Of course, when were witches ever tamable?

Thessaly's economic strength always lagged behind that of their southern neighbors in mainland Greece. Tyrannical rulership helped many of the *poleis* to have stabilizing power, which assisted in furthering their developments. However, such was not the case for Thessaly, which remained a tetrarch, or region divided into four states. For orators, thespians, playwrights, and philosophers of the south, Thessaly was the place of the barbaric, or "babbling foreigners."

To sum it up, one author describes Thessaly's reputation thus: "Thessaly never became completely Hellenized and was regarded rather as a bulwark against the barbarian north than as a genuine and fully privileged member of the Hellenic world."[25]

WITCHCRAFT AND SHAMANISM

Despite its negative caricature, Thessaly was also the home to many medicinal plants. According to Theophrastus, a student of the Greek philosopher Plato and a contemporary of Aristotle, the mountains of Ossa and Pelion were known to have on their slopes powerful drugs. Mount Pelion (known for centuries as "Woody Pelion" due to its thick forests[26]) was the home of the centaurs: half-human, half-horse beings. Their leader, Chiron, was a wise teacher who tutored many young heroes of Greek legend, including Apollo's son Asklepios. Mountains are and have been symbols of the *Axis Mundi*—that is, the central mountain in the scheme of the Three Worlds. Thessaly was surrounded by these mythic mountains, specifically Olympos, Orthys, and Pelion. There were smaller peaks, of course, but these three garnered the attention of mythmakers in ancient Greece.

The Axis Mundi is a place where Sky connects with Earth, creating a liminal boundary. The caves of the mountains create an entrance to the underworld, and in these areas pharmakeia, magoi, Strix, and other practitioners would have abundant access to the gods and spirits by using hallucinogens. In this context, there is no clear boundary between the sacred and mundane, between magic and medicine. Both are united on these mountain slopes.

It is for this reason that many Athenians feared the magical feats of the witches and magical practitioners in Thessaly. Using their crafts, they were able to symbolically climb the Axis Mundi

---

25. Westlake, 20.

26. Clark.

and astral project to the heavens, or, through the caves, descend to the underworld below. Here their alliance with the gods and spirits made them formidable.

The magic of the Strix and other practitioners of Thessaly was what some people called "shamanic." In ancient Greece the name for a shaman was frequently "iatromantis."[27] I believe in using terms native to a culture rather than imposing one. Shaman comes from the Tungus word šamān, describing an individual who communed with spirits for healing, prophecy, and counsel, and who remained as a tether between their tribe and the spirits. In ancient Greece, however, there were different spirits and functions that served the shaman. That is why in their native language it would be iatromantis, or one who is a "physician-seer" ("medicine man").

A demigod who was native to, and instructed in, the arts of healing in Thessaly was Asklepios, the son of Apollo, described as an iatromantis. Part of the repertoire of an iatromantis was to induce *ekstasis* through meditation techniques in a process known as incubation. Ekstasis, or ecstasy, is a state of extreme trance in which one alters one's state of consciousness through vigorous emotional, mental, and/or physical actions that excite the muscles and nerves. This leads to a "crash" in which the aftereffects of such rigorous excitement create a type of active stillness, leading to astral projection and other gifts. Incubation was a method whereby an individual descended into a cave—resembling the darkness of the underworld—and entered into a deep trance state. This allowed one to enter the Dreaming: the Gate of Horn. In Greek literature, the Gate of Horn was said to be the realm of true dreaming, and the Gate of Ivory is the realm of false dreaming. I liken the latter to

---

27. Kingsley, *In the Dark Places of Wisdom.*

everyday stress-inducing dreams and weird "what did I eat?" dreams (what I collectively call junk dreams).

Aside from the incubation states and herbal concoctions that were made for spirit work and healing, the witches of Thessaly were also renowned for performing a ceremony known as the "drawing down of the moon." The phrase is now borrowed into the language of Wicca, describing a high rite in which the high priestess of the coven ritually trances to embody the spirit of the goddess into her. It is typically performed at the time of the full moon, when the goddess is said to be at her peak lunar cycle, and thus more easily accessible. But in Thessaly, the drawing down of the moon ritual was the highlight of what made the Strix the witches that they were.

Drawing Down the Moon

According to some Greek and Roman writers from the late Classical age (e.g., Aristophánes, Sosiphanes, Plutarch, Pliny the Elder), the Strix of Thessaly were able to perform a ritual known as the drawing down of the moon. They were also known by the Greek word *phármakis*, meaning someone who practiced herbal magic (both remedial and poisonous). While in ancient times the words may have meant different things, today many of us who practice these ways can use them interchangeably. In modern times, our practices are not meant to keep us apart, but to unite us. Therefore, we who practice the ways of the Strix merely use these various labels to separate our specialties within the modern craft, but we are all still Strix.

The drawing down of the moon was considered by many ancient writers to be the most powerful feat the witches of Thessaly were able to accomplish. The first mention of this feat in ancient Greek writings comes from a comedy called *The Clouds*, written in the fifth century BCE by the Athenian comic playwright Aristophánes. This play is said to also be the thing that brought the reputation of Socrates low, and subsequently led to his death.

In the play, the central character and antihero Strepsiades tries to avoid paying his son's debts. Aristophánes writes of an exchange between Strepsiades and Socrates:

Strepsiades: Now tell me this, pray; if I were to purchase a Thessalian witch, and draw down the moon by night, and then shut it up, as if it were a mirror, in a round crest-case, and then carefully keep it—

Socrates: What good, pray, would this do to you?

Strepsiades: What? If the moon were no longer to rise anywhere, I should not pay the interest.[28]

While a joke, this exchange nonetheless points to a legend among the Athenians about the reputation of women in Thessaly, a land not under Athenian influence. Though it was written in the fifth century BCE, I estimate that the legends must go back further by at least a hundred years or more. Drawing down the moon was said to be hazardous to the women of Thessaly; they were thought to lose their eyes or their feet, or even a family member.[29] Roman writers such as Apuleius and Lucan were even more afraid of the women of Thessaly than the Greeks were. The latter saw them as nothing more than barbaric and backwater foreigners who were uncivilized. Thessaly was wild, chaotic, and (gasp!) did not listen to the voices of the very patriarchal Athens. Athens, you see, was a city-state named for the goddess Athena. However, women had no rights: they could not participate in voting, be leaders, and could

---

28. Aristophánes, *The Comedies of Aristophánes.*

29. Anonymous, *The Suda.*

not even testify on their own behalf. In fact, in the medical corpus of Hippocrates, young girls who hit puberty were said to suffer from hallucinations and to bring madness upon themselves. This is the reason why girls were married off as soon as they hit puberty.[30]

THE HEALING ARTS OF THESSALY

Recall that there were various practitioners of magic in the ancient world. Our focus has been on the iatromantis, the physician-seer. They originated as priests dedicated to the Greek god Apollo Oulios ("Healing"). These traits were passed down to his son Asklepios, who was renowned for his abilities to heal medically and mystically. An iatromantis who performed thaumaturgy and was a pharmakos, he established "dream temples" known as asklepions, where many ill were cured. *Katharmos* (purification) was performed in these temples regularly.

Many of these asklepions were built outside of a town, on a hill, or otherwise near a spring. Since illness incurred miasma, and plagues were frequent, the asklepions functioned as hospitals, where the ill could be treated without spreading illness to the local city-state. Such were the renowned arts that Thessaly presented for its magical practitioners.

This is important to take into account, because the shamanic aspects of an iatromantis are also part of the repertoire of a Strix. I have participated in incubation ceremonies where sacred herbs were mixed with drinks such as milk and, upon imbibing, it did not take long to trance. I ended up lying down, and traveled to the underworld, the place beneath the Axis Mundi (the World Tree). Located here, in the dark places, lies the wisdom that the philoso-

---

30. Blundell, 98–99.

pher seeks, and the health that the iatromantis brings with them to the patient.

Three major asklepion "dream temples" were built: one in Epidaurus, one in Pergamum, and one in Cos.[31] The entire ordeal began with a series of purification rites, including bathing in the cold sea. This cleansing helped prepare the patient for the healing ordeal they were going to undertake, and made sure that they were also, in a way, hygienic before entering this mystical hospital setting. Offerings to the gods ensured favor, and fed the deity involved so that the patient would be blessed by a visitation from Asklepios himself. It was portended that he would come in a dream-vision to the patient, entering through the Gate of Horn and revealing the treatment plan that the patient needed. This was a holistic concept, allowing for peace to the patient. The iatromantis might interpret the dream, and assist the patient in becoming aligned. From these traditions we the Strix are inspired to help others in uniting the mind, spirit, and body of those who come to us. We will explore healing methods further in Chapter 8.

SUMMARY

Strix Craft is rooted in the traditions of Thessaly, from which our spiritual ancestors come. Strix are concerned with the work of healing and assisting in bringing forth the power of the gods in the form of the drawing down of the moon. While a dangerous rite, nonetheless drawing down of the moon is a sacred rite. Perhaps the warning from others that a Thessalian Strix would lose a body part or a family member was an outsider's perspective on the danger of the magics involved. Perhaps it was a rumor spread by the Strix themselves to keep others away from the practice. Whatever

---

31. Kelly, Rees, and Shuter, 22.

the case may be, the drawing down of the moon is a holy act that brings the attention of the moon goddess down to the land and to the herbs that will be blessed and used in subsequent rites.

Heavy magics are the aim of this book, and with that emphasis comes responsibility for how our behaviors may cause ripples throughout our immediate microcosm into the macrocosm beyond. In order to better grasp the concepts of how, why, and when we use Strix magic, let us explore the implications and consequences of our ethics.

CHAPTER 3
ETHICS OF STRIX CRAFT

Ethics, simply speaking, is defined as the study of right and wrong.[32] The question of just what ethics entails has long been a debated topic. Just what is right and wrong? Is there a universal human truth? What about other tribes and peoples who have radically different lifestyles? Are there regional ethics? How do we implement them? Just what makes our standing correct? How does this affect love spells and hexing? Let's explore the topic of ethics in Strix Craft.

THE AIM OF ACCOMPLISHMENT

All things begin with a goal, a target in mind. These aims for your workings—whether they be for love, sex, wealth, or health—all have consequences. The consequences we aim for are to be better and good. Yes, rare exceptions exist because human nature can be bent toward good or evil; I am discussing those aspects of people who long to live life to the fullest, and who want to have their accomplishments bring about good effects. Impact. Nurturing. Positive consequences. These are the aims that the Strix look for.

---

32. *Webster's*, 392.

Think of the aim or target like a target in archery. Only by creating tension when pulling back the bow and releasing the energy so that the arrow hits the target right will satisfaction be accomplished. There must be a natural right and natural wrong in certain instances, and for the Strix there is nothing more pressing than to understand the notion of right and wrong.

NYX AND THE DIVINE WITHIN

In Strix Craft, there is a belief that we are all part of the divine energy that pervades the cosmos. I call it "Nyx." Nyx is the star goddess who is responsible for continual creation. She is the Primordial Being in which everything lives, moves, and has its own being. We will explore more about Nyx and the various deities in Chapter 6. For now, suffice it to say that Nyx is the thread that binds us together: animals, plants, fungi, humans, bacteria, and all that exists. She binds the cosmos within itself, and allows the gods to exist inasmuch as we, too, exist.

By contemplating that we are connected to her in all ways, we are affirming our own penchant for life. We, too, have the potential to create beauty in the world, and to add on to what the power of nature has instilled into us. Recall in Chapter 1 that Aelian stated that nature herself is a sorceress, a phármakis. The Divine and the world are sacred. Recall also that it is via alliances that the Strix gain their power to accomplish the aim that they seek. The spirits have their own rules for how they are to be petitioned and interacted with. The spirits include those of our ancestors, the nymphs, and the daimones.

The spirits instruct us on the various boundaries that they have, and also teach us about our own boundaries: what is acceptable and what is not. An example of personal acceptability that readily comes to mind concerns how if a person is very well educated on a certain subject (e.g., video games, engineering, chemistry, anthropology, religion, etc.), they are able to perfectly make an informed judgment on that topic as to what may be factually right and what may be factually wrong. In other words, by educating ourselves we form mental boundaries on what we know is suitable to that subject and what is not—especially as we follow the facts of what is given to us.

FACTS AND PASSION

But while we look for the facts in the subject areas we are able to judge, we as humans are also animals of passion. We want to view happiness and truth with the subject of pleasure. Aristotle writes that pleasure is "the reason why [people] love the life of enjoyment."[33] Pleasure is the aim, too, of the Strix.

The ethics of the Strix lie in the pursuit of pleasure and happiness. But they are also balanced by our relationship with our deities and spirits: they exist. They are as real as you and I. In a polytheistic mindset then, we have a reality filled with plural possibilities. Why plural? Polytheism is a lens by which to view multiple deities, multiple realities, and multiple truths. Poly means "many," and many are the ways of the Strix.

CONSEQUENCES

What does this mean for you? If you seek to practice love magic, for example, then there will be consequences to your magics. But there always is. Any time you put your energy out there and petition the gods, no doubt there will be ramifications to some things. Petitioning the gods and spirits is not a buffer for you either. Whatever you ask for and whatever you work toward, you need to know

---

33. Aristotle, Book I, Chapter 5.

the consequences. This is true for anything in life. Gods aren't our parents or guardians to watch over us each time to make sure we are making the best decisions we can for our lives. We make mistakes. We can lose ourselves. It happens. This is why magic is so important to also work introspectively as a theurgist. Please be very careful with your petitions and what you decide to put energy toward.

The ethics we hold are to understand the results of our every action. It is to understand that when we aim our vision and desires with the power of the deities and spirits, we calculate the response both to ourselves and those around us. It is like a pebble being dropped in a still pond. There is potential there, and when dropping a pebble, the effects ripple outward immediately before disappearing. The environment is never the same. The ecosystem has changed. This might seem banal, but it is paramount. Along with the question of consequences comes the inevitable talk in Hellenic polytheism about what is known as hubris.

HUBRIS

What is hubris? In Strix Craft, we have three definitions of hubris. First, it is excessive pride and boasting. Yes, we can be proud of our accomplishments and many other things. Yes, we can boast of our exploits and successes. But the pride I refer to is dangerous overconfidence. One example is when, despite cautionary and real warnings of factual consequences to actions, our leaders act like they are above such things. They create real danger to those beneath them on the economic ladder, and they sacrifice others for their foolishness. Second, another example of hubris is victim-shaming: this is when victims come forward detailing abuse and yet, for their own selfish gratification, many will bully and attack the victim. This is hubris. Third and finally, hubris is the insolence to compare yourself to, and even state that you are greater than, the gods themselves. In the ways of the Strix, we are not only polytheistic but also pantheistic. There is a divine energy through Nyx that we all are One. There is a prayer: "Nyx, I am you and you are I. I am you like myself, and you are me." What this prayer and statement means is that we all carry the Divine within us in some form. Yet, the gods are more powerful than us. They are powerful natural forces of our planet, and even beyond it. To defy the natural order is to defy them: climate change is a real threat in our times, and unless we do something about it, we will have defied the natural order of our world and will reap the punishments of our hubris. Destruction without thought of reaping what we sow and the notion that we can live this way—whether as an individual or within a corporate setting—are what bring down the punishment of the gods and the wrath of the spirits we work with.

VIRTUES

Along with the question of ethics and right behavior, the Strix also have virtues. While the question of ethics is the debate about what is right versus what is wrong, virtues are the boundary lines that help us build our character in order to make the best decisions possible. Has someone trespassed on our character? How does this define who we are? Should we fight back or bring peace? According to these teachings that build our mindset, where does the target lie? Where do we draw our boundary lines in collaboration with the question of ethics? These are just a few of the constant self-inquiries we should be contemplating when living, moving, and having our being. So then just what are our virtues? The virtues of the Strix are fourfold:

Arete: Excellence. Striving toward excellence in all things. Do your absolute best, whether it is working, magic, taking care of your hearth, raising children, or whatever projects come your way. The Greeks felt a passion for arete, or excellence, in what their hands produced. It could range from artistic pursuits to harvesting beautiful fruit and wheat. Whatever it was, it encompassed everything. In the ways of the Strix, arete is bound up with Nyx, who seeks to ensure that she knows herself in all of her ways. We, being children of Nyx, want to be her essence made manifest, for the knowledge and wisdom that we gain will one day return to her, and become part of a much larger matrix.

Xenia: Hospitality. This sacred contract between people is rife with so many implications about how we treat strangers and one another. Hospitality is encouraged in our pursuit of arete, and it is said that sometimes gods will come to households or people in disguise to test our xenia. Inhospitable people and places are to be punished. When we are employers or employees, we achieve arete by showing xenia to customers and the people we work with. We treat each other right, and give compensation equal to what we are worth. We are humans, and we all deserve the opportunity to be treated with kindness and dignity, as well as to show it in return.

Eusebia: Piety. In ancient Greece, piety was something that encompassed so much more than the modern concepts of humility, fidelity, and "holiness." Piety, in short, is based on right action. It is a contract of right practice when it comes to our relationship with the gods and also right action when it comes to our relationship with our fellow human beings. By behaving outwardly within right choice, we are showing the gods and spirits that we are worthy of attention and blessing. With the gods, piety is shown when we engage in proper religious practices toward them by adhering to the laws that they have passed to gain gnosis ("inward knowledge"), blessing, and the cycles of life and death. By giving, they give. We give back. It is reciprocity.

Sophia: Wisdom. Wisdom is not merely having a way of thinking. It is the striving for knowledge of everything around us so that we might grow within. It involves things such as critical thinking, questioning, and having a love, awe, and reverence for the worlds around us. It means striving to learn as much as we can, from our failures as much as our successes. Wisdom is the all-encompassing virtue that teaches us the occult wisdoms of magic and myth. If we are not growing within, it is not wisdom. That is simply intelligence. Intelligence gets us nowhere if we cannot apply what we learn and absorb to better our lives in some way.

These fourfold virtues are what we live for as Strix.

SUMMARY

In this chapter we have discussed the beginning of the philosophical underpinnings of modern Strix Craft. Questions will lead to more questions, and that's okay. Ultimately, you will have to take the information presented herein and really contemplate how your actions lead to the penalties you reap. Keep in mind that self-reflection is never ending. Your knowledge and wisdom will grow and change; this is only natural. As we explore topics such as hexing and binding, we will return to these teachings of ethics, hubris, and virtues. Now let us get started with the necessary preparations.

SECTION 2
GETTING STARTED

CHAPTER 4
TOOLS

We begin with gathering the necessary tools of our craft. Tools help us to understand the symbols of how we practice. They are also living entities—spirits, if you will. Each tool is imbued with life, and a contract is made when it comes to how we utilize them. This makes our tools very susceptible to different energies, and as a result I do not allow just anyone to handle my tools. They are sacred beings. When they are not in use, I always cover my working altars where my tools are placed. I will go into altars and shrines in Chapter 7.

Suffice it to say for now that the gathering of these tools may vary. You may make them on your own, in which case they can be considered to be more yours since they are uniquely endowed with your energy. Or they may be purchased. Neither, however, is in my opinion better than the other. I merely mention that making them may grant you a perspective of greater ownership because they are crafted by your hands.

So just what are the tools of the Strix? How do we use them? How are they imbued with living spirits? What do they symbolize? Let's explore them in greater detail. But first, let's start with the understanding of sacred space.

SACRED SPACE

People frequently ask how we define sacred space. For example, for many Neopagans the entire world is sacred, and not limited to a specific place. While this may be true to them, there are places that are hallowed because they are homes to specific spirits. Shrines, of which you will be taught in this book, are homes. If you want to have a temporary home, then create an altar. But shrines are permanent spaces in your dwelling for a specific deity. One way, however, to make it easier to house multiple deities in Strix Craft is to use consecrated and activated tiles with sigils engraved or painted on them. We will go into more detail in the chapters on magic and the deities associated with it.

Grottoes, wells, cliffs, groves, and temples were and are homes to the gods and spirits. When we talk about the creation of sacred space, we are referring to a temporary altar to the gods and spirits we invoke. Of course, in some places we enter their space, and when doing so there are precautions to take because these are the demands of the gods and spirits prior to entering their homes. It's like when some of us were told to not track mud into the house: we take off our shoes at the doorway lest we be penalized. Or we make an effort to be clean and well-dressed prior to meeting someone for a date. There are social graces and demands when we are in someone else's territory. We must adapt to them, whatever our misgivings.

In performing a ritual to create the living temple not made with hands, we are in effect stating affirmatively, "Gods and spirits, we call your attention to us now in this place." Whether it is demarcating the space by flowers, cornmeal offerings, a blade, or some kind of physical or spiritual barrier, the purpose is to call attention to your place of worship.

BÔMÓS

Every deity that was worshiped had one. A *bômós* is a raised platform. There were different kinds of tables to deities. Chthonic (or underworld deities) most likely had a type of pit or some kind of low platform with a hole in it so that the land could receive offerings such as honey, bread, milk, or even blood.[34] *Bômói* could have any shape (e.g., cylindrical, square, rectangular, etc.), as long as the top was flat. According to the size of the sanctuary, the bômós could be as simple or as grand as one wanted, but usually the grand ones were more of an exception in the large temples rather than the norm. For our purposes, you may use anything from a table to a block of stone (for outdoor areas). The table may be any shape, so long as it is flat, and large enough to hold the objects mentioned herein. A bômós is a sacred place, so be sure to treat it as such.

TEMENOS

The *temenos*—that is, a place marked off by some kind of barrier—is the designated space of the sanctuary. Some people have marked theirs off permanently by use of a fence, cement blocks, or even tiki torches and a patio in the center. However, not all of us have such opportunities. I know of some who have taken their rooms or small apartments and created a temporary barrier by simply using the energy from a blade or finger. They use their mental space to create such a living temple. Some will use the old European witch ways and use a cord to mark out the nine-foot circle. Some use a special rug. Use your imagination. Do not be limited by the "can't" and "have not." Remember that the gods and spirits fuel our creativity. As much as you want to draw near to them, they also want

---

34. Mikalson, 5–7.

to draw near to you. It is the dance of Eros that creates such a living desire.

The Blade

You may use a single-, double-, or triple-edged blade. The symbolism of the blade as a sacred object comes from Central Asia, in places such as Mongolia and Tibet. From this place, a kathartai and iatromantis by the name of Abaris came. Abaris carried a golden arrow or blade, and he spoke to it often as if it were a living thing. He was the teacher to Pythagoras, to whom he handed the sacred arrow in a gesture of trust and respect.[35]

Pythagoras is widely known for the mathematical theorem known as the Pythagorean theorem. But he was also a philosopher, an iatromantis, a kathartai, and the founder of a mystery tradition located in Crotona in Southern Italy.[36] Here Pythagoras taught a form of reincarnation known as metempsychosis ("in soul"). The earliest references to this teaching come from the first half of the fifth century BCE; sources during this time credit the doctrine to Pythagoras,[37] who lived a century earlier. Metempsychosis is the belief that the soul is eternal, and it will come back into human form. In the afterlife, each soul is treated as an individual, subject to rewards or punishments. After a time, the soul may be freed. In addition, metempsychosis also taught that the soul of an individual may leave the body at any time; soul and body were fluid, rather than in a fixed state (a teaching in some Orphic cults as well).

The blade is a link back to these mystery traditions of Pythagoras, Orpheus, and Abaris, who came from the East. There is a

---

35. Kingsley, *A Story Waiting to Pierce You*, 3–14; 35–36.

36. Kingsley, *Ancient Philosophy, Mystery, and Magic*, 331.

37. Johnston, 43–49.

link there, a golden thread that binds us all. The blade is to be a practical along with a ceremonial tool. As a practical tool, it is to remain sharp and clean. As a ceremonial tool, it is used for directing energies, banishing unwanted entities, creating alliances with certain spirits, and symbolic bloodletting. Bloodletting is when you carefully prick your finger, and the blood is used as a substitute sacrifice or to call forth certain entities in a prescribed manner; please note that you should always use a sterile lancet or diabetic needle for any actual bloodletting, and prick your finger only. It is paramount to keep the blade sharp and clean, and sheathe it when not in use so as to keep it away from others.

The blade symbolizes the ability to conduct a sacrifice (not an actual one with a living animal mind you). Sacrifice means to make holy, not to surrender. As a result, the blade is able to consecrate and make holy what it touches. Made in the fires of a forge, the blade symbolizes the element of fire and its alliance to the underworld powers.

When you have a blade to your liking, the following is a formula used to make it a living spirit. Begin by assembling some amber and some poplar leaves. Take a mortar and pestle, and grind the amber to powder. Mix it with poplar leaves and place it in a thurible, metal bowl, or ceramic bowl. The species of poplar does not matter, as long as it is from the family Salicaceae in the genus *Populus*. For those in the Southern Hemisphere, in places such as Australia, consider the resin from the genus *Xanthorrhoea*, whose resin has been used as incense for churches.[38] Light a charcoal, and place the charcoal in the thurible or bowl. Now place the incense mix onto the charcoal. Allow it to burn. Wave the blade in a figure eight pattern in the smoke as it rises.

---

38. Williams, 101.

Now, find a place to sit comfortably outside. You may sit on the ground (ideal) or in a chair. As long as you are comfortable, that is what matters. Beneath the sun in the afternoon facing south (or north in the Southern Hemisphere), take the blade and with both hands raise it to the sky pointing at the sun. Feel the energy of warmth, healing, vitality, and transformation entering the blade. Do this for a minute or two. Next, burn some more of the incense mix. Now hold the blade in front of your chest, both hands grasping the handle of the blade while it points up. Be very careful. Chant the following nine times:

> Blade of sun,
> Blade of power,
> Blade of fire,
> Awake desire.
> Living spirit,
> Underworld being,
> Dwell within.[39]

After each chant, wave the blade in a figure eight pattern into the smoke. After the ninth time, stab the blade into the ground. Now wait until sunset, and then remove the blade. It is alive and ready for use. On the working altar, the blade is placed in the south (or north in the Southern Hemisphere).

THE TWO CHALICES

Also known as a *kylix*, a chalice is typically a goblet: a cup with a stem and base. In ancient Greece the kylix was more of a wide-

---

39. Unless otherwise indicated, all prayers, chants, and formulas are written by me.

brimmed bowl with two handles atop a stem.[40] Each type of chalice is used for drinking, but with separate symbolisms. One is what is called a "blood chalice," and the other is a "water chalice."

The blood chalice is a specific kylix used for wine. In fact, this was the most common use of a kylix in ancient Greece. The blood chalice holds wine for the ceremonies, and represents the blood of Dionysus. The Dionysian mysteries from Southern Italy and Sicily play a major role in modern Strix Craft, Dionysus being the bringer of salvation and the source of life in the mysteries.

To consecrate a blood chalice, simply wash it and make it clean. Then, after it dries, set it beneath the dark moon. Draw forth a sterile lancet or unused diabetic needle, and request of the spirit that what you are about to do gives life to the blood chalice, making it a receptacle of the god. You may say something like this: "Sacred blade, I whisper to you: O spirit, as I prick my finger, allow crimson kisses to awaken the blood chalice."

Prick your forefinger. Now beneath the stem of the goblet, draw an Invoking Earth Pentagram. Touch the center, and leave your finger there for a moment. Concentrate on the spirit of the blood chalice drinking and coming to life from your blood. When you are done, put a small bandage on your finger if necessary. Remember to keep the blood chalice covered when not in use.

In the rituals, the blood chalice is filled with wine and blessed in the following manner:

With your power hand, perform an Invoking Earth Pentagram, which is done in the air over the blood chalice once it is filled with wine. The power hand is your dominant hand. If you are ambidextrous, feel free to use whichever is most comfortable for you. Upon completing the drawing of the Invoking Earth Pentagram,

---

40. Faas, 93.

say the following: "From the soil to the vine, from the vine to the grape, from the grape to the wine. Blood of our god, return unto thee in thanksgiving and praise. Let it be acceptable in your sight. So be it!"

Now pour half of the wine into the ground or an offering bowl. This is known as a libation. A libation is an intentional pouring of liquids such as wine, honey, or milk into the sea, onto the ground, or over objects such as bowls, tombs, and altars.[41] When you do this, you are basically sharing and remembering the meaning behind the symbol of the wine. You are also inviting the spirits to partake in this "feast." On the working altar, the blood chalice is placed to the south next to the blade (or north in the Southern Hemisphere).

The water chalice is another goblet. As its name implies, it is filled with water and used for either divination or drinking— sometimes both. While the blood chalice symbolizes the blood of the god Dionysus, the water chalice symbolizes the life blood we have within us from the womb of the Earth Mother Gaia—that is, the waters of the ocean, springs, rivers, and rain. We are connected to her and her to us via the waters of the world. Gaia is 70 percent water, and so is the human body. We are a microcosm of the macrocosm that is the Earth Mother Gaia.

While the blood chalice is an invitation for the spirits to feast with us, the water chalice is an invitation for the participants in the rituals (i.e., Strix) to share liquids with one another. We affirm our right to life, and our right to connect with one another in the spirit of love, unity, and the energies that pervade through us via Gaia. The drinking of the water chalice is done right after the blood chalice ceremony.

---

41. Gaifman, 1.

To consecrate the water chalice, simply wash it and make it clean. Then, after it dries, set it beneath the full moon. Get a clean dish of water. With your power hand, draw over it the Invoking Pentagram of Water. Raise both hands over it and whisper, "Goddess of the Moon, I beseech you to give life to the kylix before me. Awaken, Holy One, and may we never thirst." Now take some of the water from the clean dish and gently wash the chalice nine times. When it is done, place the chalice on your working altar. Cover it when not in use.

When preparing the water chalice prior to sharing it, bless it with the following words: "In return may we receive your divine illumination! Let us hear your voice, O sacred ones! Come unto us, even as the rain fertilizes and blesses the earth. So be it!" On the working altar, the water chalice is placed to the right of the blood chalice.

THE WAND

Wands are depicted in ancient Greek art and lore. Examples of such wands include the caduceus of the god Hermes, and the wand of the sorceress Circe. Another wand example is the pine-cone tipped *thyrsus* of the ancient Dionysian thiasoi.

The caduceus is a short staff around which two serpents entwine themselves, with two wings spread near the top. It is a symbol of the god Hermes, and is known as the "herald's wand."[42] Hermes is the messenger god of the Greeks, and is the walker between the worlds of gods and mortals (both the living and the dead). He has a knack for being a trickster deity: someone who likes to make jokes at others' expense, but only to bring powerful lessons and to help create what is needed. In fact, in Homer's

---

42. Friedlander, 5.

"Hymn to Hermes," the god is described as a "wily child with a seductive mind—a robber, cattle rustler, guide of dreams..."[43]

Circe is a sorceress featured in Homer's epic *Odyssey*, an adventure tale of a man, named Odysseus (king of Ithaca), who with his crew leaves to go back home to Greece after the ten-year Trojan War. However, the god Poseidon is offended, and Odysseus and his crew spend twenty years at sea and find themselves in a variety of locations. One of those locations is the island of Aeaea, a mythical place where Circe makes her home. She is a daughter of the sun god Helios, and is considered by some modern practitioners as a goddess in her own right.

As Odysseus recounts his tale, he calls Circe a "witch-whore," a daughter of Helios, and an ocean spirit (nymph) named Perse.[44] Her home was said to be within a grove of oak and pine trees. She also had a wand made from a hazel tree, and touched the wand to each member of Odysseus's crew and transformed them into pigs.

The thiasoi of Dionysus, found throughout the Aegean and elsewhere in ancient Greece, also used wands. As mentioned in Chapter 1, the thiasoi were roving bands of women known as maenads, worshipers of Dionysus. They wore white robes and fawn skins that were worn over the robes.[45] Some carried timbrels, others pipes, and still others possibly drums. They wielded the wand known as the thyrsus, which was a short staff tipped with a pinecone. It was then ringed with ivy, a plant sacred to the god.

As you can tell, wands have a history in the practices of ancient Greek myth and cult. Gods and worshipers alike held them for a variety of purposes. The wand in Strix Craft can be made of any

43. Homer, *The Homeric Hymns,* line 19.

44. Homer, *The Odyssey,* lines 87–245.

45. Euripides, *The Bacchae,* 10.

wood or metal, but should not exceed the length between your elbow and forefinger. Why? It just makes it easier to handle. Natural materials for the wand may be preferred by some, and this is in keeping with the wands held by both Circe and the thiasoi of Dionysus.

However, it is the function of the wand that is important, and that is namely for summoning spirits, healing, and welcoming others into sacred space as an act of xenia. In bindings and hexing, the wand may touch a poppet or image of the one to be hexed and curse them. The wand is also a link to the nymphs: the spirits of the forest, springs, rivers, lakes, swamps, mountains, and other. Those Strix dedicated to the god Dionysus in particular may make their own thyrsus as a commitment to the god. It will then be a sacred covenant between the deity and themselves.

In order to consecrate your wand, hold it in your hands in a horizontal position. Beneath a dark moon, hold the wand and slowly raise it to the sky. Say the following: "In the name of that witch goddess Circe; by the magician Hermes, and the ecstasy of Dionysus, I bind this spirit to me. Circe, Medea, Hekate, Hermes, Dionysus, Pasiphaë: come forth mages of the Art Magical, and by holy powers imbue this tool with the dark and light. So be it!" It is now ready for use. The wand is connected to the elements of earth and water. On the working altar, it is placed to the west.

THE GREEN CUBE

The cube is the symbol of earth in the Pythagorean mysteries.[46] In Strix Craft, a cube is created that is four inches on each side, and painted green, the color of earth. Four is the number of earth, and the cube is one of the five Platonic solids (that is,

---

46. Rosen, 148.

three-dimensional geometric shapes that represent each of the five elements of earth, air, fire, water, and aether).

The green cube is holy by its very shape. It becomes alive naturally when it is finished. One may create the cube using wood or clay, although clay is preferable because it may be easier for some who are not experienced at woodworking. When making the cube, be sure it is hollow, because you will be placing a couple of items in it to allow an entity to dwell within it. The cube is said to be the shape from which earth arose; fire from the pyramid; air from the octahedron; water from the icosahedron; and finally, aether (symbolizing the cosmos) from the dodecahedron.

In Strix Craft, the green cube is a powerful artifact as it houses an earth entity that becomes a kind of familiar. This familiar spirit, or *daimon*, sleeps within the green cube. The green cube and the spirit within are your connection to the various land spirits. This earth daimon works in tandem with the other spirits in order to utilize harmony in your life. They will be your eyes, ears, protectors, and being from which to unleash your magic.

No incantation is needed for the green cube. However, to draw a willing entity into the cube is a different matter. To begin with, just before your cube is sealed, place a quartz crystal along with some local seeds in the cube. Seal it, and then paint it green. After it is dry, it is ready for use. Take the cube and plant it in a small pot of soil. Completely cover it and leave it beneath the moon for the three nights of the full moon (the night before, the night of, and the night after).

Each night, pour a mixture of honey, milk or cream, and your blood onto the soil. Simply feed it. After the third night, take it out of the ground and cover it gently. Once a month beneath the three nights of the full moon, cover it back into the pot with fresh soil and feed it again. Your cube will remain your connection as long as you have it. On the working altar, it is placed to the east.

LAMP OF HESTIA

In the center of the working altar is the lamp of Hestia, a designated candle or candleholder specifically for her. I use tealights, and so I have a special candleholder for her in which the tealight burns. The fire from the candle is a gateway to bring her literal presence into your dwelling. I light it whenever I have friends and/ or family over, to invoke her feelings of warmth and home. I call my home a "hearth," because that's what it is. It is her hearth, the center of all in my life. Some people choose to create a special space in their kitchen area or even the dining room where everyone meets. I think that's beautiful, as fire and food bring us back to the ancient ways of our ancestors.

Hestia is invoked before any other deity because she is the First and the Last and is the one who brings attention the hearth. She and Hermes, in my opinion, are the closest to humanity. She is the living manifestation of every fire kindled from which food and warmth are drawn. The central flame that unites us all is found in Hestia.

Find a special candleholder that will house either a taper or tealight. As I mentioned, I prefer tealights because they are convenient and they won't burn for long. But the preference is ultimately yours. The flame is her literal presence, and invoking her at the beginning of a ritual may commence like so:

"Central flame of the gods, in the house of Olympus you reign. With everlasting fire, purify the seen and unseen. By your holy light, welcome those from near and far as I bask in your presence. Bring peace and be welcome, O Lady. So be it!"

As mentioned before, on the working altar the lamp of Hestia is placed in the center.

KHERNIPS BOWL

Also known as lustral water, khernips is the sacred water that you prepare, and that you use to wash yourself before ritual or entering sacred space. Take a small bowl and consecrate it. This consecrated bowl will, moving forward, not be used for anything other than for khernips.

Fill the bowl halfway with water. Some use spring water and others use regular water. It's up to you. Then take three bay leaves and light them. When you light them, say,

"Flame of the Ruby Star."

Plunge the leaves into the water and say:

"Water of the Azure Serpent."

Now from the twelve o'clock position at the top of the bowl, make three cycles clockwise. Say the following:

"Hekas!" (Cycle 1)
"Hekas!" (Cycle 2)
"Este bebeloi!" (Cycle 3)

Although very ritualistic, every behavior means something to us. Now wash your hands and your face three times. Towel dry. Hold up the khernips to the north and state, "Chaos has no place in Order. That which is profane has no place in holiness. To the Outsiders, leave us in peace! So be it!" Take the water somewhere and dump it. If you lack property, the toilet or sink may be used. When not in use, the khernips bowl is placed beneath the working altar or simply put away.

OIL

Olive oil is sacred to the gods and spirits. Although some people may make their own oils, olive oil is best, and as pure as can be. It is worth the investment when it is for the gods and spirits we revere. This is not to say that any other kind of olive oil will not do, but if you can, aim for the best. After the washing, we anoint the forehead with oil. The reason we do this is because we are sealing our commitment to the ritual at that moment.

SCOURGE

There is a saying that goes "Washing with water cleans the impure. Anointing with oil soothes the soul. But the scourge is a reminder that even when you are cleansed and welcome, pain and suffering are inevitable from nature and from the gods." The scourge is mainly used six times per year: the Spring Equinox, the Summer Solstice, the Feast of the Dead, and the three festivals of Hekate in November.

The scourge can be any leather cat-o'-nine-tails. Its purpose is to purify and be a connection to the goddesses Hekate, Nemesis, Artemis Orthia, and the Furies, as well as Apollo in his plague-causing aspect. The scourge is a perfect tool for those Strix desiring to also become kathartai. In this capacity, the scourge is a weapon that can chase out spirits of plague and destruction. It is used to gently purify an individual or group. This is done by having everyone extend their hands, palms up, in front of them. First, the washing with khernips is performed and the hands are dried. Then, everyone extends their hands, palms up, in front of them. Clockwise, the one performing the scourging GENTLY whips the right hand and then the left hand. Finally, a drop of oil is rubbed into the palms to soothe the process. On the working altar, the scourge is placed in the west, the direction of the underworld.

BELL

The bell is a tool that is used in our rituals simply to focus the mind on the parts of the rites that are being separated. For example, from the opening ceremony of the ritual to the main portion itself, the bell is rung a number of times in order to signal a transition. It is also used to keep evil spirits (*kakodaimones*) away and keep the call to worship in the minds of the worshipers. On the working altar, the bell is placed at the top right of the table.

INCENSE

The incense is a tool wherein the rising smoke lifts our prayers and praises to the gods and spirits. We use two incense holders with incense lit: one on the working altar in the very front (it is a veil), and the other on the floor underneath it for the chthonic deities such as Hermes in his guise as the psychopomp who travels between the underworld and our world of the living.

OFFERING BOWL

The offering bowl is used to accept anything such as cake, wine, milk, an apple slice, or pomegranate juice. When receiving the offerings, the bowl is picked up and waved over the incense smoke nine times so that the gods and spirits are fed through the essence of the offerings.

VASE

A beautiful addition to any working altar, the vase can hold seasonal flowers or, year-round, roses.

The Black Mirror: The Eye of Nyx

Materials needed:

a piece of mirror or glass in a frame

black enamel spray paint

mugwort leaves

myrrh incense

The black mirror is a scrying tool used to communicate with the otherworld. It is an important component in Strix Craft, as we frequently are in contact with the blessed dead, deities, and spirits. It is called the Eye of Nyx because eyes are considered an active and passive portal between realms. It is pure black: the realm of All and Power.

Take a black mirror or make your own. To make your own, simply find a mirror of good quality and size. Some people use the glass already found in wooden picture frames at your local store. The size is up to you, as long as it is easy to handle. I say "easy to handle" because it is something you will want to carry with you for rituals and to put away. Wooden frames are best because shiny ones tend to reflect into the glass.

Purchase a can of high gloss black enamel paint that is good for glass. Remove the glass and clean it thoroughly. Let it dry. On a sunny (and as windless as possible) day, place the glass on a bed of newspapers outdoors. Spray paint the glass using quick, even passes back and forth. Let it dry (it may take a few hours). When it is dry, place the mirror in the frame. Now take some mugwort leaves and make a tea. Let it cool and strain it. Take the tea and anoint the mirror and frame with it. It is ready to be used.

Consecrate and activate the mirror on the night of the dark moon. Light some myrrh incense. Take the mirror and weave the mirror in and out of the smoke in a figure eight fashion while saying three times:

> *Eye of night,*
> *Hekate's sight.*
> *Cleanse this mirror,*
> *Spirits speak clearer.*

ICON

The icon of the deity or deities is placed in the back center of the working altar (usually facing east) with the vase in-between. These can range from statues, to paintings, to symbols. It has been my experience that their presence will respond to any of the above. Many ancient temples couldn't afford statues; only after war victories or massive tributes were large statues and grand temples able to have many.[47] I never had statues for a long time, and I thought my spirituality was inadequate because of it. But it wasn't. You can perhaps even learn to make your own! A Strix priestess made a lovely Hekate statue using a Barbie doll as a base. Remember, you are only limited by your imagination. Symbols can be such things as arrows or a small crown of laurel leaves for Apollo; keys for Hekate; grapes, thyrsus, or a mask for Dionysus; a black stone for Aphrodite; a hammer for Hephaestus; a skull or geode for Hades; a pomegranate for Persephone; wheat for Demeter; etc. Also, as a reminder, you don't always need a dual god and goddess. Some festivals are for one deity only, and others for two (or more!). As polytheists, strict dyads are unknown in our practices. When they are not in use, the images of the deities should be veiled. Once you have cleansed yourself, you may unveil them. This is so you may understand how to focus your consciousness from one realm to

---

47. Mikalson, 15–21.

another. We go from ours to theirs, in their presence. You may also add candles next to each icon of the deities. I place them behind the images of the deities. Once they are unveiled, I light the candles and call their presences down using a prescribed hymn (such as the Orphic Hymns) or one I have written. Sincerity goes a long way in Strix Craft.

SUMMARY

The basic tools of Strix Craft begin with the ones mentioned in this chapter. Some, such as the scourge, can be controversial at best. It may trigger some of you to have negative associations with it, for a variety of reasons. I would like to encourage you to explore those associations and compare and contrast them with the associations presented here. Remember, we are always asking questions about ourselves and our ethics along with our values. We are also looking for connections to the deities and spirits, and each tool is a beautiful representation of those inherent links. So write down and journal your thoughts. Mull them over. Contemplate. It may take time to perhaps come to an understanding of each tool and its use (such as the blade and blood), and that's okay. When you are ready, make that link with that spirit. I promise you the results of working and honoring these spirits in Strix Craft is well rewarding.

CHAPTER 5
HERBS

As you might have guessed, herbs play an important role for the Strix, who are also pharmakoi. The herbs are a gift from Hekate and the Earth Mother Gaia. The Strix were the early seers and medicine people who discovered the use of various plants for healing or poison. They spoke to the spirits and were taught the ancient ways. In Greek myth it was Chiron who taught the magical use of these plants to his pupils.

Plants are symbiotically linked to humanity. They have remedies and are also the homes of the wild creatures (both visible and invisible). But they have shown us the way to understand tracking, medicine, adaptation, and capturing prey. Here I will explore herbs used in the past and today by Strix. Please be aware that the more poisonous plants can be deadly. However, for educational purposes I will include them. To deny that these were ever used is to lie about our past (and present).

I'd like to also mention that herbs and plants are living spirits, and as such should be fed both physically and spiritually. A spiritual method for feeding plants is to mix three drops of your own blood into two tablespoons of goat's milk and one cup of spring water. Mix well. Pour. This can be done once a year; the new moon before the Spring Equinox is an ideal time, as is when the plant or herb is going to bloom. If it is an annual plant sacred to a deity, perhaps the festival of that deity would be a good time. Don't poke yourself to death to feed everyone at the same time! This is merely a way to help learn to take care of your green familiar spirits.

ACONITE
(*ACONITUM NAPELLUS* AND *A. LYCOCTONUM*)
Highly poisonous!

In late summer the aconite has purple flowers and grows to a height of about 5 ft. (1.5 m), and this is true for the aconite known as common monkshood (*A. napellus*). I would not recommend growing this plant in your garden, especially with children and animals near. If you decide to handle them, be sure to wear gloves. The roots, which can be mistaken for horseradish, are deadly.[48] There are certain alkaloids found in aconite that are also found in snake venom, arsenic, lead, and ammonia.[49] They are neurotoxins, and even one-fiftieth of a grain can kill a small bird in seconds.

Lore

In Greek myth Herakles went into the underworld to fetch Cerberus, the three-headed dog. Cerberus is the guardian of the underworld. He guards people who want to leave it, rather than prevent those who are going in. For the last of his twelve labors, Herakles became initiated into the Eleusinian mysteries in order to descend into the underworld. Prepared and purified, he went in and overcame Cerberus by force. As he dragged Cerberus into the daylight, the three-headed hound was brought into the sun for the first time

---

48. Atha, 92.

49. Wilson, "Is Aconite Actually Dangerous?"

and vomited bile from the shock. From the bile of Cerberus was born the aconite.[50] In the *Argonautica Orphica*, aconite is one of the plants in the garden of the goddess Hekate, grown and nurtured by Medea, her high priestess.

Magical Use

Aconite is good to ward off evil spirits, to use in necromancy rites to call forth the dead, or even to travel to the underworld itself. However, due to its poisonous nature, I must caution against it. As a viable substitute, one may use tobacco or rosemary.

AGRIMONY *(AGRIMONIA EUPATORIA)*

A perennial plant, agrimony is also known as church steeples, due to its tall column of flowers. Aromatic, it is usually found in wild places such as fields and woods. Its name comes from the Greek word *argemone*, a plant known for healing the eyes. It is a magical herb best known for its various healing and protective qualities. According to Paul Beyerl, the plant contains an oil known as tannin.[51] Tannin is a volatile oil that should not be ingested by pregnant or breastfeeding women. As an astringent, agrimony is used to help constrict tissues and dry skin in order to help treat a variety of ailments such as diarrhea, irritable bowel syndrome, fluid retention, bleeding wounds, and allergies. It is also used as a sedative.[52]

50. Rose, 177.
51. Beyerl, 54–55.
52. WebMD.

Lore

No lore is seemingly attached to agrimony, although in ancient Greece it was used to treat ailments of the eyes. Its value lies more in its uses than in any myth that may include it.

Magical Use

Due to its healing properties, agrimony may be used as a protective amulet, to help you discern the spirits, and to let you know when someone is trying to hex you.

ALOE (*ALOE VERA*)

An evergreen tropical plant commonly used in herbal medicine, aloe is a valued healer. The sap can be transformed into an ointment, face creams, and other cosmetics. The long, spiked leaves can reach up to 2 ft. (60 cm) in length. In the summer the plant may have a single stalk spiked with yellow or red flowers.[53]

Lore

Aloe is an all-around healing plant, but it is also sharply protective due to its Areian nature of having thorns to ward off predators. I had an aloe plant that was able to grow a single spiked stem with orange flowers blooming. It was remarkable. A versatile plant, its gel has been used to treat severe burns, open wounds, and intestinal issues. Planting aloe is also said in folklore to protect your home against the Evil Eye. I know my family did this.

---

53. Atha, 101.

Magical Use

Planting it near your front door is an excellent warding technique. The "spikes" from the leaves will pierce the gaze of anyone wishing you ill.

ANGELICA *(ANGELICA ARCHANGELICA)*

Angelica is a biennial plant that has all of its parts used in healing remedies. The juice is used as a tonic for the eyes. The root is commonly used for baked goods and sweets. It has tiny yellow flowers in clumps on the end of long stalks.[54]

Lore

As the name suggests, it became associated with archangels. Angelica, however, has more ancient uses. For example, in Eastern Europe, oral traditions passed down stories of unintelligible chants while the angelica was held.[55]

Magical Use

Angelica was carried by many for protection against the Evil Eye. Angelica was considered to have properties to avert the plague—and no wonder, with its diaphoretic and expectorant properties. This herb could ease coughs and fevers as a result. It may be used as a burnt offering to Apollo, the Furies, or Nemesis to avert their more wrathful aspects.

ANISE *(PIMPINELLA ANISUM)*

Anise is a flowering plant that grows about 3 ft. tall. The flowers are yellow or white, and their leaves differentiate from the base to

---

54. Atha, 109.

55. Beyerl, 58.

the stem as to how they look (simple to feathered, respectively). It is found as an ingredient in sweets and also is used in the making of a liqueur called Anisette.

Lore

Anise harbors a spirit that makes itself known in the liqueur Anisette. This is a mischievous sprite that can induce the drinker to see things that aren't there. The liqueur is also a "treat" for familiar spirits, I have found. Its medicinal qualities allow it to be used as an antiflatulent and for calming upset stomachs.

Magical Use

Magically, anise is an amulet for restful sleep against evil spirits. It can be hung over the bed and blessed in the names of Hermes, Hypnos, and Morpheus for good sleep and night visions.

ASAFOETIDA (FERULA ASAFOETIDA)

From the taproot of several species of *Ferula*, a resin can be extracted. This is asafoetida. It grows to 1–1.5 m (3.3–4.9 ft.). It has quite a pungent smell, leading to its nickname of "devil's dung."

Lore

Asafoetida was originally an Iranian plant. Thanks to Alexander the Great, it traveled to Mediterranean Europe. It is also widely used in India. It has culinary and medicinal uses.

Magical Use

In ancient Greece it was known as the "food of the gods," and was also used to invoke male gods. One of the stories is that a god's semen fell on the ground, and where it did, asafoetida was born. Which male deity this was is still unknown, although because of its connection to ritual magic, defense, and banishing of evil spirits, I choose to believe it was Priapus. Priapus is a god with an enormous phallus, and phalluses were used in the Mediterranean to ward off the Evil Eye and prevent diseases.

BALKAN PEONY (*FAMILY PAEONIA*)

Peony is a flowering plant which grows to about 3 ft. in height (1 m). The flowers come in different colors but it is recognized by its large glossy leaves. Peonies especially bloom in late spring and early summer.

Lore

The peony was named after Paian, a student of the demigod healer Asklepios, who was a son of Apollo. When Paian began to surpass Asklepios, Zeus changed him into a peony so as to protect him.

Magical Use

Collect the seeds and dry them. Thread them with a white thread and wear as an amulet for protection from disease. In similar fashion, the roots may also be collected, dried, and carved. Like the mandrake, the roots of the peony can also be used to make a poppet for a familiar.

BASIL (*OCIMUM BASILICUM*)

A bushy plant that reaches a couple of feet tall, basil has fragrant, oval leaves with prominent veins and curled edges. Purple, pink, or white flowers may grow at the tops of the stems.

Lore

It is very popular in culinary uses. In medieval times, basil was used to help freshen and scent the air in homes. Another midsummer plant, it is sacred to Apollon, Pan, and Aphrodite. Be sure to decorate your altars or shrines to them with this plant when you are worshiping these deities.

Magical Use

Used to protect the home against witches, it is also used to break hexes and bind lovers. Plant basil in your garden or have a potted plant in your home or on your altar to use the magic it brings.

BAY LAUREL *(LAURUS NOBILIS)*

Bay laurel is normally seen as a small shrub, although when left alone it can grow forty to fifty feet high. The stems sprout dark green and oval-shaped leaves that are pointed. Bay laurel has small, greenish-yellow flowers and small berries that change to blue-black when ripe.

Lore

Known as Daphni in ancient Greece, she was a fresh water nymph known as a naiad. Apollo insulted the god Eros on the latter's archery skills. As a result, Eros shot Apollo with a golden arrow to inspire him to love and lust. However, Eros then shot Daphni with a lead arrow; as a result, she swore to keep her virginity, and had a passion for the wilderness and hunts like Artemis. The lead arrow caused Daphni to hate Apollo. Chasing after her, Apollo was evenly matched with Daphni's speed. However, as he almost caught her, Daphni cried out to her father, Peneus the Thessalian river god, for help. He transformed her into a bay laurel plant. Apollo promised afterward that she would remain young and evergreen, and that she would be bestowed high honors.

Magical Use

Sacred to Apollon and the Pythia priestess of the Oracle of Delphi, crowns of bay laurel were also used for winners in the Olympic Games and other contests. As such, burning bay leaves is used to invoke purification, holiness, and the power of the sun to banish evil. It is also used in oracling rituals to enhance one's skills and clairvoyant perceptions. A specific ritual for Apollonian priestesses and priests who desire to invoke the power of the god to oracle usually follows a regimen of chewing three bay leaves daily for twenty-one days until the time of the Summer Solstice. Bay will be burned and as the smoke rises while chanting, the spirit of the god Apollon will descend and possess them.

BLESSED MILK THISTLE *(SILYBUM MARIANUM)*

A stately and beautiful plant, blessed milk thistle has sharp leaves with milky-white veins running down them. Purplish-pink flowers bloom in the second year atop a spiky stalk.

Lore

Blessed milk thistle has been connected to the god Pan, and, as an aphrodisiac, is sacred to Aphrodite and Eros.

Magical Use

An herb long known to protect the liver from poison and also used as a powerful emetic against poison in the body, blessed milk thistle is a powerful spirit. A martial and solar herb, it is used in exorcisms, for breaking hexes, and as an antidote. Burning the leaves of the plant does much to help purify the space, and keeping a potted plant nearby and fed properly will strengthen the spirit to ward your hearth. It is used to invoke the gods Pan, Dionysus, and Hermes.

CARAWAY (*CARUM CARVI*)

A plant with white flower heads and feathery foliage, its long roots can be cooked. It belongs to the carrot family and is similar to dill and fennel. The seeds are used to flavor breads, meats, stews, and even liqueurs such as schnapps.

Lore

Caraway has been used for a variety of purposes, from weddings to being thrown on coffins to keep away evil spirits. Hiding caraway in the food of your lover will also keep them faithful to you.

Magical Use

The herb can be used for fertility spells and to invoke good fortune to those gifted with such a spirit. Be sure the spirit has been cared for and fed spiritually. Pray to the spirit to lend its energy to you. Ask for its help, and ritually slice a part of the herb from root to bud. If a couple desires to conceive, they should lay this herb upon the lower abdomen of the female as she lies beneath the new moon. The partner should carve a circle around her with a black-handled knife, and then ritually have sex with her, making sure that she is brought to orgasm as well. The couple should then place the caraway as a dried amulet over their bed until the birth of their child, and afterward, burn it as an offering to the spirits of fire and smoke, who will return part of its essence back into the land. If you desire to protect a gestating infant, then lay this herb upon the lower abdomen of the female as she lies beneath the full moon. Carve a circle around her with a black-handled knife, and invoke the goddesses Artemis Orsilokhia and Hekate Eileithyia to protect the mother and the child. After the prayers, lay the dried-up piece over the bed until the birth of the child. Burn it when its purpose has finished.

CATNIP *(NEPETA CATARIA)*

Do not ingest while pregnant!

Possessing bluish-gray leaves, this plant has tufts of flowers that grow alongside long stalks. The plant can grow to a height of two to three feet (45–90 cm). The flowers are lavender-blue or lilac-blue.

Lore

Blooming from July to October, this herb has always been popular for culinary and medicinal purposes. Its oil is a feline aphrodisiac, and bruising it just brings the oil out more. It is used in healing for calming an upset stomach, or as a mild sedative.

Magical Use

To induce headaches and fevers in an enemy, take some of the catnip and make a small crown; affix it to the brow of the *kolossos* (poppet) who represents your enemy. Leave it there for as long as you desire for the effect to be done. If you change your mind, burn the crown of leaves. You may also use a fed spirit to help link your consciousness with that of a cat who has claimed you as their own.

CELANDINE, LESSER *(RANUNCULUS FICARIA)*

Highly poisonous!

Considered a weed, lesser celandine is actually a useful herb (note: most herbs are considered weeds). It has shiny, heart-shaped leaves that are tooth-edged. The flowers are small yellow buds with four petals. However, there are varieties that exist that have different colored flowers. It can grow to a height of 18–36 in. (45–90 cm).

Lore

A member of the poppy family, lesser celandine is sacred to the goddesses Rhea, Demeter, and Persephone. The plant is named for *chelidon*, the Greek word for "swallow." [56] The legend goes that if the eyes of a baby swallow are removed with a needle, then the mother will simply replace them with the sap of the lesser celandine.

Magical Use

It can be used in healing rituals and exorcism rituals. For healing rituals, one can use the roots in a ceremony to rub on a poppet in the lung area. In an exorcism ritual, simply create a circular barrier of lesser celandine in dried herb form and the energy will irritate the evil spirit, causing it to vanish; this will leave the individual exhausted and weak. The individual should be placed in the center of the circle, or perhaps even the poppet of their likeness if they cannot be brought to the circle. Be sure to not break a fresh plant because the sap is highly irritating to the skin.

CHAMOMILE (*CHAMAEMELUM NOBILE*)
Use with caution if pregnant!

A daisy-like plant, chamomile is a low-growing plant with leaves and flowers approximately a foot high (31 cm). Chamomile is a very well-known herb, and it is used in some regions as a lawn. A popular tea, fresh chamomile tea is good for calming and clarity.

---

56. Atha, 142.

Lore

No mythic connection is known, although Hippocrates does cite it for its use to relieve cold symptoms and for protection.[57]

Magical Use

Chamomile tea can be drunk before seership rites such as incubation rituals. The essential oil is used to relieve swelling. Place it on a poppet for distance healing.

DEADLY NIGHTSHADE *(ATROPA BELLADONNA)*
Highly poisonous!

A member of the potato family, deadly nightshade has trumpet-like flowers and large, shiny black berries. It reaches three feet tall (90 cm). The plant, like aconite, contains alkaloids that have sedative and diuretic properties. *Atropa* is the name inspired by the goddess of fate who cut the ties to life.

Lore

Strix made ointments out of deadly nightshade and flew to the witches' sabbats in the Middle Ages. In ancient Greece, this plant was known as strigum (note its associations with the word Strix).[58]

Magical Use

On no account should any part of this plant be used or cultivated where children or domesticated animals will be. Its association with Hekate and sorcery rendered this popular herb a place in forbidden history. Concoctions used to poison enemies were created, and in the Middle Ages (although at other times I am sure) women

---

57. Moumita.

58. Hatsis, 135–139.

used juice from the plant to dilate their pupils. It is appropriate (though not encouraged, due to safety concerns) to use this plant to consecrate all tools used in hexing, or to cover a poppet to be cursed. It is also a common ingredient in the witches' ointment for which Strix were very well known. A viable substitute is rosemary.

ELECAMPANE (*INULA HELENIUM*)

Growing four to eight feet tall, elecampane has long yellow flowers. It is a member of the daisy family, and is sacred to nymphs.

Lore

The plant's species name, *helenium,* is named after Helen of Troy. It was said that after she was abducted from Sparta by Paris, elecampane grew wherever her tears fell.

Magical Use

Medicinally, it is excellent in its treatment of coughs and bronchitis. In distant healing rites, make an infusion and ceremoniously baptize a kolossos (poppet) of the individual by immersing the kolossos into the infusion fully and completely. Baptize it nine times, followed by breathing gently into the chest (as if to give life into the lungs) three times.

FENNEL (*FOENICULUM VULGARE*)

Fennel grows three to six feet tall (90 cm–1.8 m), with tiny yellow flowers held in clusters on the stalks. The leaves are fine, lacy, and can be described as "feathery."

Lore

Fennel has a history in Greek mythology. In a fennel stalk was where Prometheus hid the sacred fire that he brought from the heavens to humanity. It was our first magic, and thus fennel has an important place. It is also the stalk that was used for the staff of Dionysus and his followers.

Magical Use

A fennel tea prepared with magic can be used as a love potion. Alternatively, fennel leaves can be burned and used as an incense while you cense yourself to break a love spell. You may also use the incense to exorcise evil spirits.

FENUGREEK *(TRIGONELLA FOENUM-GRAECUM)*

Do not ingest while pregnant!

If you are allergic to peanuts or chickpeas, do not take!

Fenugreek is an annual plant with a single stem and oblong leaves. It has a strong aroma.

Lore

Sacred to the god Apollo, fenugreek decorated his temples, and was used in religious dishes. However, as stated above, be warned that if you have certain allergies this herb is not safe to ingest!

Magical Use

Ironically, it is good in healing rites: one may use the sprig of greens and gently scourge an individual with an illness, "beating" the evil spirit from them. Scourge them gently with the greens on their back, the back of their neck, their head, their chest, their arms, their legs, and their stomach. Do this seven times, from the top of the head to the soles of the feet.

FOXGLOVE *(DIGITALIS PURPUREA)*
Highly poisonous!

A common wildflower growing four to five feet high (1.2–1.5 m), foxglove has broad basal leaves with tubular-shaped purple, white, and pink flowers. All parts of the plant are poisonous.

Lore

A man named William Wittering recorded the use of digitoxin and digitalin from foxglove leaves to treat congestive heart failure in the eighteenth century. Wittering, a young medical student, was called on to give his opinion of a recipe that helped to treat dropsy (now called congestive heart failure). An old wise woman had a recipe that contained about twenty ingredients, but Wittering deduced that it was the foxglove that treated CHF. He began to administer the herb himself and became very famous,[59] and even cited 163 cases in which the herb had worked! Sadly, the old wise woman's name eludes us. Had it not been for this "village witch" (as she would be called nowadays by many, even though she was most likely a Christian folk healer), Wittering would not know about the plant's healing properties. He took full credit for his success, and never named the woman.

Magical Use

This plant is sacred to Hekate and Persephone, and is used in ancestral venerations and necromancy. In fact, an underworld pit should have a small border of foxglove. An underworld pit is a triangular hole in the ground (or in a pot) lined with dried foxglove and having three black candles at each corner. As a magical substitute, I highly recommend agrimony.

---

59. Castleman.

GARLIC (*ALLIUM SATIVUM*)

Related to the onion, garlic can be known either as a vegetable or an herb. An annual bulb, the plant itself grows 6–12 in. in height with a single head of greenish-white or pale pink flowers.

Lore

Garlic is sacred to the goddess Hekate. It was one of the offerings served to her on the nights of the dark moon. These servings were called "*deipnons*," meaning "suppers." The night of the dark moon was called Hekate's Deipnon.

Magical Use

A solar-based herb, garlic is a natural ward against evil spirits and banishes revenants. It is most powerful when the dried leaves are braided, creating a rope of garlic that is strung from the ceiling over a doorway or entranceway. Sacred to Hekate and Apollo Oulios, garlic wards and is used in exorcism rites. Medicinally it is very much a healer.

GREEK SAGE (*SALVIA FRUTICOSA*)

Greek sage is a perennial shrubby plant growing a foot high (31 cm) with hairy leaves that grow in clusters. The flowers grow in a whorl form with pinkish flowers.

Lore

The ancient Greeks felt that sage was a valuable plant. It was said to be capable of warding death and conferring long life.

Magical Use

It is a sacred aromatic plant and the burning of this herb creates a "ground zero" of space devoid of any energy, whether good or ill. It can be used to banish everything in a hearth or area. This is also good for creating a magically "sterile field" around stones, crystals, and ritual tools. Keep in mind that burning Greek sage, because of this nature of this herb, will banish ALL spirits, both good and ill. If you don't want this result, then petition your good spirits for help in keeping evil ones away. Always remember to make an alliance with your local spirits.

HENBANE (*HYOSCYAMUS NIGER*)
Highly poisonous!

Growing up to three feet tall (1 m), this plant has bell-shaped flowers with purple centers and purple splotches. Though beautiful to look at, the plant can have a bad odor. This plant should not be grown where you will have children or domesticated animals.

Lore

Henbane was an herb that was probably used by the ancient Greek priestesses of Apollo to induce trance states, as it was known as "Herba Apollinaris." However, as *Hyoskyamos*, it was holy to Persephone. The dead were also thought to be crowned with henbane leaves as they wandered hopelessly along the banks of the river Styx, not having had proper burial services to usher them over to the other side.

Magical Use

Oddly, only pigs are said to be able to eat the plant without it negatively affecting them. An underworld pit with some henbane next to it makes a great attraction to the spirits of the underworld. A crown of henbane leaves can be used in rites in which a skull is used for an oracular rite with the dead. Remember that contact with the skin may cause an irritation. A viable substitute for henbane is tobacco.

HYSSOP (*HYSSOPUS OFFICINALIS*)

A member of the mint family, hyssop has been used as a purification and consecration herb for millenia. Reaching about two feet (.06 m) in height, hyssop has dark green leaves that are shaped like lances. The flowers are rich blue and two-lipped, growing in whorls.

Lore

No known connection to any ancient Greek myth is known. However, this plant was known to the ancient Greeks. They used it for purification and protection purposes.

Magical Use

It is used to create sacred space, either by burning it or using it as an aspergillum. Taking a bath with hyssop is perfect for purification and consecration. Make a tea or use it as an aspergillum to anoint your altars and shrines when cleaning them on the new moon. You may also lightly "scourge" your home in case there is a spirit there that is unwanted, or perhaps needs to return somewhere rather than banishing it altogether—a mischievous sprite, for example.

IVY (*HEDERA HELIX*)

Growing about 66 to 98 feet high (20–30 m), this plant with aerial roots is able to wind its way up on cliffs, walls, and trees. It has greenish-yellow flowers that are rich in nectar. The ivy yields berries that range from black and purple to orange and yellow.

Lore

An evergreen vine with woody stems, ivy is sacred to the god Dionysus. Crowns of ivy were created to crown artists (particularly poets).

Magical Use

Wind some ivy around a poppet to bind it and induce "drunken confusion" for that person's mental state. Alternatively, allow it to grow outside of your home both as a natural shrine to Dionysus and as a repellant against evil. To induce ecstasy, perform a ritual frenzy with a crown of ivy, chanting the name of the god.

LAVENDER *(LAVANDULA OFFICINALIS)*

A perennial shrub with lavender, blue, white, or pink flowers that grow in small spikes, the shrub grows about 2–3 feet tall (0.6–1 m). The leaves are gray or grayish-green.

Lore

Honey bees are highly attracted to it, and so it is sacred to the Melissae and Demeter.

Magical Use

Used in medicine for centuries, lavender has an aromatic scent popular as a tea and in aromatherapy. As a tea it calms the nerves and helps one to ground, focus, and ease tension and stress. Avoid large amounts of the oil as an application or ingestion, as then it becomes poisonous! Unlike Greek sage (or common sage) and other herbs that banish, lavender is grown to welcome spirits. Feeding lavender only strengthens its aura, which helps to flourish the hearth and cover it in a mantle of blessing.

MANDRAKE (MANDRAGORA OFFICINARUM)

Highly poisonous!

A small perennial herb that grows six inches in height, the flowers grow in clusters of pale white to purple and are bell-shaped. The most famous feature of a mandrake is the root. The root has an odd resemblance to the lower parts of a human body.

Lore

Associated with Aphrodite by the ancient Greeks, the mandrake was called the "love apple." However, due to its association with witchcraft, I associate it with the goddess Hekate and the witch goddess Circe.

Magical Use

There are a wide variety of uses for mandrake, and in the ways of Strix Craft it is used as a powerful familiar to trap souls or house spirits. As such, the root is used as a cage, and only when slicing it open to release the spirit does it "shriek." It is also an ingredient in the famed witches' ointment that the Strix used.

MARJORAM (ORIGANUM MAJORANA)

Marjoram is a tender evergreen shrub that grows to 80 cm (32 in.). It has tubular pink or white flowers and grows in the sunlight or light shade; the plant flowers in the summer (so be sure to bring it inside in the winter).

Lore

It has culinary uses to flavor stews, fish, or soups. The oil is also used in liqueurs and soaps. Marjoram is popular at weddings, where it is woven into a wreath for the newlyweds. It is used in healing treatments for insomnia and bronchial issues. Using the oil in massage therapy is wonderful. Due to its uses to flavor and bless love, the Romans said it was sacred to the goddess Venus. Ancient Greeks planted it on graves to nourish the beloved dead.

Magical Use

It can be used in ancestral veneration by placing some on your ancestral shrine to help nourish the beloved dead. Carrying it on your person is said to protect against lightning.

MARSHMALLOW (ALTHAEA OFFICINALIS)

The marshmallow plant grows to 4 ft. (1.2 m) and has pale lilac flowers growing on the stem. The foliage is gray-green with soft, hairy leaves. They naturally occur near streams and in marshes.

Lore

Marshmallow was used in funerary works, and was ingested as a preventative to disease. As a result of its chthonic connections and its growth near water or the marshes, it is sacred to Dionysus Limnais (Dionysus of the Marshes, where he had an oracle located).

Magical Use

A chthonic plant, it can be planted to ward off spirits of disease. It is also used in rituals to Dionysus. The flowers can be laid out in a circle or can be used to decorate a thyrsus (Dionysian wand), to invoke his spirit.

MINT (MENTHA)

Mint is a very large family of perennials.

Lore

Minthe, a river naiad of the underworld river Cocytus, was in love with Hades and shared his bed. But when Hades fell in love with the young Kore, Minthe was cast aside and wailed her grief, entering into hubris when she declared that she was even more lovely than Kore/Persephone. As a result, Demeter trampled upon the nymph, and she grew into the mint plant.

Magical Use

Sacred to Hades and Demeter, a drink mixed with barley and water was said to be sacred for those about to enter the underworld during the Eleusinian mysteries. Keep mint away from shrines sacred to Persephone, as she was not too keen on this nymph. Nonetheless, mint can be used to break love spells. Simply give the afflicted individual a cup of mint tea (peppermint) to break the spell.

MUGWORT (ARTEMISIA VULGARIS)
Potentially toxic!

Mugwort is a perennial herb that grows six feet high and has aromatic, fine, silvery foliage. The flowers are small and reddish-brown. It is a member of the wormwood family, and is sacred to the goddess Artemis.

Lore

The herb is sacred to Artemis in her guise as the mountain maiden who hunts.

Magical Use

Make an infusion and use it to anoint scrying tools such as the Eye of Nyx (a black mirror). In fertility spells, place a sprig of mugwort under the bed where the mother sleeps so that the spirit can easily help the labor. In this sense of midwifery it is sacred to both Hekate and Artemis.

PATCHOULI *(POGOSTEMON CABLIN)*

This plant grows well in warm climates, but does not do well in direct sunlight. It is a bushy herb that grows about 2.5 ft (75 cm) tall, with pink-white flowers.

Lore

Patchouli is a well-rounded herb, being used in cooking and incense making, and is used as an insect repellant.

Magical Use

Anoint yourself to awaken sexual energy. This herb may be used in any rituals where sex magic is to be done.

ROSE *(ROSA)*

A perennial shrub that can grow up to three feet in height (1 m). It has dark, wrinkled leaves and cupped, single pink or red flowers.

Lore

In Greek myth, there was a nymph by the name of Chloris who was the wife of Zephyrus the West Wind. She loved flowers and it was due to her that they blossomed and flourished. She lived in the Isles of the Blessed, islands far to the west. She one day came upon the lifeless body of an unnamed nymph. Stricken with grief, Chloris took her and transformed her into a flower. Aphrodite blessed the flower with beauty; Dionysus, with nectar. The Three Graces bestowed charm, joy, and splendor. Thus was born the immortal rose.

Magical Use

Sacred to the goddess Aphrodite, dried roses are used to perfume a home and welcome good spirits in. The ultimate flower of love, the rose is used in love spells to attract lovers. However, the thorns are used to make someone suffer until they fall in love with the sender. Thorns are used to prick the fingers and the blood is given as an offering to familiar spirits.

ROSEMARY (ROSMARINUS OFFICINALIS)

A perennial shrub growing about six feet in height. The leaves are short, stiff, and look like needles.

Lore

Rosemary is sacred to the goddess of memory—Mnemosyne—and scholars wore chaplets of rosemary on their heads to aid in memory recall.

Magical Use

One may burn some and place it in water to make holy water. Crowns of rosemary can be made to bless and heal someone suffering from depression. To break a hex, make a tea of the rosemary and also burn some in your hearth. Feeding a spirit of rosemary and keeping it at your front door will serve as a powerful ward.

Rue *(Ruta graveolens)*
Highly toxic!

Physical contact with rue can lead to blisters, and so gloves and protective clothing should always be worn when handling this plant. Rue grows to a height of three feet with small yellow-green flowers. The leaves are blue-green, waxy looking, and very divided with many lobes. The leaves are aromatic.

Lore

The ancient Greeks considered rue to be a plant that can uncross hexes, negate any magical workings, and serve as an antidote to poison.

Magical Use

To hex someone with an illness, take the kolossos (poppet) and pin rue on the "body" beneath the dark of the moon. Alternatively, using this herb by planting some near your door or windows is perfect for warding. Wear a dried sprig on your person to negate magical attacks and break curses.

Wormwood *(Artemisia absinthium)*

Wormwood is a perennial herb with fibrous roots. It grows to a height of just under 4 ft. (1.2 m), with a rigid stem that is grooved and silvery-green. The flowers are a pale yellow. It is found naturally on hardy ground such as rocky slopes and the edges of fields and footpaths. It flowers from early summer to early autumn, and needs plenty of sun.

Lore

This bitter herb is used in flavoring wines, mead, and beer, but it is more famous for being the main ingredient in absinthe. A patron herb of herbalists and wortcunners, Artemis gave the wise centaur Chiron this herb for healing.

Magical Use

This herb is sacred to the goddess Artemis and the goddess Isis. The stalks can be used to make a circlet, and provide excellent protection from wild spirits. Using it as a flower essence, it is used in incubation, divination, and dream work.

SUMMARY

Herbs and plants are a fascinating subject. There is so much depth, and what I have presented here is a sampling of how these are used by the Strix in modern times. You'll have noticed that a couple of plants have been listed as ingredients in the famed witches' ointments. Unfortunately, I will not be able to give out the exact recipe in this book. It is potentially deadly, and the wrong mix on a tired day could kill you. There are substitutions, however. These are just as potent even if they don't contain the exact chemical makeup that the forbidden herbs would. We will explore the witches' ointment further in later chapters.

CHAPTER 6

DEITIES AND SPIRITS

People tend to think of ancient Greece as a monolith of myth—that is, that all gods were worshiped together all of the time by everyone. This is simply not the case. Instead of Greek religion, it would be more accurate to say there were many Greek religions. Mystery cults, temples, hearths, and other places had their own manifestations of deities and spirits as well as their origin myths. For example, in the city-state of Lokri in Southern Italy, Persephone and Aphrodite were said to have an annual mystery cult that involved the death and resurrection of a figure named Adonis. Here Persephone is simply the queen of the underworld and not Kore, the maiden daughter of the earth goddess Demeter as celebrated in the Eleusinian mysteries. In Kypria, the birthplace of Aphrodite, she had a warlike aspect, something absent in the classical myths of ancient Athens. Bearing this in mind, the deities and spirits of the Strix are unique to the modern practice of Strix Craft and this cultus. We have our own myths and language. Some of these interpretations may surprise you, but they are specific nonetheless.

Deities usually have two natures: *ouranic* (that is, a "sky" or upperworld deity), and *chthonic* (that is, an "earth" or underworld deity). In addition to Hekate, who is but one who transcends both the ouranic and chthonic categories, other deities are actively worshiped by the Strix. Below, I present them to you. The inclusion of some in our pantheon may surprise you, as does their story. Again, there were multiple manifestations of Greek religion, and multiple pantheon hierarchies depending on many factors. For myself, I worship deities such as Dionysus, Hekate, Pan, Pasiphaë, Circe, Hermes, Zeus, and Apollo. Strix are polytheistic, and we open ourselves up to various deities and spirits however they may call to us.

Before we explore the list of deities, I would like to present the story of creation and the cosmos. Journey with me as we start at the beginning…

In the lap of Erebos arose Nyx, the first mother, god herself. She awoke (or reawakened?) and traveled the cosmos. At the very end she came upon the curved black mirror of space. Here she saw herself: the first awakening. She fell in love with the complete wholeness of what she was seeing: the first desire. She began to masturbate and lo! Upon orgasm all came into being that was primordial. And the firstborn were the sacred twins Eros and Thanatos: Desire and Death. They were born in sexual embrace: now male, now female, now neither, now both. And Eros sits in the heavens playing his flute whereby the sacred music of the heavens whirls. Thanatos dances about the heavens, his blade slicing the music where life is.

Nyx desired to know herself again, to find her way back to the wholeness she once knew. In order to do so, she transformed herself and manifested into the sea of the cosmos. Evolution is the story of her love, her desire for gnosis. In the order of evolution came the first primordials, or first born. They are the primal beings whose power and influence are cosmic. Then came the Titans. The Titans are the earliest gods who were worshiped before the rise of

the gods. They are connected to the olden path of pre-Greek sha-
manism; beings covering themselves in gypsum clay echoing an
old initiatory ritual.[60] Finally, we have the gods themselves—the
Theoi.

The list below is not exhaustive. It only covers major figures
that play a role in the creation mythos, the rise of the Titans,
and the stories of the gods. There are countless spirits and other
beings, but they are not named because there are too many.

THE PRIMORDIALS

Nyx

Nyx, or "Night," is the first mother. She is the star goddess: innu-
merable and the progenitor of all gods, spirits, and beings in the
cosmos. Her milk feeds the beings of the galaxies and can be seen
by us when we view the Milky Way. Her orgasm is what gave birth
to all of creation. She is imaged as a starry veiled goddess with
dark skin and with prominent breasts and an open vulva. She is
crowned with brilliant blue stars, fiery and alive.

There is no shrine or altar that can be dedicated to her, as she
is a part of all. She is within and without all that exists: firstborn,
Titan, god, nymph, animal, and human. That being said, if you
would like to represent her, black tourmaline or obsidian are perfect. Their darkness is reflective of the night, which is the meaning
of Nyx's name.

Erebos

The lap of darkness in the depths of the world, Erebos is the
manifestation of the underworld and also the dark energy of our
space-time continuum. He is the primordial consort and cosmic

---

60. Harrison, 491–494.

potential for Nyx. Like her, Erebos has no sacred connection to any particular object. He exists in all.

Eros and Thanatos

The firstborn sacred twins, born in sexual embrace, are the embodiment of desire and death. Each one has a purpose. Eros sits upon a blue lotus in the center of the cosmos playing his flute, which harmonizes and brings together the energy and matter of life. He also will ejaculate sperm that creates fertility in the great expanse of space. Thanatos whirls about Eros with his blade, cutting away what does not serve.

Eros is envisioned as a blue childlike deity who plays his flute while sitting upon a blue lotus. He is crowned with peacock feathers. Eros enjoys offerings of grapes, apples, chocolate, roses, or lotuses. You may depict him as a simple stone, which was his depiction in Thespiae,[61] and his sacred stone is the lapis lazuli.

Thanatos is envisioned as a purple child-like deity who whirls about Eros in a circle dance while wielding a blade. He is crowned with black feathers and carries a necklace of skulls. His offerings include snakeskins, white lilies, poppies, or bones ethically gleaned from certain animals. Be sure to check the laws in your state as to what can be harvested and what cannot. His metal is iron, particularly black iron.

Ourania

Ourania is born from a mixture of the juices from Nyx and star matter. She arose from the cosmic foam, and with a spindle in hand began to weave the record of creation itself. She takes the music of Eros and threads it into the formation of what is and what shall be.

---

61. Pausanias, 9.27.1

She was known by various names, but her better-known epithet was that of Ananke, or necessity.

She is envisioned as a woman surrounded by white stars, rising from the depths of the blackness of space. Her crown is nebulous. She is dark, reflecting her parentage of Nyx and Erebos.

Offerings to her include roses and sea or lake water (ideally captured under a starry night). Her sacred stone is the blue sapphire.

Hekate

In our teachings of O(r)phic Strix,[62] Nyx manifested herself in all of these ways: every god and spirit is a manifestation of her essence. But there needed to be a deity of balance, one born of Nyx who could also take over some of her functions and skills. So, Nyx reached deep inside and touched her heart: the primordial heart pounding with the blood of a hundred thousand stars. She split the heart, and from the destruction came the goddess Hekate. She was the azure rose, the primordial heart. After she was born, Hekate slashed her tongue and from the drops that landed in Thessaly grew poisonous plants that nurtured the first Strix. Nyx gave over to Hekate the rulership of our world's three realms of land, sea, and sky. Hekate is the divine mother of all of the Strix, and if you have ever felt a calling, then you are one of hers. Strix are guided to remember their path, their ways, and their traditions. We are the torches of the great mother and the owls that screech beneath the moon as we draw it down.

---

62. There is a particular tradition of Strix Craft known as the Ophic Strix, named so because the initiates are known to honor the serpent (*Agathosdaimon*). However, some have also named it the Orphic Strix in honor of the Orphic mysteries that influenced the Dionysian teachings within the tradition. Either is fine.

Hekate is envisioned as a triple goddess with three faces and six arms, with the lower half of her body a serpent. Her left face is that of a lion, her middle face a maiden, and her right face is a black mare. Each hand holds something significant: a pantera (offering bowl), a scourge, a dagger, a cord, and two torches, one with blue flame and the other with red flame. A serpent wraps around her body.

Sacred to Hekate are black dogs, black chickens, black rams, snowflake obsidians, myrrh, owls, serpents, polecats, red mullet fish, yew trees, willow trees, cypress trees, poisonous plants, onions, eggs, garlic, and leeks.

Graiai

From the spindle of Ananke and the first drops of blood upon Thessaly were born the Graiai, the ancient mothers of the Strix. They were born with gray hair, and are named Pemphredo, Enyo, and Deino. They are guardians who live beyond the fringes of this world bordering the underworld at the river Styx, and they share between them one eye and one tooth. They are envisioned as three maidens with long gray hair, appearing to the uninitiated as terrible old hags. The claws on their hands are black with Stygian iron.

Sacred to the Graiai are onyx and black kyanite. myrrh, poisonous plants, and scrying activities.

Gorgons

They are the three gray-eyed sisters who originally came to life as masks created by Hekate to stand at the three-way crossroads. The Gorgons are crowned with serpents, and have brass wings, boar tusks, and bronze nails. They are semidivine beings, and only one—Medusa—was mortal. They dwelt in the far reaches of night and were also sea goddesses in their own right. The phase of the dark moon is also known as the *gorgoneion*, the time of the Gorgons and the underworld. Hekate rises with the mask and the dead follow in her train. Persephone, too, had the Gorgons guard the entrances to the underworld, turning mortals into stone as a punishment for trespassing into her territory. For this Persephone was also called the iron queen.

Offerings to the Gorgons include three masks depicting their faces, blue kyanite, and myrrh.

Ericapaios

Ericapaios is the light, the day, the other half of Nyx. He is her son and her complement, the bull-horned son of heaven. He is envisioned with black-blue skin and glittered in a thousand blue suns; his six golden wings shake the very cosmos. As a primordial of day, no known offerings or stones are specifically sacred to him. However, if you choose to represent him on your altar or shrine, then place a candle next to the obsidian you have for Nyx.

Metis

Metis is the wise one, the embodiment of good counsel and wisdom. It was she who helped Zeus plan the overthrow of Kronos. She made a potion that was given to Kronos, with the taste hidden by honey that she got from the bee nymph Melissa. Kronos vomited up his children. Later after the Titanomachy (the war between the Titans and the gods in Thessaly), a prophecy came forth that Metis would have a child that would supplant Zeus. To thwart the prophecy, he tricked Metis into turning into a house fly and swallowed her whole. Metis then became a part of Zeus, and Zeus thereafter was known as Zeus Metieta, or "Zeus of the wise counsel."

Metis is pictured as an old woman with white hair and dressed in a gold chiton. She holds a rolled-up scroll in her right hand. Sacred to her are tales that dispense wisdom, such as parables and fables.

THE TITANS

Ouranos

Ouranos was the firstborn ruler of the cosmic heavens. He is the son of Ericapaios and Nyx. By having duality reside within him, he became the first chief who lorded over the gods and spirits. Within the shadows of Erebos he came to Gaia, who bore him children (the first spirits).

He is envisioned as a mighty being crowned with a brass circlet. He elevates himself above Gaia, supporting himself on his arms and legs with a giant phallus. Sacred to him is brass.

Gaia

When the formation of our world began, Gaia was born. Ouranos looked lovingly upon her and came down and created the heavens that he might be near her. Gaia is the primordial green earth goddess, and mother of all. She had a prophecy from Nyx that another would come and take the place of Ouranos. As a result of this prophecy, Gaia created iron. She formed from her navel the Delphian Oracle, protected by the serpent known as Delphyne.

Gaia is imaged as a large woman, with large breasts and seated on a throne of stone. She is crowned with all manner of fruits and flowers, and veiled by a sheet decorated with bees. Her hair and body are forest green and black. Sacred to her are all manner of herbs, plants, and stones. If you would like a specific stone, I encourage you to get malachite and a Gaia stone. The latter is manufactured from the ash of Mount St. Helens, located in Washington State in the United States.

Thalassa

The sea goddess, firstborn of Ouranos and Gaia. Thalassa gave birth to various sea gods and spirits of the deep. She is the mother of the Horai. She was fertilized by the sperm of Eros and birthed a goddess with a mystery name who, when she went into the heavens, became Selene, the goddess of the moon.

Thalassa has a body made from the foam of the sea itself, her hair made of seaweed and crowned with the claws of crabs. She carries the oar of a ship in her hands and is accompanied by sharks. Sacred to her is azurite, seawater, seaweed, crab claws ethically harvested, and seashells. A beautiful offering is to clean up the beaches and the sea.

Pontos

The firstborn son of Thalassa, who also became her consort. He is the depths of the very sea itself, the mystery of the waters. He holds the secrets of all that travels within and without. His intercourse with Thalassa gave birth to all of the primordial creatures of the sea.

Pontos is also depicted as rising from the sea, covered in foam, his beard and hair made of seaweed, and he is accompanied by sharks.

Sacred to him are also azurite, seawater, seaweed, crab claws ethically harvested, and sand dollars. Like Thalassa, a beautiful offering is to clean up the beaches and the sea.

Themis

A daughter of Ouranos and Gaia, Themis became the goddess of the sight and the wide expanse of the sky. While Ouranos was the chief in the starry heavens made manifest, Themis was the sky itself of our world. She also created the luster of silver and gold. Themis is envisioned as a tall and radiant woman—one who cloaks the sky itself with radiant hues. Her hair is the wide spectrum of the rainbow colors. All things are sacred to her, and so there is no specific thing that can be attributed to her. However, an offering would be to keep the air clean and take care of her special animals—birds.

Kronos

The Titan who separated Ouranos from Gaia. He took the forged iron and slashed Ouranos so that he became a eunuch. He flung his testicles in the sea. From the blood in the sea foam was born Aphrodite Pandemos. To Kronos Nyx granted the rod of rulership from Ouranos. A prophecy from Gaia foretold that another would take his place. In an attempt to prevent the prophecy from coming to pass, he swallowed his children born of Rhea. Kronos is depicted as a giant holding in the left hand an hourglass and in the right hand a scythe whose blade is forged from iron. Iron blades and flints are sacred to Kronos, along with pyrite. Offerings include storax resin burned as incense.

Rhea

Born from the dark soil of Gaia, she became the second manifestation of the Earth Mother. Rhea is the titanic black Earth Mother and the wife of Kronos. Gaia spoke a prophecy to Kronos that a child of his would supplant him. Rhea heard the prophecy and ran to Crete, where she gave birth to Zeus on Mount Ida. It received the name "Ida" as an honorary from a similar mountain name in Anatolia (modern-day Turkey), the sacred sanctuary of Rhea. While Rhea gave birth, her hands grasped the soil, and the mountain gave forth ten spirits called the Daktyloi Idaioi, or the "Idean Fingers." The Daktyloi Idaioi assisted Rhea with the delivery of the child. Rhea then hid the youngest, Zeus, from his father. She gave Kronos a stone clothed in swaddling clothes, and Kronos swallowed it.

Rhea gave Zeus to the she-goat Amalthea to raise in Mount Aigaion in Crete. Here he was given milk by Amalthea and honey by the bee nymph Melissa. To hide the cries of the child, spirits known as the Korybantes clashed their shields with their spears in a war dance surrounding the cave. Since Kronos was the Titan who ruled the three realms of land, sea, and sky, Amalthea and Melissa raised a golden cradle hung on a tree, suspended between the realms. Zeus also played with a golden ball, a sign that he would be a future ruler of the world.

Rhea is pictured as a mother of the mysteries. Her spirits, the Daktyloi, continued to serve as magicians and blacksmiths. She is seated in a throne flanked by lions, raising a tympanon, or hand drum, in her left hand. She is crowned and wearing a red chiton. Her offerings include pine, frankincense, roses, honey mead, sex, flutes, drums, and rattles.

Selene

The secret goddess of the primordial seas who was elevated to become the moon. She is the keeper of time, the mistress of the psyche, and the goddess of our world's night. Selene is envisioned as a stately woman wearing a silver dress and crowned with seven stars. Her feet are the color of the deep blue sea, and she radiates brilliance. Sacred to her are white bulls, white horses (in particular mares), white rams, hares, jasmine, moonstones, selenite, and white roses. Offerings in the past included sacrifices of the aforementioned creatures. In modern times I encourage you to offer jasmine incense, white flowers (roses are best), and white rice.

Helios

He is the great sun. He travels across the heavens on his horse-drawn chariot. Helios has a golden body with brass armor, shoes, bracelets, and crown. From his crown proceed seven rays. Over the armor is a purple cloak. He holds in the left hand a golden whip (to steer his horses), and in his right hand a golden sword. Sacred to him are carnelian, sunstone, citrine, the heliotrope, and frankincense.

The Horai

When seasons began, the evolution of plants started. The Horai were born and they governed the rotation of the stars as signals of the seasons. As a result, three sisters were born: Auxo, Thallo, and Karpos. Each one influences various tides and times of the plants, the elders of our world.

Auxo is clothed in a light green dress and is crowned with springtime flowers.

Thallo is clothed in a dark green dress and is crowned in herbal flowers, while dark roots form her feet.

Karpos is clothed in a crimson dress and is crowned with a circlet from which hangs tiny apples, small pomegranates, and tiny pears.

Pan the Elder

When the first primordial animals came onto land, thus was born Pangenitor, the "all-giver." And when predators took their prey, he was Panphage, or "all-devourer." Pan is both predator and prey; the all of nature. He is the red king whose mysteries lie in the deep places of the land: the forests, mountains, valleys, groves, and such.

Pan is perhaps the best known of the Ancient Ones. Sacred to him are rams, deer, and pines. Burn pine incense and musk incense to him.

Chiron

The wisest and most just of all the centaurs. Chiron's home was on Mount Pelion, located in southeast Thessaly. His father is Kronos and his mother is an Oceanid (a spirit of the sea) whose name is Philyra. Chiron is known as the first healer; he taught the arts of medicine, surgery, and the knowledge of herbs for various ailments. He mentored heroes such as Jason, Asklepios, and Achilles. He was abandoned at birth for being a monstrosity, and instead was raised by Apollo. Apollo taught Chiron the medical arts, prophecy, archery and other sports, and music.

Chiron was an immortal being. Heracles carried arrows dipped in the blood of the Hydra, which made them poisonous. One night, Heracles went to a hall and was entertained by another wise centaur by the name of Pholus. Having a jar of wine entrusted to him by the god Dionysus, Heracles had the jar opened for hospitality's sake. However, the wine enraged the other centaurs, and a fight ensued. Heracles shot them with his poison arrows, but then accidentally shot one into Chiron. Chiron suffered with unbearable pain, unable to heal himself and yet unable to die. Zeus pitied Chiron's fate and took his immortality, placing him in the stars as the constellation Sagittarius.

Chiron is a centaur pictured with the head, torso, and arms of a man and the body of a horse. He holds a healer's bag. If you are in a medical profession, Chiron is a perfect patron and spiritual mentor.

Mnemosyne

Mnemosyne is memory itself. It is important to understand that some of the Titans were actually manifestations of early characteristics. With the first memory ever in this world was born Mnemosyne. She continues to live on in our lives and the lives of our world. She also works in the Titans, the gods, and the spirits. A powerful Titan, she holds all of the memories of this world ever in the mental plane.

Mnemosyne is pictured as a middle-aged woman who holds a mirror in her left hand and a small book in her right. The book is open. Things that help to preserve memories—such as photos, journals, or storytelling—are sacred to her. It does not matter whether the memories are positive or negative; she is the manifestation of all.

Maia

The earth nymph / Titan Maia never became part of the sacred assemblies of either Titans or Olympians. Rather, she was a lover of Zeus later after the triumph of the Olympians. Prior to this she merely dwelt in the dark caves of Arcadia. When Zeus came to her, it was at night. In her sacred grove located at Mount Cyllene, she became pregnant with Hermes. Maia later mentored Artemis and became the original nursemaid for Artemis and her brother Apollo. In fact, her name means "midwife."

Sacred to Maia are midwife professions, nursing, child-rearing, adoption (Maia was given a boy by the name of Arcas to be raised after his mother was killed), and sandalwood incense.

Eurynome

Eurynome is a Titan of the wide expanse of the land, water meadows, and pastures. She had a sanctuary temple in Arcadia that was only opened once a year. Her statue depicted a woman with the tail of a fish. She was a lover of Kronos and bore him Aphrodite. Sacred to her are professions such as cattle herding, farming, gardening, and keeping the land and meadows clean.

Aphrodite

Kronos castrated Ouranos when the latter used the iron sickle against the former. Ouranos retreated to the heavens and remained there; his genitals were thrown into the sea. Eventually, sea foam gathered around the penis and from this white and immortal material sprang up Aphrodite. She dwelt in the sea for some time and had a lover named Nerites. He impregnated her. When it was time for her to leave and she came ashore, she gave birth to two spirits: Himeros (sexual desire) and Pothos (sexual yearning). Her sons would henceforth accompany the goddess wherever she went. She desired for Nerites to follow along, but he refused, preferring to remain with his kin in the sea.

When she arose from the sea and came ashore to Cyprus, Aphrodite's feet caused grass and flowers to grow wherever she stepped. She was garlanded and crowned by the Horai. She was also gifted a golden girdle that enhanced her magics of love, beauty, and sex. Aphrodite can be a complex goddess, with many names and attributes. However, she has another aspect that is little known: Areia, or the war goddess. Areia is the name she took when she first felt the unquenchable loss of love. She wields armor, shield, and *labrys* or spear. Aphrodite is untamable.

She is pictured as a young woman who is every woman and yet none. Her iconography famously depicts her as rising from the sea in a cockle shell, surrounded by waves, the Horai, and the two spirits Himeros and Pothos. Doves and sea turtles are sacred to her. Offerings to her include mirrors, perfumes, makeup and beauty kits, sex, roses, frankincense and myrrh, myrtle, honey, wine, diamonds, rose quartz, small daggers, and the colors white, red, and pink.

THE GODS

Hestia

The daughter of Kronos and Gaia, Hestia is the firstborn goddess. She was the first to be swallowed by Kronos. When she was released, she took the hearth as her realm, and became chaste. In his *Theogonía*, Hesiod says of Hestia that she was the eldest daughter of the Titan-king Kronos. Hearing an oracle that his children would supplant him, Kronos swallowed all of his kids, with Hestia being the first victim. Zeus escaped punishment when his mother Rhea swapped the infant for a stone. Zeus was hidden away and when he came of age, he freed his siblings. They were all disgorged in reverse order. Because Hestia was the first victim, she was the last one freed. As a result, she is paradoxically the first and last daughter of Olympos.

In Homer's *Hymn to Aphrodite*, Hestia was wooed by both Poseidon and Apollo. All three divinities were worshiped together at Delphi, and rather than accepting any proposal of marriage, Hestia instead lay her hand atop the head of Zeus and vowed to be perpetually chaste. Zeus gave great honor to his sister and placed her as keeper of the hearth, and being the eldest has a share of every single portion of offering that is given to the Theoi. She was also venerated at Delphi where the Pythia were located. She "tended the Holy House of Apollo." [63]

Unlike the other Theoi, Hestia does not have great stories about battles or heroes. Not many myths are available aside from the *Hymn to Aphrodite*, *Hymn to Hestia*, and the *Theogonía*. Yet she was one of the most popular goddesses. Her name literally translates to "hearth." The hearth, the sacred center of a home, was her literal manifestation.

Hestia is pictured as a middle-aged woman with a white chiton and veil. She sits upon a throne with a simple wool cover. In her hands she cups a small flame. Sacred to her is the hearth—the home. Domestic duties, family raising, relationships, and any other activity that goes on in the home is sacred to her. She wants humans to have a positive impact on one another; arete and xenia are her sacred virtues (see Chapter 3).

Zeus

The son of Kronos and Rhea, Zeus is the storm god who brings the fruitful rains. He is a fertility god, virile and masculine. Zeus was born in Crete in Mount Ida and raised by the she-goat Amaltheia and bee nymph Melissa. When he was still a boy, he set out to free his brothers and sisters who were swallowed by Kronos (all but Poseidon, which will be explained later). Zeus hunted down Kronos and with cunning (Metis) he used a potion that was given to Kronos. The potion caused Kronos to vomit up his children. Afterward, Zeus and his siblings, together with other spirits, rose up against the greater Titans. Ancient stone spirits called the Hekatoncheires, and fire beings known as the Cyclops, joined Zeus and the Theoi in battle against the Titans. At the end of the ten-year

---

63. Homeric Hymn 24 to Hestia.

battle (a decisive Theoi victory, thanks to the Hekatoncheires, or "Hundred-armed Ones"), Kronos was rendered drunk with honey and relocated far to the west, to the Isles of the Blessed. Here he rules over a memory of the golden age when he ruled over Earth.

Zeus is pictured as a mature man with a beard that is dark and gray like storm clouds. He sits enthroned on a high seat carved with eagles and lightning, along with a mosaic depicting his victory. He wears a purple chiton, the color of royalty. He holds in his left hand a golden scepter and in his right hand is his lightning bolt, forged by the Cyclops. An eagle is perched on his throne.

Sacred to him are the stones azurite, blue quartz, royal plume jasper, beryl, and quartz, as well as frankincense and eagle feathers (note that in some countries, it is illegal to own eagle feathers; please check your local laws).

Demeter

The final form of Gaia-Rhea, Demeter is the yellow Earth Mother and, along with the early Olympian gods, was swallowed by her father Kronos. Demeter became the goddess who dispensed sacred law and taught humankind agriculture (hence her color yellow, for the wheat she taught humanity to plant and harvest).

Demeter is best known as the mother of Kore, who became known as Persephone in the story of her abduction by Hades (more on this later). Originally, however, Demeter was connected with the grain as the grain mother, and could shape-shift into a mare or an ear of corn. When her daughter Kore was abducted, Demeter searched the world for her. While doing so, she was pursued by her brother Poseidon. To hide from him, she turned herself into a mare and hid among a herd belonging to a ruler by the name of Onkios. Poseidon, sensing the trick, himself turned into a stallion and found her. They coupled and from this union a son and daughter were born named Arion (the black steed) and Despoine, a goddess who became a central figure in the Arcadian mysteries (the home of Pan the Younger).

After their intercourse, Demeter became wrathful and became known as the angry goddess, or Demeter Erinyes. Arion was the swiftest horse, and became owned at last by a goddess known as Adraste. Demeter is envisioned as a regal goddess with a gown depicting wheat. Her stony throne is decorated with the motif of her searching for Kore. She holds in her left hand a cornucopia and in her right an ear of wheat. In her guise of Erinyes, she wears a black veil. She is crowned with poppies. Sacred to Demeter are wheat, corn (maize), frankincense, poppies, the Virtues, flour, bread, fruit orchards, farming, motherhood, the cornucopia, geckos, serpents, and quartz.

Poseidon

The earth-shaker and the god of the wild storms, Poseidon is a shape-shifting sea deity whose domain is fraught with danger. Poseidon's lovers were many, both mortal and immortal, and he frequently found himself in the center of the heroic sagas such as the *Iliad* and the *Odyssey*. Poseidon was swallowed by Kronos but was later freed by Zeus. Casting lots, his domain became the vast ocean.

Poseidon was hidden by Rhea and given to the Telchines, a race of underworld master magicians who dwelt on the island of Rhodes. An ocean nymph by the name of Kapheira nursed Poseidon. Poseidon had many lovers, starting with a sea goddess named Halia. By her he had six sons and one daughter named Rhodes.

As Aphrodite Pandemos made her way from the sea to Cyprus, the sons of Poseidon prevented her. As a result, Aphrodite cursed them with madness, and they fell in love with their mother. For this Poseidon cursed them and they went into the land and became spirits in the east. I have already mentioned his liaison with the goddess Demeter. He did take a wife, Amphitrite of the golden spindle, who—after Poseidon married her—was finally able to lay claim to the sea itself. Animals such as bulls, panthers, lions, and tigers were sacred to Amphitrite and other sea spirits; Poseidon and Amphitrite modeled their marriage after Dionysus and Ariadne.

The Telchines gave Poseidon the trident, which became his master weapon. Gaia gifted him Delphi as a reward for his bravery. Sacred to him are aquamarine, chrysocolla, blue quartz, blue chalcedony, blue agate, sapphire, dolphins, horses, bulls, hippocampi, coral, pearls, and salt water. He is pictured as a mature man with a throne of coral, his trident in his right hand.

Hades

The brother of Zeus and Poseidon, Hades was gifted the helm of darkness and wielded a bident. He became the ruler of the underworld. In the early days, when humans died, they became shades roaming the Asphodel Fields. Hades asked Zeus for the hand of Kore in marriage, as was the custom in these times. Demeter refused but Zeus foresaw that Kore would be a great queen, and so gave his blessing and hid the deed from Demeter. Of the tale of Hades and Kore I shall tell next.

Hades was known as "Zeus Katachthonios," or "Subterranean Zeus." [64] Danaus in Aeschylus's *The Suppliants* speaks of "another Zeus." [65] Hades, in becoming the god of the underworld, also became the god of riches and wealth, as all metals, minerals, and gems belonged to him. People in ancient times feared him as they

---

64. Homer. *Iliad*, 9.4.57.

65. Aeschylus, *The Suppliants*, 231.

feared the dead. When giving a sacrifice or offerings to the underworld, people averted their gaze. Hades has a bad reputation, no thanks to Hollywood. However, he is a powerful god to call upon for wealth, for hauntings, and in times of transition when the living are about the die. He is the only god faithful to his wife, Persephone. In Sicily he was connected to the volcanic regions as Persephone was connected to the springs around them. The reasoning was that volcanoes were entrances to the underworld.[66]

Hades is pictured as a mature man in a black chiton. He sits upon a jewel-encrusted throne of skulls. He holds in his right hand a bident, and in his left he holds his helm of darkness, which radiates intense fear to all who come near it. All metals, jewels, and minerals are sacred to him, as are black rams, black roosters, and black bulls.

Kore

The daughter of Demeter and Zeus, the tale of Kore is a theme for many of the older mystery traditions throughout the Hellenic world. Kore was born to Demeter, the final form of the Earth Mother and the goddess of agriculture. She was hidden on the isle of Sicily, away from the squabbles and affairs of Olympus. Her companions were the Oceanids, the female spirits of the sea, along with Athena and Artemis. She picked flowers such as roses, crocuses, and hyacinths, and often went to a nearby spring, where she was called Kyane, the maiden of the watery springs, near modern-day Syracuse. Unbeknownst to Kore she was given in marriage to Hades, and when she went to the spring and sang a song of longing, suddenly the earth cracked open and from it came Hades. As the underworld takes all things and makes them invisible, so too did

66. Kingsley, *Ancient Philosophy, Mystery, and Magic*, 73.

the god of the underworld make Kore invisible. Her scream was heard by Helios and Hekate. Hades took her across the river Styx, the path of gods and humanity. Though Kore was surprised and afraid of the underworld, she viewed the throne and was eager to take her place there. Hades fed her his sacred food, the pomegranate, which grew only in the underworld. Knowing her fate, she said yes and acquiesced to the domain of the underworld, remaining there and bringing bright glory to the realm of the dead. She created the White Islands and the Realm of Paradise after she changed her name to Persephone.

I have seen Persephone sitting upon an ebony throne, with blue skin and veiled in black. She speaks almost in a telepathic sort of way. Sacred to her are pomegranates, apples, skulls, bones, basanite, and black opal.

Apollo

The youthful god of light, music, prophecy, and the arts. Apollo was the son of Zeus and the Night goddess Nyx. She came to Zeus in the form of a dark-gowned goddess calling herself Leto, which spoke of her origins. Apollo is bisexual, having had numerous lovers, both men and women. He gifted Helios with horses and a chariot, and as a result Helios gave to Apollo a sacred golden cup that Helios had been using to ride in.

Apollo was born of the goddess Leto, sister to Asteria, a "star goddess." Keep in mind that the influences of the Hellenic deities often overlap, and this is fine, as polytheism demonstrates that there are many that carry the function of certain deities and spirits. Whether Asteria and Leto were forms of Nyx—evolved beings who came forth and were themselves manifestations of first mother, Nyx—is unknown.

Apollo was born on the Isle of Delos, an island that was said to be a manifestation of Asteria herself (she, it was said, turned herself into a stone to avoid Zeus and grew into a mighty island that would be a sacred home dedicated to the god). Apollo was born of Leto as the second born of a set of twins, Artemis being the first born. When Artemis was born, she became midwife to her mother and helped deliver her brother. Immediately upon his birth, the Isle of Delos was ringed with golden leaves and sunlight.

Apollo wandered about, seeking revenge for his mother's troubles. She was threatened by many things as she traveled pregnant. One of the fiercest contenders was the serpent dragon Python, whose body encircled a laurel tree at Delphi. Poseidon had placed the creature there as a warning, for a sacred spring was there that, upon drinking, gave to the person the power to prophesy.

Apollo slew Python, Python's body decayed, and its stench came up from the crevices in the land. As a reward, Gaia took Delphi and gave it to Apollo for his bravery. Apollo then searched far and wide for priests; in the form of a dolphin he went into the sea and took a boat filled with Cretans. Here he initiated them, and took them to Delphi. Bee nymphs helped build the temple that housed the Omphalos (a conical stone that was said to be at the center of the known world).

Apollo is pictured as a beautiful young man whose head is crowned with the rays of the sun. He has golden hair and blue eyes, and is shown strumming a lyre with seven strings, each string for the music of the Seven Worlds. Thus he keeps the worlds in harmony with song, a pattern discovered by many peoples including the Order of the Pythagoreans. Sacred to him are swans, amber, dolphins, hyacinths, irises, and snakes.

Ares

The son of Zeus and Demeter, Ares was born to be strife unleashed. He was conceived when Demeter hid from Zeus's eyes, only to be found and mated. Her anger manifested into Ares, who fell in love with Aphrodite. From their union was born Harmonia. In the tale of Aphrodite, I believe that she was able to have an intimate union with both Ares and Hephaestus. Ares taught Aphrodite war, and so she became known as Areia. Of Areia I will explain more in the tale of Dionysus.

Ares is the unbridled god of war, battle, and civil disturbance. But, when given offerings and prayers, he was also the god who would avert war and grant peace and order in society. Ares, after all, began as an agricultural deity and spurred people to protect themselves from invasion (conversely, he is also the battle cry of the invading troops). As a god of the city, riots, rebellions, and civil disobedience are within his realm. He is the patron of the police. He helps to uphold divine and civil order, known as *Themis*. He embodies both anger and anger management.

He is a defender of women, because his daughter Alcippe was raped by a man known as Halirrhothius, a son of Poseidon. Ares then hunted down the man and killed him. Poseidon demanded a trial, and the gods acquitted Ares. He is also patron of the Amazon warrior women.

He is pictured as a young man, strong and muscular. He is armed with bronze armor, a sword (*xiphos*) at his side, and sports a javelin with a shield. Sacred to Ares are boars, civil disobedience, war, and defending women.

Artemis

The daughter of Zeus and Leto, Artemis is the twin sister of Apollo and the firstborn one. She is a chaste goddess who was called Kourotrophos, the "nursemaid," because she helped her mother birth Apollo. Artemis used the power of Selene to find the wild beasts of the night. She is asexual, not having romantic feelings for either men or women, preferring her solitude (but for the nymphs) and her love of hunting.

Artemis hides within the mountains and wilds. She is accompanied by nymphs of the mountains, bees, and forests. She who is the mistress of the animals is both predator and prey; as a result, she can have contradictory personalities. But it is all Artemis. In the city-state of Sparta young girls participated in a procession to honor Artemis, bringing her offerings and gifts. They wore bear masks to symbolize Artemis's ancient association with motherhood, mountains, and incubation. The Dance of the Bears was especially important. For young boys, however, the event was bloody: they were tied to a whipping post, and they would be flogged until the altar was filled with their blood.

Artemis is pictured as a young woman in a hunting tunic with a bow and arrow. By her side is a stag, one of her sacred animals. She shimmers in silver. Sacred to her are stags, bears, lionesses, the scourge, music, dance, and chastity. I believe that Artemis is a patron of asexual people in particular.

Hermes

The son of Zeus and Maia, Hermes is the trickster god of thieves, deception, and gambling. But he is also the god of the gym, boys, humanity in general (he is known as our friend), jobs, success, and money. As a messenger of the gods, he is also a psychopomp. Hermes is such a shape-shifting god that it is difficult to pin him down to one manifestation. He is many, yet one.

Hermes was born in a dark cave in Arcadia where his mother, Maia, dwelt. He was born at dawn on the fourth day after the new moon. Soon after his birth, he strayed out of his cradle and found a tortoise. Separating it from its shell, Hermes took the shell and fastened into it two pipe reeds. Between them he attached seven strings made from a sheep's guts. He immediately began to sing. Afterward, he placed the lyre into the cradle and made his way looking for meat, hiding in the dark as thieves are wont to do.

He came upon Apollo's sacred cattle, and took fifty of them. He had them walk backward to deceive Apollo. As he walked, he came upon an old man and told him he would prosper as long as he kept the secret of Hermes stealing the cattle. After butchering a couple of cattle, he crept back into his cradle. The next morning, Apollo went in search of the thief, sensing it was Hermes. When he found the babe, Hermes of course denied everything. But, after a little coaxing (and some threats), Hermes at last led Apollo back to his cattle. After much quarreling and even getting Zeus involved—who laughed at the whole thing and said they should reconcile—Hermes restored the cattle. He then played the lyre, and Apollo was pleased at the sound. In exchange for the lyre, Apollo gifted Hermes several things, including a three-leafed staff that bestowed wealth, a shepherd's crook, and the position of a psychopomp. Apollo previously held this office.

Hermes is seen as a young man with the wide-brimmed hat of a messenger. He has winged sandals, and he can change out his staffs depending on what he is doing. A crafty but loyal friend, Hermes is a wonderful person to turn to for nearly everything. All stones, colors, and animals are sacred to him.

Pan the Younger

The horned son of Hermes and a nymph, Pan was abandoned at birth because of his goatish looks. He was reared by Hermes, who taught young Pan masturbation. Pan in turn taught all of the shepherd boys and the Paniskoi (the satyrs) this skill as well. He is a god of the wilds and oftentimes is seen—along with Hermes and Príapus—in the entourage of Dionysus.

He is depicted as a being with the lower legs, face, and horns of a ram, and the body and arms of a man and having pointed ears. Sometimes his face is that of a man with the beard of a goat. He has an erect phallus. He is a shepherd who wanders the wilderness and the realms of the wild are his. He plays upon panpipes, luring potential lovers away from their comfort into his realm. At night he plays his panpipes and the nymphs dance in a circle, celebrating beneath the moon. Sacred to him are sex, poetry, panpipes (or wind instruments in general), and pine.

Príapus

The son of Dionysus and Aphrodite, Príapus is a dwarflike being with an enormous phallus. As a rustic and fertility god, Príapus became a tutor to the young Ares and his phallus was adopted as a symbol against the Evil Eye.

Some identified Priapus as the same as Hermaphroditus, the hermaphrodite offspring of Hermes and Aphrodite. This may also be a possibility. However, I choose to relegate his parentage to Dionysus and Aphrodite instead, since Dionysus has links to a cult of the phallus.

Dionysus

Dionysus is a most enigmatic deity, but he is nonetheless highly important in Strix Craft. Dionysus was the child of Hades and Persephone. As mentioned earlier, Hades was also known as Zeus Katachthonios (Zeus of the underworld). It is this modern confusion of "Zeus" that made some storytellers say it was Olympian Zeus who shape-shifted into a serpent and lay with Persephone. But such is not the case in our stories. In our tales, Dionysus is the child of the underworld, and at his birth he was born with bull horns in his hair and wielding serpents. As he grew into a young boy, he was in a cave where he played with various toys: dice, ball, top, golden apples, bull-roarer, and wool. Seven giants approached the cave and they painted themselves in white chalk. They leaped upon the young Dionysus and immediately he began to shape-shift into various forms attempting to escape. Finally, he turned into a bull, and as a bull he was ripped apart, each piece empowering and creating one of the Seven Worlds. Only his heart remained. As the giants began to eat the raw flesh, the goddess Areia approached, took her labrys, and began to slash the giants. She was blood-thirsty, and finally took the head of the bull and placed it upon her head as her naked body dripped with blood and sweat. The heart was given to Zeus, who placed it in the belly of Semele. When Semele was tricked into seeing Zeus's immortal form, Semele died and the infant heart was sewn into the thigh of Zeus. Here he grew, and was born of the heavenly god. He descended to the land and began to teach men the art of viniculture and the mysteries of immortality. He declared his godhood among the people and those who did not believe him or who mocked him were driven mad. He descended to the underworld finally to reunite with his parents, becoming the lord of the underworld.

For initiates into the mysteries, Dionysus claims them as his own, and initiates are guided to remember their journey through time as members of the ancient cults dedicated to the gods. He promises them a place in the afterlife, and initiates are encouraged to approach his mother Persephone and speak a series of passwords that allow them to navigate the underworld in their favor.

For example, Heraclitus—a pre-Socratic philosopher in the same school as Empedocles and Parmenides—in his fragments writes, "There awaits men after death what they neither hope nor think. And those that are there shall arise and become guardians of the living and the dead. Night-roamers, Magians, bacchanals, revelers in wine, the initiated … For were it not Dionysus to who they institute a procession and sing songs in honor of the pudenda, it would be the most shameful action. But Dionysus, in whose honor they rave in bacchio frenzy, and Hades are the same."[67] This reverses the gloomy view of the afterlife that awaits most people who aren't part of the cult; that is, the god of the underworld who is oft feared is simultaneously the god of liberation: death, life, and rebirth.

Dionysus is pictured as a young adolescent male with long, dark hair, holding a thyrsus in his right hand, and a bowl overflowing with grapes in the other. He is dressed in fawnskins and crowned with bull horns. Sacred to him are amethyst, leopards, panthers, tigers, grapes, wine (he is said to have invented it), serpents, bulls, honey, and mead. His toys are also holy, being enigmatic symbols that represent him in his various aspects.

---

67. Heraclitus, Fragment CXXII–CXXVI, 101.

SUMMARY

In this chapter we have explored the various deities and spirits of the Strix. To be sure, there are countless spirits more, for Greek religion is multiple and polytheistic. Many spirits exist throughout our world, some named, some not named. I say this to encourage you to understand that one does not need to worship all of the gods and spirits that exist, because that would be impossible.

Instead, reach out to the ones who do call to you. This is especially important—in being selective—when it comes to space, your altars, and your shrines. As mentioned before, some people just do not have the space for multiple altars and shrines, and so many are combined into a single space. That is fine.

The Hellenic deities and spirits are not jealous of one another. They will share space. Myths are not literal scriptures, but rather the songs and stories of our ancestors in which we find out about the cosmos and our place in it. Oftentimes contradictions exist, and that's okay. For example, Zeus in one area might be seen as the god of all, while in another area this is a goddess such as Rhea or Demeter. Neither are contradictory, but rely on the perceptions of the cultural lens that formulates those songs.

With this in mind, it is up to you to use the stories herein and launch yourself into a wider world of spiritual exploration. Now let us venture into the realm of magic, where we petition and make things happen.

CHAPTER 7
ALTARS AND SHRINES

Boundaries between the Divine and the mundane were readily understood in ancient Greece. Sacred space was marked off by boundary markers. An area was cut off (*temnein*) from the landscape. Such boundary markers might have been a pit, stones, a grove of trees, or wooden walls. Whatever it was, the boundary made known to all that passing the entrance of the precinct meant that you are NOW in sacred space. The territory no longer belonged to your world; it was the realm of the gods and the spirits of the place.

Now, cutting off a parcel of land for something holy may be confusing at first. Many Neopagans and witches view the entire world as one hallowed ecosystem: Gaia. It's true, too; Gaia is sacred. Every tree, stone, bug, person, and animal is blessed. But it's about focus. The ancient Greeks wanted to let each spirit and god know that the people were paying attention to them. It is a polytheistic system, where everyone has the opportunity to be the focus of veneration and worship. Demarcating sacred space wasn't about de-hallowing the surrounding area; the marked space was about giving a deity a home. In this way, an ancient Greek altar also functioned the same as a shrine.

An altar is a workplace. It is usually a flat table—round, square, or rectangular—upon which items are placed that are sacred (although other altar types exist). In short, you're actively engaged and working. It can be thought of as a tool in and of itself, helping us to focus our magic. A shrine, on the other hand, is a "house" for a deity and/or spirit. Items sacred to the deity are placed here, and the image or icon is the central focal point. It's about them, not us. The altar focuses on us and our energy, the shrine on them and their energy.

In the sacred (*hieron*) is where we become humbled before deity. Many today in the Neopagan and witchcraft communities eschew the idea of humility. To them it smacks of the pulpit, wherein we grovel before an omnipotent deity ready to chastise us for the slightest infraction and send us to everlasting torment. We beg and plead with this god to answer our prayers. That's not humility. That's humiliation. There's a difference.

Our gods are not omnipotent, omnipresent, omnibenevolent, or omniscient. They are limited. They don't see or know everything. Some know more than others (the Fates know more than Zeus, for example). Others challenge the roles that their fellow deities play (Aphrodite halts Hekate from interfering with Medea). But whatever the case, they are still limited in scope and breadth. Yet in that limitation, they are also immortal.

For sacred space, let's begin in your home. Decide where you want a small setup. It can be outdoors under a tree (preferably on your property). It can be an area where you hike frequently that is sacred to you, or perhaps a special place where you take a break from time to time and that you find beautiful, numinous, and relaxing. Perhaps it is on a shelf, or in the corner of your bedroom, or maybe on the patio in a small spot. It doesn't have to be major. In fact, I think the bigger the altar, the more responsibility that comes with it. It needs to start simple, and it will build from there. Remember, this is a focal point. Too much can overwhelm you. Also, you may think you're not "doing enough" if you don't have the decked-out altars complete with a ten-foot amethyst geode, a seven-foot wand alchemically mixed from St. Germain's ashes, and an athame the size of a Bowie knife. Start small. Start simple. It works.

Now that you've picked your spot, demarcate it. Outside you can surround your tree or spot with a set of stones in a circular fashion. If it is surrounding a group of trees it is known as a grove. Here where I live we have a few palm groves. Find something that is comfortable for you, and that speaks to your spirit. If it is on a flat surface like a shelf, perhaps put a potted plant near it. If, like me, you kill plants, then a simple cloth will do. It doesn't have to be a particular color, but if you want one, may I suggest white, blue, green, or red? These are sacred earth colors in Strix Craft: white is for the purification of our minds and bodies; blue is in honor of Zeus and the Olympians; green for the land spirits; red for the heart which is the center of all. Maybe if you find some stones or crystals, put them around your surface in a nice geometric shape, and let that be a signal to your mind that what is before you is the altar. This is where the working will be. Now that we have found a small space, let us go to the next step: purification.

PURIFICATION

Purification, or katharmos, was a ritualistic behavior that appropriately cleansed one of miasma and allowed them entrance into the sacred precinct. Remember, miasma is not evil. It is not sin or pollution. It is simply an energy that is part and parcel of being mortal. It is who we are. It doesn't take morality into account. You don't have to keep away from sacred space if you cuss, listen to heavy metal, play D&D, call on Satan, or trip your baby brother (just don't do it lest I be blamed for encouraging violent sibling rivalry). It is about hospitality: *theoxenia*. It's about separating the things that make us human: bodily fluids like semen, vaginal fluids, birth, afterbirth, blood, and such things as death.

Purification can take many different forms. Before the entrance of some sacred spaces (*temenos*), sometimes a small basin stood filled with water. The basin was called a *perirrhanterion*, and sprinkling some water on yourself symbolically cleansed you. It's like the basins of water in front of some churches (like the Anglican, Eastern Orthodox, and Roman Catholic). You sprinkle some on yourself and then enter the church.

Depending on the severity of the miasma, some priests and oracles might instruct the person or persons to simply sprinkle, wash their hands, or even bathe in a sacred spring or river. The requirements can also change from deity to deity. Some deities might have stricter rules because they have greater functions, and others have minor rules because they might be more limited in scope. It's a rough guess, but by no means true across the board. Different deities and spirits will simply have prescriptions. It may not make sense to us, but to them it does, and it is, after all, all about them. Ultimately, research, meditation, and divination will help you to know what to do. If you ever have any doubts about what your deity may want, find someone you trust who is a diviner, and ask. It's that simple.

Making Lustral Water

In my temple, I teach the following prescription for purification. First, we make what is called khernips. Khernips (also known as lustral water) is simply some water with burnt herbs or an incense joss stick that has been lit and plunged into the water. Making it is simple: grab a bowl and fill it with cold water. Some people like to use spring water, and that's fine too. I take a bowl with water and then I light a couple of bay leaves. I recite the following traditional Orphic Strix prayer:

Flame of the Ruby Star...

(I plunge the bay leaves down into the water.)

Water of the Azure Serpent...

I then slowly, clockwise, circle the bowl with the herbs three times. Each time I come full circle I say:

"Hekas (circle 1), Hekas (circle 2), Este Bebeloi (circle 3)!" ("Afar! Afar! O ye that is Profane!")

Voila! Khernips. Some make it simpler than this. For example, some merely light some incense and plunge the joss stick into the water. What I have presented is the format my temple uses, which is slightly more ritualistic and meaningful for us. Having done all of this, I will wash my hands, wash my face, and then anoint my third eye, lips, and heart using the traditional Orphic Strix prayer.

Anoint your forehead and say, "By the Mind of the Azure Flame [68] I consecrate myself." Anoint your lips and say, "By the Mouth of the Sacred, I consecrate myself." Anoint your chest and say, "By the Heart of the Goddess, I consecrate myself." Fully anoint your left hand and then your right and say, "By the Touch of the Godself, I consecrate myself."

---

68. In our system, it is taught that when Prometheus brought physical fire to humankind, he also brought down a metaphysical flame to awaken humanity to magic. This blue fire sits just above the crown of our heads.

I will then remove the bowl with the water and place it elsewhere as an offering to the spirits of chaos. I will say the following traditional Orphic Strix prayer:

"Chaos has no place in Order. Profane has no place in Holiness. Leave us in peace, and accept these offerings in appeasement."

A word of caution: Once I use a specific bowl for this ritual procedure, I will always use it for this purpose. It is a sacred tool, and should not be used mundanely.

THE HEARTH MOTHER

While the above prescriptions can be used for altars and shrines alike before approaching the gods, let me turn our focus to a Strix altar. We come to the first deity honored by the Strix: Hestia. Hestia is a unique goddess, and far too often downplayed if you ask me. After purifications, I light a candle that stands in the center of the altar, and I invoke the hearth mother by lighting the candle and tending the flame. I welcome her to purify the space with her holy flame, and bring the warmth of home and security to the sacred. I will say the following traditional Orphic Strix prayer:

Eternal Fire,
Deep calls unto Deep,
Thanksgiving and Praise unto Thee,
The Ruby Star shines forth from within,
The blossom of the Spring Rose comes forth.
We approach Thy sanctum with respect.
Bless our rites and attend unto us, we pray.
Let your holy flame light within our hearts.
Let our souls be made purified even as You are.
Khairete [hail] Hestia!

The family unit (*oikos*) was the central place of religion in ancient times, and it still rings true to this day. We may think of the ancient temenoi and the mystery cults as the defining religious atmosphere, but to do so would ignore how much of a role religion played in the home. For many ancient and modern cultures, spirituality is inseparable from the everyday activities of the household: bathing, eating, raising children, cooking, making love, fixing the house, tending to the needs of strangers and loved ones alike—these were central to religious duty (remember xenia!). Spirituality was not measured by how often you went to the temples, nor by how many sacrifices you performed, nor limited to a room. To live and breathe was—is—the embodiment of holiness. To be human is to be sacred. Indeed, there were even Theoi of the oikos who watched over and protected them. Part of the household gods were also the ancestors, who were invited regularly to important family occasions such as births, weddings, or funerals. Due to the vast amount of literature on the ancestors, I'll be dealing with them in a later chapter. I would simply like to emphasize that the home was as important as any temenos.

The hearth is the central fire in a home where cooking was done, while in colder months it also provided warmth to the oikos. As a result, it was the primary focus for family gatherings. Some modern-day hearths may be kitchens with dining room tables, mantels, and fireplaces, or a combination. In my home, my central area is the living room, where I have a candle set aside for Hestia. At the slightest invocation, she is there. She is there when cooking and cleaning are done in the kitchen, and it is in my kitchen where conversations take place and sometimes religious veneration is held.

In the mystery traditions, Hestia tending the eternal flame that was the hearth was extended to her tending the central flame of the cosmos. At the very epicenter of our universe was the first spark of creation that gave birth to all. Here the virgin goddess presided over the cosmic hearth. This was probably deduced from the *Hymn to Hestia*, in which she dwells within the Temple of Delphi, the navel of the world. (Delphi was said to be established when the god Zeus released two eagles at opposite ends of the world. They met at the center [navel] and here the Oracle of Delphi sat, the nexus between all worlds.)

THE CULT OF THE HOUSE SNAKE

Extending to Hestia is also the domestic cult of the house snake.[69] Among many European folk customs, most notably Greece and the Balkans, a snake is welcomed into a dwelling with reverential words such as "Welcome, lady of the house," or even "Welcome, guardian." Greek homes were often built on an earthen floor, and offerings were frequently left out to feed the nonvenomous serpents that fed on the rats. In doing this, harvests were protected and plagues were kept away. Interestingly enough, serpents graced the asklepieions, the dream temples of Asklepios. I believe that the serpents served the same purpose there as they did at the hearths of the oikos: to prevent plague and bring healing. The shedding of the snake was considered an apotropaic device against the Evil Eye and disease.

Coiled serpents were discovered in earthenware jars and other objects used for the home. In certain parts of modern-day Greece, Albania, Italy, Russia, and Sweden, peasants will offer milk and breadcrumbs to the snakes living beneath the floorboards. A hole in the floor is used to dump the offerings in the belief that this will nourish the snake and, in doing so, will extend to the "sacred

---

69. Nilson.

lady."[70] The serpent, the virgin of fire incarnate, is also addressed as the "house mother."

In my temple, we create a clay snake and have a sanctified candle in the name of the hearth mother. The serpent is the spirit of the home, and the guardian of the dwelling. In Hellenism, this serpent is called the *Agathos Daimon*, or "Good Spirit." After the purifications, Hestia's candle is lit and the icon of the serpent is coiled around it, being careful not to touch the dripping wax. We say:

Hestia,
Lady of the Living Flame,
Come and dwell here,
Purify this space in Your Name,
Come and dwell here,
Lady of the Living Flame,
Hestia.

Remember that the flame that burns bright is her made manifest. Treat her as such. She is here to bless your oikos and to consecrate it, to guard and protect it. Whenever I feel the need to cleanse my space from toxic energy, I will do a house cleaning, but at the end I will be sure to light a candle to Hestia to invoke her presence into the space. She makes it a home. People coming to my home can tell the difference, and I believe you will be able as well. Remember: you are the priest or priestess of your home. Treat it as a temple. "Enter in peace and be welcome."

You have made a shrine/altar, performed the purifications, and lit the candle to Hestia. What now? Let us turn a moment and explore the various magics and rituals that pertain to our Strix path.

---

70. Salem.

SECTION THREE
MAGICS AND RITUALS

Chapter 8

Healing Magic

Healers were as integral to the ancient Greeks as they were to any other society. In fact, the modern West's demand for integrity and compassion for health professionals stems from the ancient healers of Greece. But we cannot begin to speak about healers without discussing the demigod Asklepios, the son of Apollon and the Great Doctor.

In ancient Greece there were a variety of modalities committed to the healing arts:

- *Pharmakeia*: the herbalists
- *Kathartai*: the purifiers who administered cleansing rites
- *Iatromanteia*: medicine healers devoted to Apollon Oulios
- *Thamauturgeia*: the miracle workers
- *Strix*: the witches who might be a combination of many of these

The healing these practitioners worked was not limited to the physical body, but wholeness. Scholar Peter Kingsley informs us that healers, such as the iatromanteia, dictated not philosophical reasoning but a holistic sense of the cosmos as it relates to the individual.[71] They were dream walkers, able to understand and speak in dark riddles in order to convey important information.

Iatromanteia, in particular, were considered sons of the god Apollo in his guise as Oulios. Using chants and breathwork, they were able to control their senses and were highly regarded as healer-mystics. By performing their sacred work, they were able to perform thaumaturgical applications to the sick and dying. They were literally physician-seers, and Asklepios might have served as the premier example of an iatromantis.

Mycenean inscriptions demonstrate that the Asklepion traditions go as far back as 1500 BCE.[72] However, it was the poet (or poets?) Homer who first relayed the tale of Asklepios circa 900 BCE. According to the Homeric tradition, Asklepios's relationship to Apollo is never mentioned. Instead, his sons Machaon and Podalirius travel with the Greeks in the *Iliad*. They are prized by Nestor, who states that "a leech is the worth of many other men." (A leech is the old word for physician.)

However vague Asklepios's relationship was (and there is also no mention of any godhood conferred), fragments of the poems of Hesiod that mention Asklepios survive dating to 700 BCE. The story included seems to be corroborated by the historian and writer Apollodoros. The tale written by him seems—in my opinion—to be part of an oral tradition, since Apollodoros is a son of one Asklepiades Pharmakion. I believe that this latter individual is probably from a lineage of priests in the Asklepion traditions.

Different authors have different tales. According to the Greek geographer and traveler Pausanias, in his *Description of Greece*, the Oracle of Delphi relayed that Asklepios was born in a town known

---

71. Kingsley, *In the Dark Places of Wisdom*.

72. Bailey, 257–263.

as Epidauros.[73] In this tale, which I believe has more truth in it, Asklepios was the son of Apollo and Koronis. Koronis accompanied her father on a journey, and she gave birth to Asklepios on a mountain. He was left there, and a she-goat came and nursed the demigod. A watchdog who oversaw the herd protected the infant. A shepherd found the infant and saw a luster about the child that resembled the brightness and crackling of lightning. Later found by Apollo, the boy was taken to Thessaly to be reared by the centaur Chiron, who taught the boy the healing arts.

Asklepios was a wonder worker who was able to cure the sick and even raise the dead. Regarding the latter, in one tale it is said that he was shut up with the mortal Glaukos. While Glaukos was ill, Asklepios meditated and a serpent appeared. He killed the serpent and entwined it on his staff. Then a second serpent appeared with an herb in its mouth. He administered the herb to Glaukos, who became well and immortal. Glaukos then went to the sea and became a sea spirit whose oracles were said to be even more accurate than those of Apollo. The herb was then cultivated and given to the dead so that they might revive.

Asklepios founded dream temples, the most famous of which was in his birthplace of Epidauros. Dream temples, called *asklepieions*, were places where the priests of Asklepios gave medicines and potions to the sick. They were then led to a room where they slept the night. In the dream world via the Gate of Horn, Asklepios (or a daemon impersonating him) visited the sick and gave them an answer as to how to heal properly. The dreams would be interpreted by the priest. Asklepieions frequently had mineral springs and a gymnasium, along with perhaps a library and a theater.

---

73. Pausanias, 2.26.7.

However, there was another purpose to the temples, and that was the practice of incubation.

Incubation was a technique (or set of techniques) that allowed an individual to trance and visit the otherworld. I believe that the influence of incubation came from the east in Egypt where sleep temples were established dedicated to the demigod (or god) Imhotep, a similar being to Asklepios. Whatever the original influence, however, it was a tried and true method. Kingsley informs us that the philosopher Parmenides used such a method to travel to the underworld. In my experience with incubation, it is a powerful technique in finding your way to Persephone, the goddess of the underworld.

BUILDING A SHRINE TO ASKLEPIOS

Materials needed:

dark green or yellow altar cloth

image of a serpent

marshmallow root

mandrake

elecampane

Balkan peony—seeds and roots

burdock root

poppy seeds

valerian root

small jar

gold or dark green tile

A shrine to Asklepios includes the following steps:

Find a place you can house him permanently. It can be whatever space you have on a shelf or in a nook. The grander the better, but work with what you have. As time goes on and he gives you more success, you can always add more space, but it isn't necessary. Boundaries and devotion get you a long way with him. You may also use your Strix shrine, working it as an altar by switching out deities. This is perfectly acceptable.

Asklepios Sigil

In this space you may use a dark green or yellow cloth. Place on it a clay image of a serpent (or a serpentine image). In a jar place the following herbs: the root of marshmallow (*A. officinalis*), mandrake (*M. autumnalis*), elecampane (*I. helenium*), the seeds and roots of Balkan peony (*P. officinalis*), the root of burdock (*A. lappa*), seeds of poppy (*P. somniferum*), and the root of valerian (*V. officinalis*). These seven herbs are a reminder and attractant to the daemons of sleep and incubation.

Place an image of Asklepios in the back center. It can be a picture from the internet, a tarot card you associate with him, a painting, a mask, or a statue. When you clean the shrine (and a major cleaning should take place on the dark moon for every one of your shrines), DO NOT WASH anything you've drawn down a spirit into. A simple wipe and anointing with four drops of wine and khernips should suffice. You may wrap implements in red or white silk so as to keep them free of dust. Such implements may include a wand that looks like a serpent.

To call down his presence into the shrine, take a gold or dark green tile and write the sigil of Asklepios on it. The sigil is a double circle with the name Asklepios between them. In the circle is a staff with serpent entwined. To the right is an eye, symbol of Oulios. To the left is a small jar, symbolizing the blood of the Gorgons that Asklepios carried, used for either healing or death.

Burn some poppy seeds in a thurible and wave the tile in the smoke by grabbing the tile in both hands and slowly waving it in a figure eight motion in the smoke (be sure it is a well-ventilated area). Anoint your forehead, heart, and hands with some oil such as those containing lavender. Get comfortable.

Now begin a Fourfold Breath: Breathe in the count of four. Hold your breath to the count of four. Exhale slowly to the count of four. Hold to the count of four. Repeat this procedure four times, purposefully lowering your blood pressure and relaxing your muscles. Be aware of your body, in its entirety. Mentally bring your awareness to your body, beginning with the top of your head. As you breathe, intentionally continue to bring your awareness to your temples, then jawline, and then your neck. Note parts where you are stressed and need to relax. Stretch, yawn, and SLOWLY circle your neck. Continue to bring your awareness to your shoulders, and intentionally relax. Rotate your shoulders and loosen up your stance. Continue to scan your body, bringing your awareness to your torso, your pelvis and groin, your thighs, your calves, and finally your feet. Continue to intentionally relax your muscles and be aware of yourself. Once you feel grounded and relaxed, it is time to begin.

Begin in silence. If you need noise-cancelling headphones then so be it. Turn off your phone, pull the shades, and lock your doors. Be sure you will not be disturbed by any sudden noise or distraction while in the middle of this rite that might jerk you back to your body and may temporarily unbalance your spirit. This results in you feeling confused, angry, unbalanced, and shattered.

As you breathe, envision a white flame encompassing your feet (or if you are sitting, the coccyx and sacrum touching the ground). The more you breathe slowly and focus, the brighter it becomes. This flame swirls upward, from your feet, to the back of your solar plexus, to the front of your heart, to winding its way to the back of your throat, and finally twirls to your third eye. It "hums."

"SSSSSSSSSSSSS … SSSSSSSSSSSSS … SSSSSSSSSSSSS … SSSSS SSSSSSS …"

Continue to chant the sound of a snake. Take the tile and hold it in your hands, and then hug it against your solar plexus where the white flame is. When you feel ready, cry "IT IS DONE!" Drink some mead, juice, or mineral spring water, a bottle of which should also be on the shrine. Relax. You did well. When you're ready, place the newly anointed tile with lavender oil underneath the image on the shrine. As long as it is there, it has been activated and will live there. Continuing to care for him will enhance your relationship with Asklepios. Daily prayers, offerings, and holding special times for him, such as Sundays and the eighth day after the dark moon, will increase your benefits. Sundays are dedicated to the sun, the source of light, vitality, and healing.

CLAY EFFIGIES

When you want to heal a particular malady on a certain part of the body, use clay to mold the shape of that body part (e.g., an eye, liver, gallbladder, leg, etc.). (The making of a clay effigy applies to anyone other than you as well, including pets.) It has been used with success using this operation. Leave the clay body part in a bowl, or somewhere on the shrine. As it lies there, offer up your prayer. Be sure to give offerings daily if you can, each time waving the clay effigy through the smoke in a figure eight fashion. Offerings for Asklepios include frankincense, poppy, cypress, and cedar. Sandalwood may also be used. As the smoke rises, so too do your prayers rise to the deity. When you have been healed, write a letter of testimony along with the date and time you are writing. Afterward, roll it up into a scroll and find a place for it on the shrine.

WAX POPPET

For you or someone else who needs healing, make an effigy (called kolossos in Greek) of wax. You'll need the following:

some wax, such as paraffin or beeswax (the latter is my personal go-to as it is more natural)

a double boiler or a large saucepan along with a clean, stainless steel pitcher (such as a coffee can or smaller pitcher)

olive oil

one blue pin

something that links the person to that kolossos: an image, unwashed clothing, nails, or hair

herbs such as chamomile (*Chamaemelum nobile*), St. John's wort (*Hypericum perforatum*), valerian (*Valeriana officinalis*), or feverfew (*Tanacetum parthenium L.*)

Fill a large saucepan with water halfway. Let it boil on medium heat. While this is going on, place your wax amount—which should be a little over the size of your hand—in the clean coffee container or pitcher. Place the smaller container in the larger saucepan. Watch it carefully, and wait until the wax is completely melted.

Once the wax is melted, remove its container from the saucepan and pour it into a heat-safe container. Let it sit for a moment, just long enough to cool but not to be too stiff. Rub your palms in some olive oil. A couple of drops on each palm should do. This is so the wax does not stick to your hands. While still pliable, shape the wax into a human figure. Knead it as you go. If it cools too much, simply reheat it over medium heat in your pitcher or can inside the saucepan until it is pliable again. It may take some practice for you to get it to the point where this is happening. Continue to knead until it looks like a human effigy. (Note: it does not have to be perfect. However, be as creative and thorough as you can.) While making the kolossos, repeatedly whisper the name of your target. This aids in your focus.

Shape the wax image into the figure of a human being. If it is for a woman, enhance the chest to make breasts; if it is for a man, add a phallus. The wax image may also have hair, nail clippings, and/or a photo of the person attached to the image. This procedure also applies to animal loved ones. Just roughly shape the wax in the form of whatever animal it is you are healing. With the blue pin, write the legal name of the person to whom the healing is being sent to. If it is for a pet, write out their name.

On the back of the image, carve the sigil for Och, the Olympic spirit of healing. The sigil for Och is a double circle with his name between them. Inside the circle is his sigil, which looks like a trident with a circle at the base. Wave the effigy through incense smoke in a figure eight fashion and recite the Orphic Hymn to Asklepios:

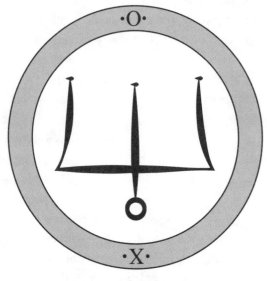

Och Sigil

Healer of all, Asklepios, Paian
the lord, who touches humans with magic
soothing the agonizing suffering
of disease, strong one, may you come and lead
down Health, ending sickness and the hard fate
of death. You are a helper, promoting
growth, and keeping evil away, sharing
blessings. Strong child of Phoibos Apollon,
your fame shines and you hate disease. You hold
Hygieia as your blameless spouse. Come,
blessed one, savior, send a good end of life.[74]

---

74. Dunn.

When you or the other individual is healed, take the wax poppet and remove the implements of hair, nails, and/or the image. Cover everything in salt, dissociating yourself from the kolossos. Ritually bury the body parts and burn the image if you used one. Take the kolossos and, if you live near a stream, place it there. You may also opt to leave it somewhere outside or in a garden to decompose naturally. If none of these are options, then simply ritually break them into smaller pieces until they are small enough to spread somewhere unnoticeable such as a nearby park. Be sure to have a testimonial written that will stay on the shrine to show the healing powers of Asklepios. Always writing a testimonial will increase your faith and the faith of others in his healing abilities.

THE SERPENT WAND

If someone is feeling physically or emotionally ill (i.e., depressed, out of balance), then this wand technique is for them. I must stress, however, that this technique is no substitute for medications if necessary, depending on the severity of the illness. Asklepios was and is the god of physicians, and so medical practitioners are hallowed healers even today. Remember that. Please keep in mind to always seek professional help in situations that merit it. If you are in doubt, then ask for help. Never underestimate the power of modern medicine.

Take a wand that you have either carved or been given and bless it in the name of Asklepios. This wand can be different from the one on your Strix shrine. This wand may be shaped serpentine for emphasis. What is important is that it is dedicated to Asklepios and to him alone. To dedicate it if not already done, simply paint or carve the name of Asklepios on the wand. Then, wave the wand through the smoke in a figure eight fashion. Sprinkle it with mineral water. Now it is ready for use.

Have the person lie down comfortably on their back. Have them perform the Fourfold Breath as described below; by doing so you are inviting them into the healing process. This is paramount—healing is a participatory event. If the person does not want to heal, then it will not work. Have them imagine an Azure Flame above the top of their head, as you envision one on yours. Perform a Fourfold Breath: breathe in the count of four...hold to the count of four...exhale to the count of four...hold to the count of four. Do this four times; focus the blue fire so that it extends from the crown of your head to the wand itself. As you focus, the flame becomes brighter and hotter. The fire is the link of magic between us and the gods. It is our living cord to the Divine, from whose source all that we manifest occurs.

When you are ready, slowly use the wand to "scan" the person's body. You do this by slowly starting from the top of their head, and holding the wand a few inches from their body. Close your eyes and carefully see the wand become a living snake in your hand; it is the power of Asklepios coming alive. The serpent is the devourer, and will devour any illness that is present in the body. As you go over the body down toward the feet, focus on the living serpent in your hand. When you "detect" a spot, focus the wand over it. This sense could manifest as a throbbing in your palms, a cold spot, an unusually hot spot, or just erratic energy. It may even be felt in a part of your body, a pain or sensation not your own.

The illness might manifest as an animal form to your eyes: a scorpion, a spider, a rat, etc. Whatever it is, these are not real animals but simply forms that the various illness daemons (called the *Nosoi*) take. The serpent, however, is powerful and effective enough to "eat" the illnesses and bring harmony back into the body. Keep in mind that if this method seems shamanic (for lack of a better term), it is. Remember that the iatromanteia are physician-seers, able to see the plague and render it harmless through a variety of procedures including medicine, hot and cold baths, herbal ingestion, and energy work.

Once the serpent has crawled and devoured the spirit, you render the wand "clean" by waving it over the incense smoke in a figure eight fashion and crying, "Hekas, Hekas, Este Bebeloi!" It is done. Always remember that when the individual is healed, a testimony is written out and left on the shrine of Asklepios.

CANDLE MAGIC

This working is also appropriate for pets. Take a blue candle and use khernips and incense to cleanse it. Inscribe the name of the person or object you wish to heal. Take some oil such as lavender or olive oil, and dress the candle appropriately; you do this by anointing the candle with the suggested oil from the top of the candle downward to the bottom. Do this nine times, intentionally and slowly while focusing on the name of the person or object. (By "object" I mean the specific anatomy in need of healing, e.g., lungs, liver, heart, etc.) Take an image of the individual, and place it beneath the candle or behind it (depending on if it is an actual photo you don't want to ruin or just a printed image). Now call upon Asklepios and Och to bless your rite. Light the candle. Say the following: "As with the god's/goddess's aid I melt this wax, so straightway may my malady melt away." In combination with this spell, you may also burn lavender, frankincense, or poppy leaves. When you light the incense, say, "As you burn, so also will you burn away the ailment of my affliction." Focus on the individual, yourself, or the pet and the intensity of the love and healing you want to send to them. Once the candle is done and the incense is burned down, leave the image where it is. When successful, take the image and hide it away somewhere. Be sure to always write a testimony of healing and leave it on the shrine.

MEDICINE

I cannot write about Asklepios and emphasize enough the sacredness of medicine. The medical field has changed rapidly since the late nineteenth century, when there was a radical shift from orthodox medicine to "back to nature" movements that emphasized a holistic view of the body as well as encouraging the body to heal itself. While seemingly moronic today in the face of Western science, keep in mind that when these reactionary practices emerged, Western medicine wasn't exactly at its best. Although Louis Pasteur discovered what would become known as the germ theory of disease, it was still commonplace for physicians to saw off a limb and then deliver a baby—without washing their hands or sterilizing their equipment. Anesthesia was hardly ever used and there were times when women were tied down and had a gag of wood in their mouth while their cancerous breast(s) were removed with a sharp implement. This was the world that these practices—naturopathy, homeopathy, chiropractic, and herbalism—came from. It is easy to understand why these were created.

The essential component that unites these practices (along with acupuncture, ayurveda, and Traditional Chinese Medicine) is the belief that there is a vital force within the human body, whether it is called prana, pneuma, qi, chi, or simply the vital force. The imbalance of this force is what creates "dis-ease." It is the purpose of the practitioner to bring this force back into harmony and to encourage the human body to revive its innate ability to heal. While perhaps not scientifically sound, nonetheless there are plenty of instances in which it works. The usual prescription from these modalities includes rest, sunshine, proper diet, proper lifestyles, and positive environmental changes.

Interestingly enough, the priests of Asklepios felt the same. The centers were often connected to gymnasiums, mineral springs, and theaters to assist patients to have good lifestyle changes and entertainment. Herbs were and are currently used in various ways to help with healing. In our current society we are surrounded by an ever-increasing build of chronic illnesses, most of which are caused by the unhealthy "Western diet," a decrease in physical activity, and an increase in polluted waters, soil, and atmosphere. As a result, we are encouraged to change our lifestyle and return to the prescriptions and principles of our medical ancestors such as Hippocrates, who advocated for such techniques in order to walk in divine health.

SUMMARY

We have explored Asklepios and his power of health and healing. Some workings such as kolossoi, candle magic, and serpent wands are ideal methods. But we must not forget the healing power of modern medicine. Asklepios is the patron of medicine, surgery, and healing. How that healing comes doesn't matter; it comes. It will happen. The mystical and the medical can work in tandem to create a powerful effect on the body. I encourage you not to forget this.

CHAPTER 9
EROTIC MAGIC

Love magic appears in nearly every aspect of ancient Greek life, from Homer until the advent of Christianity.[75] Even the gods use such magic. For example, Aphrodite possesses a golden girdle that has the power to seduce anyone. Circe uses potions. There are famous examples of erotic poetry, statues, and spells that existed in ancient times. Sappho, in her *Hymn to Aphrodite*, asks the goddess to relieve her of her unrequited love for another woman. However, Aphrodite appears and says that Sappho's love will be returned. The question remains as to how this is supposed to happen. One of the epithets of Aphrodite is the name *Epistrophia*—that is, deviser. She is cunning in her arts, and love magic and eroticism belong to her. She taught Jason how to seduce Medea, the priestess of Hekate. What does this mean for you? Just what do I mean by erotic magic? It is a corpus of rites and actions that infuse oneself or another with the intent to instill and/or maintain various levels of affection and desire. There is evidence that men frequently performed rituals and actions on themselves to increase their libido (not much has changed in thousands of years). I feel the need to explain what erotic magics are because it is the intent that defines

---

75. Faroane.

it. For example, if you want to curse your ex to fall in love with another woman who is a living nightmare, that isn't love magic. That is a curse. Your motivation and goal are what define it, along with the alliance you create from your deities and spirits to help you achieve that goal.

Eroticism would not, in my mind, exist without Aphrodite and Pan. Before we get started on doing love magics, there are a couple of things I would like to mention. First, as a devotionalist Strix who has experienced much success in my magic when I set aside a home for a deity or spirit and begin a reciprocal relationship with them, I encourage you to begin with a shrine dedicated to Aphrodite and/or Pan. Remember that shrines are permanent homes, and as such love and care must be given to upkeep. It isn't simply making an altar (or not) and doing the work. Second, respect must be given to the deities and spirits whom you will be contacting. This means also following proper protocols such as purifications prior to entering their space; this includes making khernips and washing oneself to remember you are entering sacred ground.

The Greeks had different words to describe the different types of love magics:

- *Philtron:* "Love incantation." A potion or drug. That which brings "philia," or affection
- *Stergēma:* "Love charms"
- *Charitēsion:* "Beauty charm." Spells to make oneself more charming
- *Saturion:* Derived from the word "satyr." Commonly used throughout the Roman period to mean a person who was using certain plants in the orchid family that produced male lust and made erections more possible

- *Agōgimon:* "Spell that leads." That is, spells designed to force young women from their homes
- *Philtrokatadesmos:* "Love binding tablet." A spell written on a tablet that details binding someone to fall in love with you and punishing them in various ways until they do so
- *Phusikleidion:* "Genital key spell." A spell that is used to enhance one's libido, particularly used by men

Both men and women made use of these various types of love spells, and I would like to add that spells of these types also had inscriptions for same-sex lovers.

Love magics are tricky, and as we discussed in Chapter 3 on ethics, we need to know the consequences of our actions. Gods aren't beings we can lay blame on. We are all interconnected through and by Nyx; what we aim to do, we will no doubt accomplish, but there will always be consequences. Allow me to discuss a couple of points.

Aphrodite is the goddess of love, beauty, and—as Areia—war. She is not to be trifled with, and Ares is a god who defends women and rape victims. If you decide to perform a spell for someone to have sex with you, you will need to contend with Ares energy as a consequence for the motivation to rape someone. However, if you would like to work toward becoming someone who someone can desire to have sex with, then that is okay. You're working on yourself.

Let me be clear: There is nothing wrong with pleasure. It is the aim of accomplishment for the Strix to be a part of this world and experience all that she has to offer. But pleasure and hubris—excessive pride—can be dangerous. Nonetheless, what follows are magical acts for love magics, because they exist. There is inherently no shame in desiring to have it. Love, after all, is one of the most primal things we as humans crave. With it comes acceptance and fulfillment.

I would also like to add that the target of your aim may experience what is called an "erotic seizure." It feels like the flu but is in fact the working of the deity/spirit on that individual. Anacreon states that Eros "struck [him] with a massive hammer, like a bronze worker, and then doused [him] into a frigid stream." Sappho in her poetry sings that Eros "shakes my heart as a wind falls upon a tree."

I would like to include one more topic: the subject of sex and masturbation. This chapter encourages using sex magic via masturbation to connect with spirits. However, I realize that many people do not or cannot perform masturbation when worshiping and working with a deity or spirit. For that reason, I encourage you to skip that part and go directly to the chant given. The power of breath and chant is effective. What orgasm does is enhance that working, but there is no reason why one cannot perform the working without masturbation. I include sexual acts such as masturbation because we are dealing with eroticism specifically. Find what you are currently comfortable with, and go from there.

With that in mind, let us explore erotic magics.

BUILDING A SHRINE TO APHRODITE

Materials needed:

pink, red, or white altar cloth

image of Aphrodite

perfumes, mirrors, or seashells; recommended herbs and resins

an apple

black or red tile

For Aphrodite, find a place you can house her permanently. If you can't, that's okay. I understand that space can be very limited for many of us. It can be whatever space you have on a shelf or in a nook. The grander the better, but work with what you have. As time goes on and she gives you more success, you can always add more space, but it isn't necessary. Boundaries and devotion get you a long way with her.

You may also use your already built Strix shrine. If you haven't built it, do it now. The instructions and implements can be found back in Chapter 7. This main shrine can be used for any working you will be performing, and you can change out your symbols and deities easily with each working.

When performing love magic, place a pink, red, or white cloth on the shrine. Place an image of hers in the back center. It can be a picture from the internet, a tarot card you associate with her, a painting, a black conical stone that might be magnetized (early representations of Aphrodite were aniconic), a mask, or a statue. Decorate the shrine with things that she loves, such as perfumes, mirrors, and seashells. You may even add small bottles or jars of herbs and resins sacred to her such as saffron, storax, myrrh, frankincense, cinnamon, cypress, marjoram, and myrtle. Remember to always keep her space clean (of course, this goes for any shrine or altar).

When you clean the shrine (and a major cleaning should take place on the dark moon for every one of your shrines), DO NOT WASH anything you've drawn down a spirit into. Why? Washing something in which a being has been called down into will negate that being's energy. Washing creates a clean slate, and we'd rather treat a spirit with respect. A simple wipe and anointing with four drops of wine and khernips should suffice. You may wrap implements in red or white silk so as to keep dust from settling on them.

Once a week, preferably Fridays, leave an offering of an apple and some delicious wine. Fridays are sacred to her; in Latin, Friday was named after her Roman counterpart, Venus. After twenty-four hours, dump out the wine and leave the apple for animals to feed. You may anoint her shrine with perfume and incense throughout the week.

INVOKING HER PRESENCE

Once the setup is done, it is now time for actually calling down her presence to inhabit the image and the shrine itself (one of her daemones will be sent) and preparing to do your work.

Aphrodite Sigil

To call down her presence, take a small square surface painted black (or red) and inscribe the sigil of Aphrodite Pandemos. This sigil consists of a double circle in which the name of Aphrodite is written. A dove sits upon a branch from which roses and thorns sprout. This symbolizes the holy goddess and her aspects of beauty, and the reminder of the pain that comes from pursuing that beauty.

The reason we are using a small tile (or any surface) is because we need a physical anchor for her presence. We need somewhere for her daemon to live. The tile can be made of any substance, although wood would be the easiest to obtain. A simple 3" x 3" item is fine (I use this number merely for an example of size and not for any esoteric reason).

Now find a comfortable place to begin the working. Be sure to have your curtains closed, your doors locked, and your phone off. If you want to play some music appropriate to the rite, go ahead. Be sure all of your tools are gathered together prior to starting … including a lighter or match for candles.

Burn some of her herbs in a thurible and wave the tile in the smoke. I'd advise against burning the cinnamon, though. Anoint your forehead, heart, and hands with some lotion that is pleasing to you (again, avoiding cinnamon, as it burns), perhaps lavender. Slice an apple crosswise so you can see the pentagram. Get comfortable and get naked. If you are not comfortable being naked, that is fine. Find clothing that is comfortable to wear, whether a special robe, or just shorts and a shirt. Ancient Greeks might have had special clothing for certain times, but that was mostly for the wealthy. Everyday people wore what they had, except perhaps for special occasions like weddings. But going to the temples wasn't necessarily like going to church and dressing in your "Sunday best." The importance was placed on washing and doing, not necessarily clothing or belief. I choose to be naked during erotic rites, but for others I might be clothed. The choice is up to you and your comfort level.

Now begin a Fourfold Breath: Breathe in the count of four. Hold your breath to the count of four. Exhale slowly to the count of four. Hold to the count of four. Repeat this procedure four times, purposefully lowering your blood pressure and relaxing your muscles. Be aware of your body, in its entirety. Mentally bring your awareness to your body, beginning with the top of your head. As you breathe, intentionally continue to bring your awareness to your temples, then your jawline, and then your neck. Note parts where you are stressed and need to relax. Stretch, yawn, and SLOWLY circle your neck. Continue to bring your awareness to your shoulders, and intentionally relax. Rotate your shoulders and loosen up your stance. Continue to scan your body, bringing your awareness to your torso, your pelvis and groin, your thighs, your calves, and finally your feet. Continue to intentionally relax your muscles and be aware of yourself. Once you feel grounded and relaxed, it is time to begin.

Place the tile upon which you have inscribed the sigil of Aphrodite Pandemos near your genitals. This is so when you reach climax, you will have anointed the tile itself. Also place one half of the apple you cut onto the tile as well.

Begin to masturbate. As you do so, envision a crimson flame encompassing your heart. The more you breathe slowly and focus, the brighter it becomes. This flame swirls, "hums," and beats in rhythm to your own heart. At a certain point, begin to chant:

"PANDÊMOSSSSS … NEPHERIE'RIIIIIII … PANDÊMOSSSS … NEPHERIE'RIIIIIII …"

Continue to chant these names, masturbating. Bring yourself closer to orgasm. Make love to yourself and remember that it is your energy and actions that are drawing down the daemon. When orgasm is reached, some of the fluids will anoint the tile with the sigil where you will exclaim, "IT IS DONE!" Some of it will also anoint half of the apple, while you take a bite out of the other half. Drink some wine, juice, or water. Relax. You did well. When you're ready, place the newly anointed tile underneath the image on the shrine. As long as it is there, it has been activated and will live there. The fluids will dry, and that's fine. That's as it should be.

Continuing to care for her will enhance your relationship with Aphrodite. Daily prayers, offerings, and holding special times for her, such as Fridays or the fourth night after the dark moon, will increase your benefits. This was a sacred time for Aphrodite as well on the lunar calendar. Moving forward, whenever you want to worship Aphrodite or work with her spirits, the tile is your focal point. When not in use, cover it in a red silk cloth. Color is important, as it will distinguish various spirits as we move forward.

Pan, the patron of same-sex love in men, is also petitioned in these various spells. Again, I would advise caution, as "Pan" is the root of the word "panic," and as such, people who are being targeted may experience an anxiety that something is missing in their lives.

Building a Shrine to Pan the Younger
Materials needed:

image/representation of Pan

syrinx

statue of a tortoise

cologne

Pan is a wild god of the forests and mountain wilds, and so if you can make an outdoor shrine all the better. The following instructions I give for an indoor shrine.

No cloth is necessary. Place an image of Pan, such as from the internet; a tarot card; a statue; a phallus made of clay, wood, or glass; the skull of a goat (taken ethically with zero harm to the goat, such as if it has died of natural causes); or a mask. Clean the area thoroughly. Place a *syrinx* ("Pan pipes"), a statue of a tortoise, some cologne, and perhaps even a jar of pine leaves on there. If you have beech trees near you, consider making a wand of beech and leaving it on the shrine to use when calling upon Pan or one of the spirits associated with him. Again, you may switch out your main Strix shrine and use it as a temporary altar for Pan when specifically worshiping him and working with his spirits.

When you clean the shrine (and a major cleaning should take place on the dark moon for every one of your shrines), DO NOT WASH anything you've drawn down a spirit into. Washing something into which a being has been called down will negate that being's energy. Washing creates a clean slate, and we'd rather treat a spirit with respect. A simple wipe and anointing with four drops of wine and khernips should suffice. You may wrap implements in red or white silk so as to keep them free of dust. Remember to always keep his space clean.

Once a week, preferably Wednesdays or Saturdays, leave an offering of cream, milk, butter, mead, and/or honey on his shrine. Leave it there for a few hours and then dump the offering out. I usually leave an unopened bottle of honey on the shrine. Ants can easily get to an open bottle, so that's something you might want to consider. You may also make masturbation or sex a ritual offering to Pan, as he is extremely fond of that energy. Moving forward, whenever you want to worship Pan or work with his spirits, the tile is your focal point. When not in use, cover it in a black silk cloth. Color is important, as it will distinguish various spirits as we move forward.

INVOKING HIS PRESENCE

To call down his presence into the shrine, take a tile and paint or draw the sigil of Pan. The sigil is a double circle with the name of Pan inscribed between the circles (much like Aphrodite Pandemos). Within the sigil is a horned head of a ram, a flame at the crown of its head, and a beard coming from it. Beneath is the Tau symbol, a Greek letter whose meaning is life. Burn some pine leaves in a thurible and wave the tile in the smoke. Anoint your forehead, heart, and hands with some oil such as those containing some musk. Get comfortable and get naked (if you wish).

Pan Sigil

Now begin a Fourfold Breath: Breathe in the count of four. Hold your breath to the count of four. Exhale slowly to the count of four. Hold to the count of four. Repeat this procedure four times, purposefully lowering your blood pressure and relaxing your muscles.

Be aware of your body, in its entirety. Mentally bring your awareness to your body, beginning with the top of your head. As you breathe, intentionally continue to bring your awareness to your temples, then your jawline, and then your neck. Note parts where you are stressed and need to relax. Stretch, yawn, and SLOWLY circle your neck. Continue to bring your awareness to your shoulders, and intentionally relax. Rotate your shoulders and loosen up your stance. Continue to scan your body, bringing your awareness to your torso, your pelvis and groin, your thighs, your calves, and finally your feet. Continue to intentionally relax your muscles and be aware of yourself. Once you feel grounded and relaxed, it is time to begin.

Begin to masturbate. As you do so, envision an emerald flame encompassing your feet (or if you are sitting, the coccyx and sacrum touching the ground). The more you breathe slowly and focus, the brighter it becomes. This flame swirls, "hums," and begins to connect your spine and body to the ground like a network of vines. At a certain point, begin to chant:

"PAAAAANNNN … NO'MIIIIUUUUSSSS … PAAAAAN-NNN … NO'MIIIIIUUUSSSS …"

Continue to chant these names, masturbating. Bring yourself closer to orgasm. Make love to yourself and remember that it is your energy and actions that are drawing down the daemon. Take the tile and place it near your genitals so that when you reach climax the juices will anoint the tile itself. When orgasm is reached, some of the fluids will anoint the tile with the sigil where you will exclaim, "IT IS DONE!" Drink some mead, juice, or water. Relax. You did well. When you're ready, place the newly anointed tile underneath the image on the shrine. As long as it is there, it has been activated and will live there. Let it dry. Continuing to care for him will enhance your relationship with Pan. Daily prayers, offerings, and holding special times for him, such as Wednesdays or Saturdays, will increase your benefits.

MAGICS

We now turn our attention to the workings and various techniques to use for love magics.

THE ROSE CHALICE

Sometimes love magics are as simple as consecrating an object toward that purpose. A cup that dates back to the late eighth century BCE has an inscription that translates thus: "Whoever drinks from this cup, desire for beautifully crowned Aphrodite will seize him instantly." This is perfect for couples (or more) who are having troubles and need to find their zest and love again, or for people in relationships who need to feel erotic and beautiful again. To be reminded of their self-worth. The rose chalice also works as a charm to hypnotize others into falling in love with the first thing they see when Aphrodite's spell works on them. So be very careful with this potent philter.

Take a chalice, preferably one you may have made with clay or wood (as examples). If you don't know how to make one, any goblet with a stem will do. Underneath the stem, inscribe the sigil of Hagith, and around the chalice itself in Greek write the aforementioned inscription. You may also create a tile for Hagith. Hagith is an Olympian spirit under the domain of Aphrodite. The sigil is a double circle with the name Hagith inscribed between them. Within is the actual sigil.

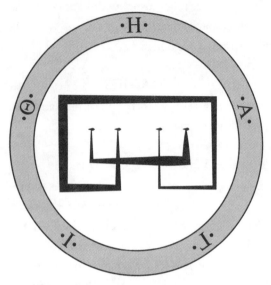

Hagith Sigil

To activate Hagith, uncover the silk covering of Aphrodite and place the tile of Hagith on top of the tile of Aphrodite. Place both hands on Hagith and say the following:

Aphrodite,
Bring forth thy spirit,
Hagith lives within thee.
Aphrodite,
Hagith lives within thee,
Bring forth thy spirit.
So be it!

On the fourth day after the dark moon (during the waxing part of the lunar cycle) take the chalice to your shrine of Aphrodite. Prepare yourself with khernips.

Perform the Fourfold Breath: Inhale to the count of four. Hold to the count of four. Exhale slowly to the count of four. Hold to the count of four. Repeat four times. Be aware of your body, in its entirety. Mentally bring your awareness to your body, beginning with the top of your head. As you breathe, intentionally continue to bring your awareness to your temples, then your jawline, and then your neck. Note parts where you are stressed and need to relax. Stretch, yawn, and SLOWLY circle your neck. Continue to bring your awareness to your shoulders, and intentionally relax. Rotate your shoulders and loosen up your stance. Continue to scan your body, bringing your awareness to your torso, your pelvis and groin, your thighs, your calves, and finally your feet. Continue to intentionally relax your muscles and be aware of yourself. Once you feel grounded and relaxed, it is time to begin.

Visualize a crimson flame where your heart is. The more you focus on it, the brighter it becomes. The flame swirls, "hums," and beats in rhythm with your own heart. Remember you are calling down the spirit of Hagith into the chalice itself: whoever drinks from it will be smitten with love. Hold the chalice in your hands and, while breathing, place the chalice upon the uncovered sigil of Hagith. Now say the following:

By she who is the Girdle of Love,
By she who is the Rose that Blooms,
By she who is the Thorn of Blood,
I call to thee Pandemos,
I call to thee Hagith,
Anoint the Chalice,
Here blooms the Rose,
So be it!

Periodically, anoint the cup with four drops of wine. You may keep the chalice wrapped in red or white silk until it needs to be used.

CANDLE MAGIC

Take a red candle and use khernips and incense to cleanse it. Inscribe the name of the person whom you desire to fall in love with you. Take some oil, such as rose, myrrh, lavender, or olive oil, and dress the candle appropriately; you do this by anointing the candle with the suggested oil from the top of the candle downward to the bottom. Do this nine times, intentionally and slowly, while focusing on the name of the person. Take an image of the individual, and place it beneath the candle or behind it (depending on if it is an actual photo you don't want to ruin or just a printed image). Now call upon Pan or Aphrodite to bless your rite. Light the candle. Say the following: "As with the god's/goddess's aid I melt this wax, so straightway may ___ melt with love." In combination with this spell, you may also burn myrrh. When you light the incense, say, "Myrrh ... as you burn, so also will you burn ___." Focus on the individual and the intensity of the love you want them to feel toward you. Once the candle is done and the incense is burned down, leave the image where it is. When the magic has been successful, take the image and hide it away somewhere. When you want the infatuation to stop, simply tear the image in half and bury it somewhere.

EFFIGY WORKING

An effigy, or poppet, is known as a kolossos in ancient Greek. Not just a substitute for the word "colossal," which refers to size, it originally was used to denote a tutelary image.[76] The idea of using effigies (aka poppets) to inflict curses and other spells is ancient, and we will explore hexing in Chapter 10. Here, we will make an effigy to use in love spells.

In order to make one, you can use one of the following ways. First, there is a wax effigy. In order to make one, I must caution you to watch for burning hot wax. Please be careful as you make it. With that warning, here is how you make a wax poppet. You'll need the following:

some wax like paraffin or beeswax (the latter is my personal go-to as it is more natural)

a double boiler or a large saucepan along with a clean, stainless steel pitcher (such as a coffee can or smaller pitcher)

olive oil

14 thumbtacks/pins (at least one of which is red)

some dried rose petals

something that links the person to that kolossos: an image, unwashed clothing, nails, or hair

some perfume or cologne

herbs such as calendula (*Calendula officinalis*), lavender (*Lavandula angustifolia*), oregano (*Origanum vulgare*), patchouli (*Pogostemon cablin*), or rosemary (*Salvia rosmarinus*)

Fill a large saucepan with water halfway. Let it boil on medium heat. While this is going on, place your wax amount—which should be a little over the size of your hand—in the clean coffee container or pitcher. Place the smaller container in the larger

---

saucepan. Watch it carefully, and wait until the wax is completely melted.

Once the wax is melted, remove the container it is in from the saucepan and pour it into a heat-safe container. Let it sit for a moment, just enough to cool but not to be stiff. Rub your palms in some olive oil. A couple of drops on each palm should do. This is so the wax does not stick to your hands. While it is still pliable, shape the wax into a human figure. Knead it as you go. If it cools too much, simply reheat it over medium heat in your pitcher or can inside the saucepan until it is pliable again. It may take some practice for you to get it to the point where this is happening. Continue to knead until it looks like a human effigy. Note: it does not have to be perfect. However, be as creative and thorough as you can. While making the kolossos, whisper the name of your target repeatedly. This aids in your focus.

Once it is done, affix an image to the front of the kolossos. If you have any bits of unwashed clothing or other anchors such as nails or hair, add them now in the appropriate places. If you don't have anything, then with the red pin simply inscribe their full legal name on the poppet. It doesn't matter where. The point is to create an anchor of some kind, and names have power. Knowing a name can give you power over that individual. You might want to do this anyway even though you may have an image, anchors, and herbs.

Now roll the kolossos in some perfume or other sweet-scented oils. When you are done, roll the effigy in the herbs mentioned, whether one or many. Continue to whisper the name of the target. Now burn some incense sacred to Aphrodite (for women) or Pan (for men), and wave the kolossos over the incense. I should note that if your target is a nonbinary individual, any of the aforementioned deities will do. As you do this, petition Aphrodite or Pan to inflame the target with love and lust. You may say something akin to the following:

Incense,
Smoke of the Gods,
Food of the Ancient Ones,
Feast, O Aphrodite,
Feast, O Pan,
Hear my words and cast forth thy love and lust.
Feast, O Pan,
Feast, O Aphrodite,
Upon the name of my target, who is [name].
So be it!

Now place the kolossos on the tile of either Pan or Aphrodite.

If you want to make a cloth effigy, then simply get material in the appropriate color, such as red, pink, or white. Cut the pattern into roughly the shape of a human. It doesn't have to be perfect. The effigy need only be a little larger than the size of your hand so it isn't cumbersome. Leaving some space, stuff the effigy with the appropriate herbs. Wave it over the incense and repeat the words you said for the wax effigy. Finish sewing it closed, and it is done.

If you have any items such as fingernails or hair belonging to the person, place them in the appropriate areas of the poppet. If it is a cloth effigy, simply stuff the cloth with the appropriate herbs (remember to also cleanse the cloth you are using). If you do not have nails or hair, then place a photo of the person on the effigy. Now, carefully take thirteen pins that have also been cleansed, and place one each in the following areas: anus, genitals, feet, hands, forehead, eyes, back, heart, mouth, and solar plexus. With each pin inserted state, "Rouse yourself, O (wo/man). Be thou roused in every place I pierce. Fire of love, bring passion upon mine and let them think of me always. Be thou roused in every place I pierce."

When you are finished piercing the entire poppet, say the following:

"Rouse yourself, O ____. Be thou roused in every place I have pierced. Fire of love, thou shalt not sleep or have any experience with anyone else except me alone. Be thou dragged by thy hair, thy guts, and in all thy places, until thou dost not stand aloof from me. Until I hold (her/him/them) in my arms, being loved and in turn loving them always and forever."

When the ritual is finished, put the effigy in a hidden place on the shrine. Once the ritual has been successful, take the effigy and ritually take it apart, lovingly and saying, "This is done. Mine has come hither. I ritually offer this to you, Aphrodite/Pan. Take these, I pray, and let the magic return. For this is completed, my prayer done, my wish granted. Now we are bound forever."

Note: remember, when you are bound together, you are fully responsible for that individual's energy, life, and blood. I offer this as a warning. If you do not want to be bound, then simply do not say the words.

THE WHEEL OF TORTURE

In ancient times, animals were sacrificed in bizarre rituals that were meant to use blood as the life force along with the principles of sympathetic magic ("like for like"). That is, by performing a certain act of magic, it was believed that the energy would repeat itself upon the individual either in a physical or some other way. I add this bit of information here for educational reasons; to deny that our ancestors used blood magic is to erase their identity. We own it, we accept it, and we move on. Some magical paths do entail some form of animal sacrifice, such as the African-Diasporic traditions. However, for us it is not necessary. Not for any superior motive (for we are not that), but simply because for our magics here we don't need it. I must stress that this "don't need" phrase does not imply that we are somehow more evolved in our spirituality. Please be respectful of different initiatory magical systems and their contributions to their own cultures.

The Wheel of Torture historically involved a live bird known as an *iunx* (a type of woodpecker). The movement of their head and the flick of their tongue was said to be the reason they were used, as they seemed to be under some sort of "love madness" in seeking out a mate. For our purposes, we will use instead a clay or cloth effigy of a bird. You will attach it to a small wheel or disc with its wings outspread. Begin to whip the bird with a scourge, summoning the spirit of "love madness." Repeat the following:

"As I whip this bird, may [Name] be whipped with frenzy in love for me, Cyprogeneia.[77] Hasten, O wingéd one, and let [Name] not be allowed to sleep or eat until they have come to me in my bed."

Then the effigy is burned while saying, "As you burn, burn in your heart for love of me. Do not forget me, but come to me in my hour of want." The ritual is ended.

THE APPLE OF APHRODITE

Materials needed:

apple

image of the desired person

red candle

olive or rose oil

---

77. An epithet of the goddess Aphrodite Pandemos meaning "Cyprus-born."

incense containing rose, sandalwood, frankincense,
   and / or marjoram

In our myths, Aphrodite Pandemos took seeds gifted from Gaia the Earth Mother and planted them in good soil far in the west. What arose was the first apple tree, and it sprouted the golden fruit in her garden. Aphrodite enjoyed the color red in particular, and so she plucked a golden apple and sliced open the fruit. Inside was her mark, the five-pointed star, a symbol of the lemniscate (the infinity symbol) by which all things were ordered. The gold was reflected by the noonday sun. As dawn came upon the world the very next day, she dipped the apple into the rosy red colors and thus was created her favorite red apple.

I share this story to inform you that apples are indeed sacred to Aphrodite Pandemos. The following is a ritual of love. Take an apple and slice it in half crosswise to reveal the pentagram inside. Take out the center portion that contains the seeds. Do not leave them anywhere if you have pets or any animals nearby, as they are poisonous.

Within the cavity of one half of the apple, place an image of the person, such as a small photograph. Above it place a red candle dressed in olive or rose oil. Lavender oil and cypress oil will also do. Remember to anoint from the top of the candle to the bottom nine times. Inscribe the name "Cyprogeneia" into the red candle. This marks it as hers. In the other half, light some charcoal and use incense that has a combination of rose, sandalwood, frankincense, and marjoram. Now burn it. As the smoke rises say:

"[Name] is the apple of my eye, and I am theirs. O Cyprogeneia, Lady of the Golden Fruit and the Scarlet Flame, I call upon you now to assist me in erecting the heart, mind, and soul of [Name] to me. I

command thy daemon to conjure lust and love toward [Name] as they hunger for me. Come, Peitho, and do Thy work." Repeat this prayer *nine times. Now watch the candle go down and burn the incense as it wanes.*

SUMMARY

We have explored erotic magics, and seen how these ancient ways can be used powerfully for our times. These methods do work, and so I caution you once again to be careful when operating them. The powers of Aphrodite Pandemos and Pan are primal and alive, and their energies will work with yours in aiming to accomplish that which you set your desires to.

CHAPTER 10

BINDING AND HEXING

I cannot write this book without touching on binding and hexing. In ancient Greece, cursing was a serious act of magic that could call down vengeance spirits such as the Furies; the spirits of those who sputtered curses out of hate and spite could also become vengeance daemons.[78] Before continuing with this chapter, as with the previous one on erotic magic, I encourage you to go over the ethics chapter (Chapter 3). Look at our virtues and pay attention to what you are about to do.

MEDEA

Strix follow their own conscience and sense of right and wrong. Divinity is not needed, and neither are thou-shalt-nots. As a reminder, the basis for our ethics is that Strix Craft can be and is political in nature. We have our own personal power. In fact, I teach a saying: *Never surrender your personal power*. Political battles over the right to autonomous authority in our conscience and right to our own bodies is something that frightens much of the patriarchal establishment. The Strix need only look to Medea, the

---

78. Luck, *Arcana Mundi*, 29.

high priestess of the goddess Hekate, in her dealings with being used and scorned by Jason.[79]

Medea is a granddaughter of the sun god Helios. She is also a niece of Circe the enchantress. Medea's tale in the epics of Jason were already known by the eighth century BCE in Hesiod's *Theogonía*. But one of the most complete surviving accounts of Medea is found in the *Argonautika*,[80] written by Apollonius Rhodius in the third century BCE. In this account, Medea is a priestess of the goddess Hekate and lives in the kingdom of Colchis, located in what is now the nation of Georgia. This suggests that the cult of Hekate was non-Greek in origin, but where exactly it originated is still unknown.

Medea was a powerful phármakis. Argos, the builder of the eponymous ship the *Argo*, said, as they headed to Colchis "There is a maiden, nurtured in the halls of Aeetes, whom the goddess Hecate taught to handle magic herbs with exceeding skill all that the land and flowing waters produce. With them is quenched the blast of unwearied flame, and at once she stays the course of rivers as they rush roaring on, and checks the stars and the paths of the sacred moon."

Medea helped Jason and the Argonauts steal the Golden Fleece, a powerful magical relic that was guarded in the sacred grove of Ares by a serpent-dragon who never slept. Jason vowed that if Medea helped him, he would marry her. She makes it back to Greece with him after a series of adventures on the voyage home.

To take the tale further, Euripides, a fifth-century Athenian playwright, wrote the tragic play *Medea*. In it, the tale informs us that Medea was abandoned by Jason and merely was going to be

---

79. Euripedes, *Medea*.

80. Rhodius.

relegated to the position of a mistress. Jason married a wealthy Corinthian princess instead. Medea laments the betrayal by Jason and cries, "By that dread queen whom I revere before all others and have chosen to share my task, by Hecate who dwells within my inmost chamber, not one of them shall wound my heart and rue it not. Bitter and sad will I make their marriage for them; bitter shall be the wooing of it, bitter my exile from the land. Up, then, Medea, spare not the secrets of thy art in plotting and devising; on to the danger." [81]

What does this have to do with personal power? Simple. Medea was not ashamed to feel sadness, betrayal, and pain. She had reason to. She insisted on using what she knew, and that was her magical skills. Nowadays many would chide anyone like Medea who called herself a priestess for daring to use her magical skills to attack her partner—who abandoned her and relegated her to the position of a mere mistress, replacing her with someone younger, wealthier, and "Greek." Jason was a misogynist. He used Medea for his own ends. She betrayed her own family, left behind all that she knew.

Be that as it may, the main point is that many witches of old had no qualms about using their magic for political ends. Like Aradia of the Middle Ages who cursed the Church and noble status quo for their treatment of the poor,[82] Medea teaches us the lesson that our magic is ready and to be feared. We can use it to our advantage and to another's disadvantage. If this frightens you, then I encourage you to face your fears and come into your own personal power.

---

81. Euripedes, *Medea*.

82. Leland.

PERSONAL POWER

Personal power is a sacred trait many witches fail to develop. Personal power is coming into your own spirit and knowing deep down that you can accomplish anything. It is knowing that you don't have to be enslaved to the minds of others. It takes breaking yourself from deadly habits and the establishment that wants you to be downtrodden, bitter, and trapped. You are not any of these. Strix develop their personal power through knowing they are children of Hekate and a manifestation of the god Nyx: god herself.

You are divine, and the Divine exists immanent within you. This means that you have a lot of potential, and you can make your visions come true. Note that I said "vision" and not "wish." Wishes are fleeting; here today and gone tomorrow. Wishes are the product of a fantastical mind and magical thinking.

But through the agency of Hekate, the power of the spirits and the support of your ancestors, you are able to accomplish your vision. What is a vision? It is the direct focus of what you practically desire to have in your life. It is an awareness of something you want manifested, and your passion doesn't let it go. Do you want to be an artist? An actor? A musician? Perhaps a doctor or a lawyer? Are you feeling strapped for cash and even like a failure because you doubt your intelligence? Do you want children? How about success in your current job? A job? How about being free to be yourself? What about connecting with Divinity and coming into your own?

All of this and more is achievable through coming into your personal power. It is a cornerstone of a Strix's focused ability. Use your skills. Meditate. Incubate. Journal. Get in touch with the gods, the spirits, and the ancestors. You'll be surprised at what comes through.

BRIMO AND PRAXIDÍKE

Sometimes, though, obstacles come in your way. Pain and trauma shatter your soul. You become broken. You cry until you can't cry anymore. You scream until your throat burns and feels like it is about to burst, until you feel like you can't breathe. When this happens, and you feel powerless, it is time to call upon the gods for empowerment and a reminder that they are immanent.

The goddesses Brimo and Praxidíke are two powerful goddesses to turn to during these times. They are able to help you focus and release the pain you are feeling. Brimo is an epithet of the goddess Hekate. By epithet, I interpret it to mean a gift: a mask that she uses to supply us with a gift of anger. Hekate Brimo was popular in the magical land of Thessaly.[83] *Alexandra*, a play by the tragedian Lycophron, records the following exchange between Cassandra and her mother Hecuba:

O Mother, O Unhappy Mother!
Thy fame, too, shall not be unknown,
But the maiden daughter of Perseus,
Triform Brimo ...[84]

Here Hekate's name is Brimo, and Jane Ellen Harrison identifies Brimo as the Thessalian Kore. Prior to getting a specific root from the underworld for Jason, Apollonius Rhodius said of Medea:

Seven times bathed she in living founts,
Seven times called she on Brimo, she who haunts.
The night, the Nursing Mother. In black weed
And murky gloom she dwells, Queen of the dead.

---

83. Harrison.

84. Callimachus, Lycophron, & Aratus.

BUILDING A SHRINE TO BRIMO

A shrine to Brimo includes the following:

a small tile roughly the size of the tiles you have been using
   throughout this book (approximately 3" x 3" is fine)

a small, sterile lancet or clean, unused diabetic needle

black or blue silk cloth

comfortable clothing (or naked)

suggested herbs

thurible

charcoal

suggested décor for the shrine

image of the goddess

a silk cloth to wrap the tile

Find a place you can house her permanently. It can be whatever space you have on a shelf or in a nook. The grander the better, but work with what you have. As time goes on and she gives you more success, you can always add more space, but it isn't necessary. Boundaries and devotion get you a long way with her. You can even use your Strix shrine, changing out images and tiles to worship and call upon different deities at various times.

On your shrine place a purple altar cloth. On this, place an image of Hekate Brimo in the back center. You can make a mask, buy a statue, use a tarot card you associate with her, or make your own. If you use a statue, place a purple veil over the image. Decorate the shrine with images of serpents, vultures, a purple or scarlet throne, or simply a purple candle. When you clean the shrine (and a major cleaning should take place on the dark moon for every one of your shrines), DO NOT WASH anything you've drawn down a spirit into. A simple wipe and anointing with four drops of wine and khernips should suffice. You may wrap implements in purple or black silk so as to keep dust from settling on them.

Brimo Sigil

To call down her presence into the shrine, take a purple tile and write the sigil of Brimo. The sigil of Brimo is a double circle in which her name is written in between the circles. Within the circle is a cauldron with a flame, above which is crossed in an X manner a key and a torch. Light the charcoal in the thurible. Burn some mugwort leaves in a thurible and wave the tile in the smoke in a figure eight fashion (be sure it is a well-ventilated area). Anoint your forehead, heart, and hands with some oil, such as those containing lavender or myrrh. Get comfortable.

Now begin a Fourfold Breath: Breathe in the count of four. Hold your breath to the count of four. Exhale slowly to the count of four.

Hold to the count of four. Repeat this procedure four times, purposefully lowering your blood pressure and relaxing your muscles. Be aware of your body, in its entirety. Mentally bring your awareness to your body, beginning with the top of your head. As you breathe, intentionally continue to bring your awareness to your temples, then your jawline, and then your neck. Note parts where you are stressed and need to relax. Stretch, yawn, and SLOWLY circle your neck. Continue to bring your awareness to your shoulders, and intentionally relax. Rotate your shoulders and loosen up your stance. Continue to scan your body, bringing your awareness to your torso, your pelvis and groin, your thighs, your calves, and finally your feet. Continue to intentionally relax your muscles and be aware of yourself. Once you feel grounded and relaxed, it is time to begin. Begin in silence. If you need noise-cancelling headphones then so be it. Turn off your phone and be sure you will not be disturbed by any sudden noise or distraction while in the middle of this rite that might jerk you back to your body and may temporarily unbalance your spirit. This results in you feeling confused, angry, unbalanced, and shattered.

As you breathe, envision a white flame encompassing your feet (or, if you are sitting, the coccyx and sacrum touching the ground). The more you breathe slowly and focus, the brighter it becomes. This flame swirls upward, from your feet, to the back of your solar plexus, to the front of your heart, to winding its way to the back of your throat, and finally twirls to your third eye. It "hums."

When you are ready, chant the following:

"BRIIIIMMMOOO ... ADRAMANTEIAAA ... BRIIIIM-MMOOO ... ADRAMANTEIAAA ..."

Continue the chant and grab the tile. Place it on the ground in front of you. Reach toward the tile with your hands and extend your palms, focusing your energy into the tile. When you sense the energy is raised, take the lancet or diabetic needle and prick your right forefinger. Allow nine drops of blood to fall on the tile, the blood awakening the sigil. It is done. Be sure to wash your finger and place a small bandage on it if needed. Drink some wine, juice, or water. Relax. You did well. Allow the blood to dry on its own. When you're ready, place the newly anointed tile underneath the image on the shrine. As long as it is there, it has been activated and will live there. Continuing to care for her will enhance your relationship with Brimo. Daily prayers, offerings, and holding special times for her, such as Saturdays or the actual night of the dark moon, will also help.

Note: I highly suggest keeping tiles with dried blood on them away from where children and animals can reach them. Perhaps purchase a small box or container and place them inside with a lock and key. Take them out when you want to honor these deities and spirits and perform certain magical workings. They are sacred vessels, alive. Remember to take them out during their special times and feed the spirits their drops of wine.

Building a Shrine to Praxidíke

We also have the goddess Praxidíke. According to Orphic sources, Praxidíke is a mask of the goddess Persephone in her guise as the exacter of justice and retribution. In order to start your shrine and activate the tile, you'll need the following:

a small tile roughly the size of the tiles you have been using
    throughout this book (approximately 3" x 3" is fine)

a small, sterile lancet or clean, unused diabetic needle

black or blue silk cloth

comfortable clothing (or naked)

suggested herbs

thurible

charcoal

Suggested décor for the shrine

Image of the goddess

A silk cloth to wrap the tile

The following is the hymn as translated by Patrick Dunn in his *The Orphic Hymns: A New Translation for the Occult Practitioner*.

Orphic Hymn to Persephone:

Come, Persephone, daughter of great Zeus,
blessed one, only begotten goddess.
Accept these gracious offerings to you.
Many-honored wife of Plouton, you give
life diligently, and control the gates
of Hades, beneath the depths of the earth.
Praxidíke, with lovely locks of hair:
Holy child of Deo, and the mother
of the Furies, queen of the underworld,
maiden whom Zeus sired with ineffable
seed—you are the mother of loud-roaring and many-formed Eubou-
leus. The shining
and luminous playmate of the seasons,
honored and mighty, maid bursting with fruit.
Mortals long for you alone, bright, horned,
springtime goddess, who is delighted with
meadow breezes, revealing your
holy body in the green and yellow new shoots.
In autumn, you were seized and forced to wed.
Now you, Persephone, alone are life
and death to toiling mortals, for you feed

us always, and also kill everything.
Hear, blessed goddess, and send up the fruits
from the earth, blossoming in peace and with
the soothing hand of health, and a rich life
that leads old age, sleek and shining, downward,
queen, to your kingdom, to mighty Plouton.

Find a place you can house her permanently. It can be whatever space you have on a shelf or in a nook. The grander the better, but work with what you have. As time goes on and she gives you more success, you can always add more space, but it isn't necessary. Boundaries and devotion get you a long way with her. You can also use your Strix shrine, alternating tiles and images to fit in with the deity or spirit you are honoring at any given moment.

In the space place a black altar cloth. On this, place an image of Persephone Praxidíke in the back center. You can make a mask, buy a statue, use a tarot card you associate with her, or make your own. If you use a statue, place a dark blue veil over the image. Decorate the shrine with images of serpents, three skulls, a dark blue throne, or simply a dark blue or black candle. When you clean the shrine (and a major cleaning should take place on the dark moon for every one of your shrines), DO NOT WASH anything you've drawn down a spirit into. A simple wipe and anointing with four drops of wine and khernips should suffice. You may wrap implements in a dark blue or black silk to keep them free of dust.

To call down her presence into the shrine, take a dark blue tile and write the sigil of Praxidíke. The sigil is a double circle with the name Praxidíke in between. In the center is a scale, beneath which is a sword with its blade pointing up known as a *xiphos*. Burn some myrrh in a thurible and wave the tile in the smoke in a figure eight fashion. Anoint your forehead, heart, and hands with some oil, such as those containing mint or myrrh. Get comfortable.

Praxidíke Sigil

Now begin a Fourfold Breath: Breathe in the count of four. Hold your breath to the count of four. Exhale slowly to the count of four. Hold to the count of four. Repeat this procedure four times, purposefully lowering your blood pressure and relaxing your muscles. Be aware of your body, in its entirety. Mentally bring your awareness to your body, beginning with the top of your head. As you breathe, intentionally continue to bring your awareness to your temples, then your jawline, and then your neck. Note parts where you are stressed and need to relax. Stretch, yawn, and SLOWLY circle your neck. Continue to bring your awareness to your shoulders, and intentionally relax. Rotate your shoulders and loosen up your stance. Continue to scan your body, bringing your awareness to your torso, your pelvis and groin, your thighs, your calves, and finally your feet. Continue to intentionally relax your muscles and be aware of yourself. Once you feel grounded and relaxed, it is time to begin. If you need noise-cancelling headphones then so be it. Turn off your phone and be sure you will not be disturbed by any sudden noise or distraction while in the middle of this rite that might jerk you back to your body and may temporarily unbalance your spirit. This results in you feeling confused, angry, unbalanced, and shattered.

As you breathe, envision a white flame encompassing your feet (or, if you are sitting, the coccyx and sacrum touching the ground). The more you breathe slowly and focus, the brighter it becomes. This flame swirls upward, from your feet, to the back of your solar plexus, to the front of your heart, to winding its way to the back of your throat, and finally twirls to your third eye. It "hums."

When you are ready, chant the following:

"PRAXIDÍKEEE ... MENATHOOUUSSS ... PRAXIDÍKEEE ... MENATHOOUUSSS ..."

Continue the chant and grab the tile. Place it on the ground in front of you. Reach toward the tile with your hands and extend your palms., focusing your energy into the tile. When you sense the energy is raised, take a small, sterile lancet or diabetic needle and prick your forefinger. Allow nine drops of blood to fall on the tile, the blood awakening the sigil. It is done. Be sure to wash your finger and place a small bandage on it if necessary. Drink some wine, juice, or water. Relax. You did well. When you're ready, place the newly anointed tile underneath the image on the shrine. As long as it is there, it has been activated and will live there. Continuing to care for her will enhance your relationship with Praxidíke. Daily prayers, offerings, and holding special times for her, such as Saturdays or the night of the dark moon, also help. Recite the Orphic Hymn to Persephone as part of your devotions.

Note: I highly suggest keeping tiles with dried blood on them away from where children and animals can reach them. Perhaps purchase a small box or container and place them inside with a lock and key. Take them out when you want to honor these deities and spirits and perform certain magical workings. They are sacred vessels, alive. Remember to take them out during their special times and feed the spirits their drops of wine.

THE FURIES

Praxidíke is Mother of the Furies. These are vengeful spirits that haunted anyone who committed certain crimes or wrongs upon an individual. The Furies were called upon to go after criminals who committed homicide, violated xenia, committed patricide or matricide, or attacked the vulnerable, such as children or the elderly.

While these are traditional roles that were ascribed to them, it is my experience that the Furies also go after the perpetrators who have committed abuse and neglect; murdered in cold blood; and violated other humans by rape, abuse, and death. They are not concerned with right and wrong necessarily. They are primal forces who haunt the guilty. When called down, they have extreme power and are dangerous to handle. Before you do so, be sure to perform a ritual to purify yourself both before and after. Also be sure to journal your thoughts and emotions after the crime has been committed toward you. They will not go after someone who has robbed you or done minor things like lie to you for whatever reason. Rape, abuse, murder, neglect, and violation are their purview.

Please note: if a crime has been committed, please go to the police and have the law take care of it. The following is an adjunct to, not substitute for, justice.

BUILDING A SHRINE TO THE FURIES

On a space or shelf place a black altar cloth. This is your designated space for the Furies. Grab a black tile and on it place the sigil of the Furies. It is a double circle with the name Eumenides, or "Kindly Ones," an epithet they were known by. In the center are three masks with serpents. The mask on the left has stable, closed lips. The one in the center has their lips slightly parted. Finally, the one on the right has a crooked smile. These creatures are not to be disturbed except in times of great need, so keep the tile covered until that time. To activate the sigil, uncover the silk covering of Praxidíke and place the tile of the Eumenides on top of the tile of Praxidíke. Place both hands on the tile for the Eumenides and say the following:

The Furies Sigil

Praxidíke,
Bring forth thy spirit,
The Furies Three live within thee.
Praxidíke,
The Furies Three within thee,
Bring forth thy spirit.
So be it!

THE CURSE OF THE FURIES

Prior to calling on the Furies, there must be a period of purification to help you cleanse yourself of your own burdens prior to calling for justice. During this time, take a journal and begin to notate your thoughts and emotions considering the matter. For nine days, you must not have any sex or masturbate. It is not about the concept of sin, but miasma. Miasma, as mentioned in Chapter 1, is a sign that we are mortal and therefore of one dimension. When entering another dimension—that of the gods and the spirits—we enter into a state of deathlessness. They are immortal, and we must shed our mortal state of mind.

For each of those nine days, pray the following at sunset while facing west:

"Praxidíke, I submit to you. Golden one below, mistress of the land above, I pray you accept me as your servant."

On the ninth day, take a ritual bath with cold water. Use the herbs hyssop, rosemary, lavender, and mint in the bath by tying them into a muslin bag and letting the bag soak into the tub so that the oils from the herbs fragrance the water. Get in the water, and sit for a moment. Then prepare to baptize yourself nine times. The following is a line to say before each immersion:

"In the name of Praxidíke, I cleanse my past." (Immersion 1)

"In the name of Praxidíke, I cleanse my present." (Immersion 2)

"In the name of Praxidíke, I cleanse my future." (Immersion 3)

"In the name of Praxidíke, I cleanse my blood." (Immersion 4)

"In the name of Praxidíke, I cleanse my bones." (Immersion 5)

"In the name of Praxidíke, I cleanse my spirit." (Immersion 6)

"In the name of Praxidíke, I cleanse my flesh." (Immersion 7)

"In the name of Praxidíke, I cleanse my bodies." (Immersion 8)

"In the name of Praxidíke, I cleanse my daemon." (Immersion 9)

This series of rituals prepares you to call upon the Furies and absolves you of your own wrongs. The addition of journaling throughout the nine-day process also will help align your focus with this ritual. Finally, it is time to call on them. Place three black candles in the shape of a triangle, and place a bowl of dirt in the middle of the triangle. Place the tile of the Furies in the center of the bowl.

Light the uppermost right black candle and say, "Alêktô, the Unceasing."

Light the bottom black candle and say, "Megaira, the Jealous One."

Light the uppermost left black candle and say, "Tisiphonê, the Overseeing One."

Repeat the Orphic Hymn to the Furies:

Hear me, Eumenides, greatly famed ones,
with a kind intention, holy daughters
of great chthonic Zeus and Persephone,
lovely maiden with beautiful hair. You
look down upon the lives of all profane
mortals and avenge all injustices.
Set over Necessity, dark-visaged

ladies, your eyes flash forth terrible rays
of shining, flesh-eating light. Eternal,
with dreadful eyes that provoke fear, sovereign,
weakening the arms and legs with madness,
grim, nocturnal, of many fates, maidens
of the night with snaky curls and fearsome
eyes, I call you to approach pious minds.

Now prick your finger with a small, sterile lancet or an unused diabetic needle. Squeeze nine drops of blood into the soil around the tile and proclaim:

(Drop 1) *"Alêktô"*
(Drop 2) *"Megaira."*
(Drop 3) *"Tisiphonê."*
(Drop 4) *"Harbingers of Justice."*
(Drop 5) *"Come at my call."*
(Drop 6) *"Rise up!"*
(Drop 7) *"Avenge my harm."*
(Drop 8) *"Hail unto You!"*
(Drop 9) *"It is done."*

Put a small bandage over the finger prick, if necessary. Allow the candles to finish burning. Please keep an eye on them. When the candles have finished burning, cover the dirt with a dark cloth and leave it out of sight until your curse work is done—perhaps under your altar or in a dark place. This curse is meant to haunt the guilty and make retribution for the wrongs they have committed. Present offerings of incense and testimonies of thanks, and honor the Furies during the dark of the moon. Reverence only is asked. Do not repeat this specific ritual for the person you intended or speak of what you have done to anyone else, knowing what a dangerous element you are working with.

THE BINDING OF PROMETHEUS

This is a binding to do when you are threatened by someone and need to stop them. It is called "The Binding of Prometheus" because the procedure nearly mirrors the kind of binding that was inflicted on him to incapacitate him. I have given out this procedure and it has always met with success. In one instance someone's ex-husband was stalking her and their children. She had every legal backing and also knew how to use weapons, but she needed something magical so it wouldn't have to come to physical violence.

The stalker eventually had a vehicular accident and ended up hospitalized for some time. It was no small matter to do this to him, yet after the abuse she endured under him, and the threats to the lives of her children, there were no qualms or guilt in the results, no hesitation to do it. I applaud her.

I have to say something first on the word "binding." There are usually three objections made to this work.

1. Binding means "binding them to you," so banish instead.
2. Binding is a dark working and shouldn't be done lest the karma of the individual be linked to you.
3. Love and light always.

I've taken each protest into consideration and here is my response to each:

1. You just want to "out of sight, out of mind" the problem for others, which doesn't work.
2. Dark things have happened to these people, and that's not what karma is.

3. Witchcraft is naturally both light and dark, and to tell people who have suffered that "love and light" is the answer is coming from a place of privilege and of not wanting to deal with one's own trauma and pain.

There, plain and simple. I realize my responses will be polemical to some, but we use the tools of our ancestors and guides to get things done. Witchcraft is dirty, earthy, and not just love and light. It is the soil and roots that hide beneath the sun. It is a holy power from Nyx and Hekate. We are the ones who get to wield this power and see its effectiveness occur. It is meant for the people to use against oppression and evil. Witchcraft has always had a political bent and remains so to this day. "Binding" is meant to incapacitate a victim, weaken them, or else cause them to behave against their own wishes.[85]

In order to perform a binding spell, you will need a kolossos of the person. This may be of wax or cloth. To make a wax kolossos, you'll need some of the following:

Some wax like paraffin or beeswax (the latter is my personal go-to as it is more natural)

A double boiler or a large saucepan along with a clean, stainless steel pitcher (such as a coffee can or smaller pitcher)

Olive oil

A black pin

Something that links the person to that kolossos: an image, unwashed clothing, nails, or hair

Herbs such as asafoetida (*Ferula asafoetida*), which smells like heavy dung, so be careful; rue (*Ruta graveolens*), patchouli (*Pogostemon cablin*), or wormwood (*Artemisia absinthium*)

---

85. Marston.

Fill a large saucepan with water halfway. Let it boil on medium heat. While this is going on, place your wax amount—which should be a little over the size of your hand—in the clean coffee container or pitcher. Place the smaller container in the larger saucepan. Watch it carefully, and wait until the wax is completely melted.

Once the wax is melted, remove its container from the saucepan and pour it into a heat-safe container. Let it sit for a moment, just long enough to cool but not to be too stiff. Rub your palms in some olive oil. A couple of drops on each palm should do. This is so the wax does not stick to your hands. While still pliable, shape the wax into a human figure. Knead it as you go. If it cools too much, simply reheat it over medium heat in your pitcher or can inside the saucepan until it is pliable again. It may take some practice for you to get it to the point where this is happening. Continue to knead until it looks like a human effigy. (Note: it does not have to be perfect. However, be as creative and thorough as you can.) While making the kolossos, repeatedly whisper the name of your target. This aids in your focus.

Shape the wax image into the figure of a human being. If it is for a woman, enhance the chest to make breasts. If for a man, add a phallus. If you have any nail clippings or hair, put those on the effigy. You may also add or use a photo of the intended, and inscribe their legal name on it with the black pin. Take the effigy to a place where you will not walk past it—perhaps an out of the way crossroads, hill, forest, marshy area, or abandoned place. Take the kolossos and the following supplies: black ribbon; black salt; gloves; a jar of poisonous leaves or flowers such as datura, belladonna, or mandrake; a small handheld shovel; six nails; a black candle; and a lighter or matches.

Once you have located the spot, dig a two- to three-foot hole. Bind the effigy with black ribbon, mummifying it and repeating these words: "As Prometheus was bound, so too art thou bound. As Zeus punished him for a crime, so too dost the king punish you for a crime." Once mummified, place the bound effigy "face" down into the hole. Be sure it fits snugly against the ground. Then take six nails and do the following:

"*I pierce thee that thou art weak.*" (Pierce right arm)
"*I pierce thee that thou art weak.*" (Pierce left arm)
"*I pierce thee so that thou cannot stand.*" (Pierce left leg)
"*I pierce thee so that thou cannot stand.*" (Pierce right leg)
"*I pierce thee so that thou art still in all things.*" (Pierce head)
"*Now I pierce thee as a feast for the Tormentor.*" (Pierce the heart)

Take the jar of leaves and cover the effigy with them. Use your gloves, as some of the leaves and flowers may get into your fingernails and that is dangerous. Pour some black salt on the entire thing. Cover it up. Now urinate over the place. Walk away and never return.

Katadesmoi: The Curse Tablets

Katadesmoi, or curse tablets, were very popular in the ancient world. Evidence suggests that it was the most widely employed form of magic.[86] Katadesmoi were written on a variety of objects including lead (which I do not recommend handling), wax, papyrus, and potsherds. The earliest katadesmoi date from about the fifth century BCE. In effect, they call upon daemons or spirits to inflict harm upon an individual. This is different than a binding or a haunting from the Furies. This is specifically to cause some kind

---

86. Collins, 64.

of physical, mental, or emotional breakdown. One can also use these to inflict generational curses upon a person or family. It is the reason these were so popular: they worked! To get started, you'll need a sheet of parchment paper, or you may make a wax tablet. For the wax tablet, you'll need the following:

- Some wax like paraffin or beeswax (the latter is my personal go-to as it is more natural)
- A double boiler or a large saucepan along with a clean stainless steel pitcher (such as a coffee can or smaller pitcher)

Fill a large saucepan with water halfway. Let it boil on medium heat. While this is going on, place your wax amount—which should be about the standard size of a sheet of paper about eight inches by eleven inches—in the clean coffee container or pitcher. Place the smaller container in the larger saucepan. Watch it carefully, and wait until the wax is completely melted.

Once the wax is melted, remove the container it is in from the saucepan and pour it into a heat-safe container. Let it sit for a moment, just enough to cool but not to be stiff. Rub your palms in some olive oil. A couple of drops on each palm should do. This is so the wax does not stick to your hands. While still pliable, shape the wax into a tablet. Knead it as you go. If it cools too much, simply reheat it over medium heat in your pitcher or can inside the saucepan until it is pliable again. It may take some practice for you to get it to the point where this is happening. Note: it does not have to be perfect. While making the tablet, whisper repeatedly the name of your target. This aids in your focus. Choose one of the aforementioned deity's epithets, such as Brimo, Praxidíke, or the Furies. Whether you are writing on the wax tablet or the parchment, write the following:

"In the Name of [Praxidíke/Brimo/Furies], by the dark of the moon and the mouth of the Gorgons; by the bite of Hekate and the froth of Cerberus, I adjure you, [Praxidíke/Brimo/Furies], to rain down upon [insert legal name of individual] and their line restlessness, pain, never-ending hunger, and poverty. Visit and prey upon them; feast on their flesh, drink of their blood, and anoint them with your fury generationally now and always. So be it!"

Now take the tablet and go to a well, cave, spring, or stream and bury it there. Leave it for the spirits. Trust in the tablet's curse to work. It always does.

THE MATIASMA: THE EVIL EYE

The *matiasma* is perhaps the most well-known hex around the world. Numerous instruments and designs have been made to avert the Evil Eye, from mirrors that reflect light, to scissors on a window, to bracelets and necklaces with eyes on them. The Evil Eye is a very real and palpable threat for many. In fact, this hex may be the number one cause for psychic attack complaints.

Just what is the Evil Eye? The earliest belief in this phenomenon comes from Egypt and Mesopotamia.[87] It was—is—believed that the eyes are the passive and active channels for information, and that such information, which can be passed from individual to individual (like a plague), can inflict harm stemming from envy, jealousy, and/or a desire to cause death. It is rooted in greed, and envy of another's good fortune. Such was the power feared in the ancient world that oftentimes letters were written that ended with wishing the recipient to be unharmed by the Evil Eye (*abaskantôs*).

Among the ancient Greeks, it may have gone back as far as the time of Homer, if not before, approximately the eighth century

---

87. Elliott, 31.

BCE. The first known literary attestation of the Evil Eye phenomenon is from the fifth century BCE, when a Greek poet by the name of Pherecrates wrote about it.[88] A review of the literature, however, yields that mentioning the Evil Eye itself would cause harm. So, nothing was said of it. It was, in effect, a taboo. Only "the Eye," or the word *phthonos* ("envy") was uttered.

The Evil Eye was believed to manifest in the form of an evil spirit. This spirit would plague the person or persons until the spirit could be appeased. It is an example of how things start and get out of your control; in this case, the green-eyed monster really is a monster.

Children were said to be especially vulnerable to the Evil Eye, and so at birth they were swaddled and, in some cultures, given a false name so the evil spirit wouldn't have power over the child by knowing its true name.

CASTING THE EVIL EYE

To cast the Evil Eye, you must first have an emotional link such as envy, hate, jealousy, or anger toward someone. Then, target an image of that individual, whether in person or in a photo, or maybe even a physical link such as a shirt, nails, or hair. However, seeing the individual is much better, as it gives you a full view of the person and the harm you intend to cause.

Take a breath and focus on the person. As you slow down your breath, focus your emotions toward that individual. Do not blink! Stare intently at them for a good minute or two. With time and practice, you'll be able to shorten this amount. See them incapacitated. See them losing what they've gained. Inhale with each

---

88. Elliott, 53.

vision, and exhale as you force the energy toward them. Do this three times. It is done. Watch for results.

SUMMARY

We've examined the deities Brimo, Praxidíke, and the Furies. We have looked at various ways in which to bind and hex others using simple forms of imitative magic, such as the Binding of Prometheus. I feel that with each spell, we learn to gain empowerment and an upper hand over people who want to see us fail. Sometimes we can make allies of them. Sometimes we cannot. And those who desire us harm, well, they can receive back what they give to us. Remember to use these skills only when you really need them. Binding, cursing, and hexing aren't playthings. You are playing with people's lives. As such, be aware of your actions. Remember the aim of accomplishment.

CHAPTER 11

COMMUNING WITH THE DEAD

Ancestral veneration is something that the dead called me to do many years ago. As a new Pagan, I couldn't find many books on the topic. Then one night I woke up from a dream of a serpent crawling over a skull; the serpent spoke, "Blood and bone." This maxim followed me for the next several weeks. Each time it came up I felt like a restless predator walking in a cage. There was more to my magic than a simple altar and deities. There had to be more! This came not too long after my dedication to Hekate as her priest. She opened the gates of the underworld and lo! There the dead were. Ancestral veneration is now a huge part of my personal practice.

When people aren't sure where to look, or are confused because some literature in the past has stated that one must look to their own bloodline to find a pantheon of a god and goddess, I have often felt very sad. Why? Because the advice, however well intended it may be, does not take into account the various spiritual underpinnings of what a bloodline or connection to a deity really means.

In reality, we are all of "mixed heritage." None of us are pure anything. If we go far back enough, we are all related. But what exactly is ancestral veneration? How do we go about it? Why should we do it?

Let's start with the beginning: What exactly is ancestral veneration? Ancestral veneration is exactly that: veneration of your ancestors. They are a biological reality for all of us, even if we are adopted. The double-serpent DNA helix that lives within us is a modicum of our ancestral lifeline. But why should we venerate them? Simple: we are venerating ourselves when we venerate them. What we do to them ricochets back to us; they and we are mirrors that reflect one upon the other. We cannot escape who we are. Our oldest living ancestor is from Africa, and dates back about two hundred thousand years ago or so. Our ancestors are the collective repository of our soul consciousness.

If you have been reading and practicing the magics within, I will assume you are an individual who understands that there are multiple realities. In these multiple realities, gods, spirits, and other beings dwell with us. Magic is the connection that underlies all. Life continues on after our bodies cease, and whether we are living or dead, we impact one another greatly. But who are we? We are the culmination of thousands of years of evolution. And life is not done yet, and that culmination is only a fraction of ourselves. Focusing on modern Greek magic, our ancestors are the very magic that makes manifestation a reality. They are the ancient keepers of the mysteries, the gates between the worlds that can inhibit or permit blessings our way. Healing is also a major part of ancestral work.

What do the ancestors want? The same thing any of us desires: recognition. Sure, misanthropes abound, but honestly, I have found in my experience that even in family lines where some of the ancestors are misanthropic, they also are just wounded, and healing is a huge part of their reparations. Once the process begins, the otherworld gate opens and we are flooded with blessings.

THE MAKÁRIOI

I call the dead the Makárioi, or the "Blessed [Ones]." It is always a polite thing to refer to the dead or the things from the underworld in the opposite way (e.g., Eumenides ["Kindly Ones"] for the Erinyes ["Furies"]). But not all of them are blessed or well. There are ancestors who are tormented for any number of reasons: murder, abuse, or being killed and haunting our world until justice is meted out. In this case, many family lines are born with anger and bitterness issues. We have lost our identity and as a result we drink heavily or do drugs because addictions manifest as a way of coping. Unfortunately, sometimes spirits will want the family line to die because of their pull to death, and what happened to them long ago reverberates down to us; it becomes a generational curse.

Ancestors and spirits who seek to destroy the good potential in their current bloodline must be appeased and the curses broken. For those that are hurting or who have hurt, we build an altar with one black candle. This altar is for the "Lost Ones." By lighting a candle, the intention is to help use the energies in ritual to spread and heal the lost ancestors through the candle contact point.

Healing begins with us. It is such an integral part of ancestral work that I cannot emphasize this enough. It is possible that the ancient Greeks knew this and used methods such as incubation to help ancestral contact for the afflicted.

THE DEAD IN ANCIENT GREECE

The dead were memorialized in ancient Greece. The cult of the dead was well established by the sixth century BCE, when the Homeric poets sang about the underworld. In the *Odyssey*, Achilles speaks to Odysseus in the underworld about how he would rather be a poor man than the Lord of the Underworld![89] The underworld in Homeric literature is described as a gloomy place, an unseen realm. But there is also a different geography.

Let me begin by saying briefly that what I am writing now is a hint of the mystery. It is based on the notion that we wander the world as perpetual seekers of truth, and only when we come upon the spirits of our lineage do we find the path of initiation calling to us. This initiatory path is not for everyone. The mystery teachings tell us that many carry the thyrsus, but few are the true mystics. One can be an occultist, involved in other religious truths, or none at all, and still not be a true mystic. A mystic is one whose eyes have been closed. Why are they closed and not open? They were open. But what did they see? Those are the questions that lead the thyrsus bearers to go from frenzy to the silence of incubation. The path is labyrinthine into the center.

From these teachings, we assert that there are different levels of the underworld. Suffice it to say that the ancestors have a place where, regardless of their destination, they can be contacted.

The Living Power of Memory

To the ancient Greeks, memory is a living power. The dead lived on by their offspring continuing to uphold their names and deeds. Their graves would be visited often and offerings and prayers made to them. These days candles can be lit on birthdays and anniversaries, or any moments of special occasion. My family used to go to the gravesite of our passed loved ones and have a picnic there. There is a wellspring from the cauldron of memory that weaves its way from the strings of Ananke: a golden thread that weaves

---

89. Homer, *Odyssey*, XI: 489–91.

everyone together. Memory comes alive each time we commune and tell the stories and songs of our people. Whenever we share their stories, their impact, and connect with their spirits is when memory comes alive. If they did not have any blood children, the ancient Greeks would adopt others so they could be remembered, so afraid were they of becoming lost in oblivion.[90]

Some traditions teach that the walls between the living and the dead are thinned only during certain times of the year. It has been my experience, however, that when you know how to push the gates of the otherworld by awakening memory, the veil will always be thin for you.

When we talk about contacting the Makárioi, we are also talking about how rude it would be if we only got together once a year and had a conversation. Are special days set aside specifically for them? Yes. But these are feast days meant for an entire community. You're more than welcome to make your own feast day calendar as well. We all have different ones depending on memorial days, birthdays, and such. Whatever the time or day, remember that an ongoing conversation can yield many powerful results to you.

You live because of them. Your ancestors sacrificed so much so that you could exist in the here and now. You are the culmination of their dreams and hopes. That means that as you begin your ancestral veneration and healing, you'll be surprised at responses you receive from them.

THE DEATH PROCESS IN ANCIENT GREECE

Preparations were carefully made for the dying.[91] Oftentimes a ritual bath was employed first (whether by the individual or another

---

90. Mikalson, 127.

91. Graves.

female member of the oikos—household—if they were not able to do it themselves). Death was viewed as a rite of passage, in which one was leaving the hearth of the living for that of the underworld. To not give someone a proper burial was a capital offense and the eldest son was held liable.

When the breath finally left the body, the *psyche* (spirit, breath) was now in the hands of the underworld. Finally, the first of the three stages in the funerary practices came about: the *próthesis*, or the "setting forth." This is when the body was set out on a bier and the body was ritually washed, oiled, and clothed. One by one, family members came and paid their respects. The entire process was overseen by women from oikos. Terracotta art from the sixth century BCE depicts a typical próthesis rite.

The second stage was the *ekphora*, the "procession." Art from the same period depicts a body on a bier flanked by warriors or family members. This is especially shown in the Dipylon vases from the eighth century BCE. At dawn the deceased was accompanied by pallbearers and—depending on the status of the individual—on a bier with horses and accompanied by warriors. The wake was filled with mourning, loud lamentations, and music.

Finally came the interment (or cremation). Most people were buried in plots or individual graves. Contrary to popular belief, placing coins in the mouth or eyes of the deceased wasn't as popular as it has been made out to be. I certainly know of many folks who practice it, however.

Building a Shrine to the Ancestors

If you want to be successful in communing with the dead, then it begins with your own ancestors. Both new and experienced practitioners alike will benefit from the doing of the work. Remember that the blessed dead speak to us in a myriad of ways, and maintaining that relationship with them can be difficult for many, because they put a metaphorical magnifying glass upon our own shortcomings because it reflects theirs. Doing work on ourselves helps them. We are symbiotic.

Find a flat space where you can build your ancestral memorial. Remember that this is a focal point for you and your family. If you have nowhere to put it but there, then use a drape and curtain off the area. Only remove it when you are making contact. Why a drape? Simple. The dead live in a world all of their own, and the drape serves as a veil between theirs and ours. While I love venerating and working with the ancestors, I want to be sure there are boundaries in place, just as when people come over. Just because they are family doesn't mean I have time to communicate with everyone. The drape serves as a device to close the door. Place a white altar cloth on the space. Here place photos and/or mementos of the dead. These are links of memory. I always tell people to be sure that no images of a living person are in the photos placed on this altar. If you do this, the ancestors will take it that that individual is ready to join them.

Place on the memorial their favorite drinks, smokes, rosaries, jewelry, and the like. Decorate it how you see fit. It is supposed to be a sacred space of ambience and comfort. On feast days you can make their favorite food, coffee, or alcoholic drinks. Leave these on the altar between twelve and twenty-four hours, then remove them. Remember that, unlike food offerings to the deities, which are shared, food for the dead is never eaten! It is always for them. Light white candles when celebrating any special days. Saturdays, the day of the underworld, along with the new moon when the time of the dark moon is over and Hekate is placated, are perfect times for celebrating the ancestors and making household rituals.

THE LOST ONES

There are some ancestors whom we don't want to recognize. Inherently and unfortunately, they are part of our blood kin, but that doesn't mean we have to think of them when we venerate the ancestors. I'm talking about those family members who were abusive, family members you never forgave because of what they did to you and yours.

I'm not about to lecture you on love and light either. Or forgiveness. Grief and rage happen to everyone in these situations, and how we deal with it is up to each person. What I will say—and this is based on my experiences—is that we do have to be careful about how much we allow our hearts to harden (read: become bitter). Bitterness is a poison that can and will weigh us down. It is a power over us from another, rather than power from within. Remember about not surrendering your personal power. Dealing with the Shadow—that manifested Other of our deep-seated fears, traumas, depressions, and the like—is not easy by any means. But in my experience when dealing with loss, agony, pain, and rage, we are encouraged to begin a journey to find ourselves. Being out of harmony leads only to self-torment. It doesn't mean that what you're feeling isn't real or that you should be told to suppress "negative energy." Allow it to flow. Allow yourself to experience it. But rest assured that as time goes on, you can hold on to the rage without the thorn of bitterness. Yes, it is possible. Don't paint your emotions with one broad brush. With that in mind, let us look below at some techniques for communicating with the dead.

SCRYING MIRROR—THE EYE OF NYX

I gave the instructions for creating a black mirror in Chapter 4 on Tools, but I will repeat it here.

Materials needed:

a piece of mirror or glass in a frame

black enamel spray paint

mugwort leaves

myrrh incense

Take a black mirror or make your own. To make your own, simply find a mirror of good quality and size. Some people use the glass already found in wooden picture frames at the local store. The size is up to you, as long as it is easy to handle. I say "easy to handle" because it is something you will want to carry with you for rituals and to put away. Wooden frames are best because shiny ones tend to reflect into the glass.

Purchase a can of high gloss black enamel paint that is good for glass. Remove the glass and clean it thoroughly. Let it dry. On a sunny (and as windless as possible) day, place the glass on a bed of newspapers outdoors. Spray paint the glass using quick, even passes back and forth. Let it dry (it may take a few hours). When it is dry, place the mirror in the frame. Now take some mugwort leaves and make a tea. Let it cool and strain it. Take the tea and anoint the mirror and frame with it. It is ready to be used.

Consecrate and activate the mirror on the night of the dark moon. Light some myrrh incense. Take the mirror and weave it in and out of the smoke in a figure eight fashion while saying three times:

Eye of night,
Hekate's sight.
Cleanse this mirror,
Spirits speak clearer

Light a red candle in front of the mirror. Now take the Fourfold Breath: Breathe in the count of four. Hold your breath to the count of four. Exhale slowly to the count of four. Hold to the count of four. Repeat this procedure four times, purposefully lowering your blood pressure and relaxing your muscles. Be aware of your body, in its entirety. Mentally bring your awareness to your body, beginning with the top of your head. As you breathe, intentionally continue to bring your awareness to your temples, then your jawline, and then your neck. Note parts where you are stressed and need to relax. Stretch, yawn, and SLOWLY circle your neck. Continue to bring your awareness to your shoulders, and intentionally relax. Rotate your shoulders and loosen up your stance. Continue to scan your body, bringing your awareness to your torso, your pelvis and groin, your thighs, your calves, and finally your feet. Continue to intentionally relax your muscles and be aware of yourself. Once you feel grounded and relaxed, it is time to begin.

Focus on the space above the crown of your head. See the Azure Flame swirling and alive. The more awareness you bring to it, the brighter it becomes. Breathe gently upon the mirror, transferring the Azure Flame of magic to the mirror itself. Open your eyes and look at the spot in the mirror where the candle and the black color meet. Let the myrrh incense swirl its way around the mirror. Speak the following in a solemn tone:

Open for me the Ancient Caverns;
The Cavern of Sleep and Dream.
The Cavern of Dark and Night.
The Cavern of Peace and Rest.

Now wait for your messages to come through. If you have a spirit board, all the better to use this method and combine it with the spirit board for answers. Be sure to always have someone present if you plan on using the spirit board so as to record what is being said. Confirm these answers later on, or ask for some kind of confirmation. Another way is to sit and meditate. You may blindfold yourself and wear noise-canceling headphones if you must, in order to deprive yourself of your most powerful senses: sight and hearing. For those who are deaf, simply blindfolding will do.

Allow the visions to come to you as you focus on the smell of the incense. Try to move past the point of anxiety in order to "hear" the spirits speak. When you are done, remove the blindfold gently and then blow out the candle. Cover the mirror with a cloth. It is done. Record your observations.

THE PIT OF THE DEAD

For the pit, you will need your wand, your dagger, and the Eye of Nyx. Beneath a dark moon, dig a hole about three feet deep in your yard, or a foot or so deep in a large pot. Be sure it is deep enough to hold three black taper candles. The shape of the hole should be as triangular as possible. Place a black candle at each corner of the triangle. For the ditch, offerings should be puppy-shaped cookies (in the place of black puppies) covered in pomegranate and wine. Burn some incense that has the following:

1 part dittany of Crete

1 part vervain

½ part myrrh

½ part black copal

This incense will help give form to the one being called. When you are ready, place the Eye of Nyx behind the triangle and the incense in front. Take your wand in your dominant hand (right if you are ambidextrous) and point the wand at the pit. While waving it in a figure eight motion toward the pit, recite the following nine times:

Taifes kato
Kalesma mou
Prokyptoun!
Prokyptoun!
Prokyptoun!

Translation:

Wisps of below,
Heed my call:
Arise!
Arise!
Arise!

The loved one or whomever you are contacting will appear. Listen carefully. Watch slowly as the incense creates a figure—the wisp of a face, the shady figure of a person—or perhaps triggers a familiar smell. Be very careful, as the dead tend to rush in to eat the offerings in the pit. In order to control them, have your dagger out and ready. Call to the one whom you are asking to appear. Any spirit that does not identify itself as the one you called can be banished with the dagger. To close the ceremony, bid them depart and blow the candles out. Then cover the candles with the dirt by putting it all back into the hole. When this operation is finished, take a purification bath by dropping a muslin bag filled with lavender, hyssop, roses, and/or rosemary into your bathwater. Be sure to cover the mirror.

THE SKULL ORACLE

Necromancy is contacting the dead, speaking with the ancestors, and listening. These ways date back to our ancestors in Baia, Italy, where the nekromanteion was built on hallowed ground. This temple, dedicated to Hades and Persephone, guided the prospective querant below the depths into the very court of the underworld. It was a dangerous journey, and many died in the attempt. Before this, even earlier, the area was a swampy land with a single nekromanteion inhabited by a skull from which oracles spoke. Priestesses of the Graeae cared for the nekromanteion.

Find a human-shaped skull. It doesn't have to be a real one (besides, there are legal quandaries to untangle). Mine is made of rose quartz. With a marker, draw an X on the forehead and say:

As I am, you once were.
As you are, one day I shall become.
As I serve you, you serve me.
Mortality comes to all.

In a thurible, light some incense made of the following:

1 part dittany of Crete

1 part vervain

½ part myrrh

½ part black copal

Wave the skull through the incense in a figure eight fashion. Now lay it flat and look at it directly. Ask a question. Listen. A spirit board may be of use here, or automatic writing.

SUMMARY

Contacting the dead was a dangerous business in ancient Greece. Many went insane or died trying to hear the voices of their beloved dead who could reveal secrets of the past, present, and future. We have examined a few techniques in order to communicate with them. Remember that a spirit board, automatic writing, and sensory deprivation are common ways in which to hear them speak.

Whatever you do, always close the veil! Always cover the hole with the dirt. Always veil the mirror. Be sure everything is put away. Remember that the dead are desperate and desire to always communicate with the living in some way. Think of them as out-of-control toddlers and your spiritual hearth is a china shop. Control. Patience. Boundaries. Respect. These will lead you a long way in your workings.

CHAPTER 12
SEASONAL FESTIVALS

In the practice of Strix Craft, we celebrate the cycles that were birthed through the Neopagan Wheel of the Year. We merely work different magics by reenactment of the myths that speak to us. By reenacting, we bring mythos alive and are able to channel the powers of nature and the deities into our space.

It should be said that myth is not literal. The Homeric epics and the writings of Hesiod are not scripture. We do not have *sola scriptura* in Hellenic polytheism or Strix Craft, although many do interpret the myth of Nyx as a literal myth: Intelligent Design. By ascribing an androgyne deity to the mechanisms behind the multiverse, we make sense of all that was, is, and shall be.

Mythos, to me, is the song and stories of our ancestors. It is the focus of who we are and where we fit into the cosmos. It is our tales of the adventures of the gods and spirits. More so, many societies have myths that are contradictory insofar as their beginnings are concerned. One need only to read the stories of the ancient Greeks to understand the confusion behind the origins of the various deities and spirits. What are we to do then with such contradictions? It is quite simple: look to the meaning of each, and determine the teachings.

Linear stories with a "clean" interpretation of a beginning, middle, and end to myths comes from monotheism. The interpretation of this deity's followers is that no contradiction should exist in the tales, even though scholars have stated well and good that such contradictions exist. While some will clutch pearls, others have not worried about it. They see the stories as teaching parables and not facts—facts that, if denied being facts, will lead to some worshipers being ostracized by their congregation and perhaps threatened with torment in the afterlife.

BULL AND WOLF

Depending on the time of the year, it is either the Bull Half or the Wolf Half. Some may recognize these as terms for the Oak and Holly Kings, or the Light Half and Dark Half of the Year. In Strix Craft, this is a bit different. Why do we stick with these motifs? Because they work. The symbolism is rife with interpretation, and there is a lot to be said for the bull and the wolf in Hellenic mythos.

For example, the story of the god Apollo is rife with wolf and bull ritual combat symbolism. In Apollo's life, his mother Leto was led by wolves (or herself was a she-wolf). Apollo himself leads wolves to nurture his son Miletos in Crete.[92] In the tale of Danaós, the King of Libya, Pausanias relates how the bull sent by Poseidon would fight with the wolf sent by Apollo. Apollo's wolf overcame the bull, and thus a sanctuary was established for Apollo Lukeios.

Another wolf and bull story comes to us from the tale of Pyrrhus, who sees two bronze statues of a wolf and bull in combat. This depiction foretells his death, and the images were erected in

---

92. Farnell.

commemoration of the above tale regarding Danaós.[93] Another ritual combat of the bull and the wolf occurs with the contest of Minos (the Bull) and Theseus (the Wolf) in the tale regarding the Minoan bull and the labyrinth. The ritual battles between these opposing forces throughout Hellenic tales and myths brings us down to a single point: that there is an ancient competition between forces of life and death embodied in these animals. For Strix Craft, the bull is linked to Dionysus and the wolf is linked to Apollo, as well as Hekate. Therefore, the festivals that occur between the time of the winter solstice and the Summer Solstice are those linked with the energy of Dionysus. Those festivals between the time of the Summer Solstice and winter solstice are those linked with the energy of chthonian Apollo and Hekate.

This theme is relevant in that the bull represents the budding life force of fertility, vitality, and the energies of spring and summer. The bull is Dionysus, in his sacred mask as the giver of life. He is the crowned bull-horned Bacchus of the fruits and fields. His is the splendor that births creation.

The wolf, on the other hand, is life, but during the time of fall and winter. The wolf represents the opposing forces of predator, blood, sacrifice, and the gift of incubation during these harsh times. We all have a fall or winter in our lives when things become difficult, and the wolf is there to remind us that we are, indeed, still active and part of life when all around us seems to be dead.

THE CROWNING OF THE BULL
The Winter Solstice—The Triumph of Dionysus
The winter solstice is the longest night of the year, but light overcomes darkness. Satyrs and nymphs come forth in ecstatic frenzy

---

93. Plutarch.

and raise the banner of Dionysus. The raving one—an epithet of Dionysus in his mask that grants us divine madness and ecstasy—marches with thundering cries, and his maenads shout in divine madness. The transition from darkness into light is not always pleasant. Light can blind. The light that shines in our eyes is the light of life that traumatizes us as we are born into this world. Each year at the winter solstice, the energy of Dionysus upsets the status quo of increasing darkness into the quickening of the sun. The natural order is reset, and the tendrils of Dionysian fire creep out and begin to make connections beneath the land into the sky and stars above.

Tools

a blue or scarlet altar cloth

a small bottle of rosemary

sea salt

lavender

a bowl of water

a small bowl of three dried bay leaves

three cookies safe for an offering

an offering bowl (preferably wood)

incenses (frankincense and sandalwood)

central candle representing Hestia

a bell

a blade

a green cube

a vase with flowers (violets, lavender, or snapdragon)

music

grapes

a chalice of white wine/juice

an icon of Dionysus

a thyrsus

olive oil or essential pine oil

Preparing the Bômós

Clean the bômós surface with rosemary, sea salt, and lavender. Place the ingredients in the center. Leaving your hand open and flat, meditate on the Azure Flame and its purifying power. Now bring your fingers together and begin swirling the herbs on top of the bômós from the center clockwise outward, then spiral once again inward to the center counterclockwise. When finished, cry "Es'tô! [So be it!]" Place the altar cloth on top. Prepare the rest of the bômós accordingly.

Preparation

Lay out your Strix altar facing east, with an altar cloth. Incenses: one holder on the very front of the altar, and one on the ground. Bell: placed in the southeast corner. Blade: placed in front of the bell. Place the bowl of water with the three dried bay leaves on the side in the northwest corner. Place the central candle (Hestia) in the center. Behind the Hestia candle is the green cube. Place the vase in the very back of the altar. Put the plate of cookies in front of the bowl. Place the offering bowl in front of the bell. The chalice of wine/juice and water can go anywhere. The thyrsus can also go anywhere. The bowl of grapes is placed to the left of the vase, and the icon to the right of the vase. You may add a candle to either side of the grapes and icon.

Ring the bell nine times to indicate the start of the ritual.

Light the three dried bay leaves and place them in the center of the bowl. Repeat three times as you circle the bowl clockwise: "Hekas, Hekas, Este Bebeloi!" Anoint your forehead and say, "By the Mind of the Azure Flame I consecrate myself." Anoint your lips and say, "By the Mouth of the Sacred, I consecrate myself." Anoint your chest and say, "By the Heart of the Goddess, I consecrate myself." Fully anoint your left hand and then your right and say, "By the Touch of the Godself, I consecrate myself."

Take the bowl and place it outside somewhere and say, "Chaos has no place in Order. The Profane has no place in Holiness. Leave us in peace, and accept these offerings in appeasement. Es'tô!"

Light the incense. Meditate for a moment. Focus above you an Azure Flame that burns just above the crown of your head. The more you focus, the more alive and bright becomes. When you are ready, perform the Fourfold Breath and begin the next part.

PRESENTATION OF THE ICON

Starting in the east, walk clockwise in a circle and throw some petals from the flowers in the vase down before you. When completed, take the icon and walk clockwise over the flowers, presenting it to the four directions. Begin with the east. At the end make a final salute to the east by raising the image for a moment longer, and then place the icon back on the bômós. Unveil the icon. Cry, "Euphêmeíte! [Speak with silence!]" Wait a few moments and then ring the bell nine times.

ANOINTING

With the olive oil or essential pine oil anoint yourself on your forehead and state your intention: "In soundness and peace I celebrate the Triumph of Dionysus."

INCENSES

Light the incense located underneath the bômós (the chthonic incense) and say, "Spirits from below, I honor you and observe these sacred rites in your praise. Es'tô!" Light the incense upon the bômós (the ouranic incense) and say, "Spirits from above, I honor you and observe these sacred rites in your praise. Es'tô!" Spend some quiet time meditating about the deities and spirits, as well as the ritual at hand to be done.

HEARTH LAMP

Light the candle to Hestia. You may say anything you wish to her to welcome her. An example of welcoming her is below:

> *"Hail Mother!"*
> (Take a breath) *"The welcoming heat of your embrace ..."*
> (Take a breath) *"The gentle touch upon my head ..."*
> (Take a breath) *"The nurturing spirit that surrounds me ..."*
> *"Let your holy flame light within our hearts. Let our souls be made purified even as you are. Khai'rete [Hail] Hestia!"*

Let the candle flame burn and for a moment focus on the dance and the spirit of she who dwells in all living fire.

RITUAL

Be sure you give yourself enough space to not knock anything over!

Play some drumming music. Calmly ground yourself for a moment and listen to the music. Imagine yourself in a wooded area, with drums coming from wild women hidden throughout the forest and the mountain. The sensation is alluring, and you can feel heat rise within you. Anoint your thyrsus at the pinecone end with some of the white wine or juice. Gently wave it and let the drops hit you. Taste. Drink. This is the blood of the raving one, the intoxicating drink that binds us with him. Anoint and wave again. Do it once more. Now begin to dance. Take the thyrsus in both hands, and cradle the staff like you're cradling an infant. As you do so, start slow. Invoke the Azure Flame to come into your mind's eye and focus on it. As you begin to rhythmically breathe and dance, it brightens. Each time you touch the ground with your foot you release some of that energy. From the heavens you draw down to the land beneath … this is the power of the Azure Flame. As you raise energy, the flame rises and dances *with* you. Feel it surround you and penetrate you. Channel the flame into the thyrsus, and use it to strike the ground to release energy. Finally, as you dance faster, and the energy rises higher up, you increase your speed until at last you take one big breath, jump, and exhale upon landing, releasing all of the Dionysian vitality into the land around you. Yi-yi-yi-yi-yi-yi!!!!!!

Sacrifice and Offering

Take a cookie and seven grapes. Place them in the offering bowl. Open the grapes one by one, allowing some of the juice to land on the cookie. This symbolizes the rending of the Dionysian sacrifice and the recreation of the Seven Worlds (cosmos). Every myth reenacted once more channels those powers from the world back into it again, refined. The alchemy of ritual is palpable. Pour some white wine or juice into the chalice and make a libation into the bowl. Say, "From the soil, to the vine, from the vine to the grape, from the grape to the wine. Blood of our god, return unto thee in thanksgiving and praise. Let it be acceptable in your sight. Es'tô!" Ring the bell nine times.

CLOSING

Thank Hestia from your own words. But you may use the ones below as an example:

Lady Hestia,
Goddess of the Flame,
Teach us to be hospitable to one another…
Teach us to be right in our behavior toward each other…
Teach us to be of humble minds toward each other…
And teach us to honor ourselves as we honor you. Though your light
goes out in the apparent world, it remains lit within our hearts and
hearth. I thank you with a kiss.

Blow out the candle. Silently or vocally thank the other gods and spirits: "Hear my call Ancient Ones, and blessed be your names."

The rite is ended.

February 1—The Rite of Hestia

Hestia, as one can already see, is the very heart of our homes. In ancient times our ancestors huddled toward the fires to remain safe and warm. Hestia also taught the domestic arts, such as how to cook properly with herbs and spices. Hestia taught humanity how to properly use the fire that had been given to us, and how to wield it to assist us in becoming a family unit under her blessing. The taming of fire (or whatever that is we call taming) built communities and fostered a sense of responsibility toward one another and especially the welcoming and treatment of strangers. She continues to give us guidance in our homes and the sanctity of where we live. Where we reside may not be the best of places for many of us, but the magic is there. Your hearth is not just your room or your apartment or your house. It is also your heart. Your hearth is your inner dwelling, and who you allow to come in and be treated with respect may have its limits on those who have posed danger to you time and again. You, too, have boundaries. Be hospitable toward yourself. Be respectful toward yourself. But always remember, what Hestia teaches is that we are more than one. One can survive alone if need be. But more than one can help us to live.

Hestia also dwells in the center of our world: she is the central fire whose vitality nurtures the earth goddess. If we take this symbolism further, she sits at the central fire of omniexistence and is the literal star goddess who brings forth controlled fire to light up the darkness. Hestia is the First and the Last. She is the Eldest and the Youngest. All first fruits are given unto her, and she takes a portion of every sacrifice given to the gods above and below.

Tools

scarlet altar cloth

small bottle of rosemary

sea salt

lavender

bowl of water

a small bowl of three dried bay leaves

a bowl of nine dried basil leaves

three cookies safe for an offering

an offering bowl (preferably wood)

incense (frankincense)

a central candle representing Hestia

a bell

a vase with flowers (roses are best)

two candles

music

a cauldron with a red candle in the center

a chalice with water (no chalice for the wine or grape juice)

the green cube

blade

wand

olive oil or essential frankincense oil

PREPARING THE BÔMÓS

Clean the bômós surface with rosemary, sea salt, and lavender. Place the ingredients in the center. Leaving your hand open and flat, meditate on the Azure Flame and its purifying power. Now bring your fingers together and begin swirling the herbs on top of the bômós from the center clockwise outward, then spiral once again inward to the center counterclockwise. When finished, cry "Es'tô!" Place the altar cloth on top. Prepare the rest of the bômós accordingly.

PREPARATION

The altar with altar cloth faces east. Place the incense holder on the very front. Put the bell in the southeast corner. Place the blade and wand next to each other in front of the bell. The bowl of water with three dried bay leaves goes on the side in the northwest corner. The central candle (Hestia) goes in the center, with the green cube in front of the Hestia candle. The cauldron with the red candle is placed in the center in front of the Hestia candle, with the nine dried basil leaves surrounding it. The vase is placed in the very back of the altar. The plate of cookies goes in front of the bowl. The offering bowl is placed in front of the bell. The chalice of water may be placed anywhere. Two candles are placed one on either side of vase.

Ring the bell nine times to indicate the start of the ritual.

Light the three dried bay leaves and place them in the center of the bowl. Repeat three times as you circle the bowl clockwise: "Hekas, Hekas, Este Bebeloi!" Anoint your forehead and say, "By the Mind of the Azure Flame I consecrate myself." Anoint your lips and say, "By the Mouth of the Sacred, I consecrate myself." Anoint your chest and say, "By the Heart of the Goddess, I consecrate myself." Fully anoint your left hand and then your right and say, "By the Touch of the Godself, I consecrate myself."

Take the bowl and place it outside somewhere and say, "Chaos has no place in Order. The Profane has no place in Holiness. Leave us in peace, and accept these offerings in appeasement. Es'tô!"

Light the incense. Meditate for a moment. Focus above you an Azure Flame that burns just above the crown of your head. The more you focus, the more alive and bright it becomes. When you are ready, perform the Fourfold Breath and begin the next part.

PRESENTATION OF THE ICON

Starting from the east, walk clockwise in a circle and throw some petals from the flowers in the vase down before you. When completed, take the Hestia candle and walk clockwise over the flowers, presenting them to the four directions, beginning in the east. At the end make a final salute to the east by raising the image for a moment longer, and then place the icon on the bômós. Cry, "Euphêmeíte!" Wait a few moments and then ring the bell nine times.

ANOINTING

With the olive oil or essential frankincense oil anoint yourself on your forehead and state your intention: "In soundness and peace I celebrate the Rite of Hestia."

INCENSE

Light the incense located underneath the bômós (the chthonic incense) and say, "Spirits from below, I honor you and observe these sacred rites in your praise. Es'tô!" Light the incense upon the bômós (the ouranic incense) and say, "Spirits from above, I honor you and observe these sacred rites in your praise. Es'tô!" Spend some quiet time meditating about the deities and spirits, as well as the ritual at hand to be done.

HEARTH LAMP

Light the candle to Hestia. You may say anything you wish to her to welcome her. An example of welcoming her is below:

> *"Hail Mother!"*
> (Take a breath) *"The welcoming heat of your embrace…"*
> (Take a breath) *"The gentle touch upon my head…"*
> (Take a breath) *"The nurturing spirit that surrounds me…"*
> *"Let your holy flame light within our hearts. Let our souls be made purified even as you are. Khai'rete Hestia!"*

Let the candle flame burn and for a moment focus on the dance and the spirit of she who dwells in all living fire.

RITUAL

Cup your hands over the red candle. Focus for a moment on the goddess Hestia and what she means to you. What is your hearth?

Where is it that you call home? Who is it with? What does it all look like to you? More importantly, what does it feel like to you? When you are ready, take a breath, light the red candle and say:

Eternal Fire,
Deep calls unto Deep,
Thanksgiving and Praise unto Thee,
The Ruby Star shines forth from within,
The blossom of the Spring Rose comes forth.
We approach thy sanctum with respect.
Bless our rites and attend unto us, we pray.
Let your holy flame light within our hearts.
Let our souls be made purified even as you are. Khair'ete Hestia!

Ring the bell three times.

Now take each of the nine remaining basil leaves and recite the following in a worshipful manner:

I offer unto thee this fragrant spice,
(light a basil leaf and leave it in the cauldron to burn)
Holy Lady of Fire, (repeat with basil and cauldron)
Hail unto thee, thou who dwellest upon the Highest Dwellings.
(repeat with basil and cauldron)
Within thee, O Lady, the Theoi abide, and we mortals have a sure
foundation. (repeat with basil and cauldron)
Thy locks drip with lustral oil, hallowed is thy flame.
(repeat with basil and cauldron)
We worship thee according to thy names:
Hestia! (repeat with basil and cauldron, ring bell once)
Boulaia! (repeat with basil and cauldron, ring bell once)
Pyrtaneia! (repeat with basil and cauldron, ring bell once)

By whatever Name is thy delight, come sweet Lady!
Hilathi! [Be propitious!]"

Sacrifice and Offering

Take each cookie and break it in half. Eat one piece. Now lift up the chalice and say, "In return may we receive your divine illumination! Let us hear your voice, O sacred ones! Come unto us, even as the rain fertilizes and blesses the earth. Es'tô!" Ring the bell nine times.

Closing

Thank Hestia from your own words. But you may use the ones below as an example:

Lady Hestia,
Goddess of the Flame,
Teach us to be hospitable to one another …
Teach us to be right in our behavior toward each other …
Teach us to be of humble minds toward each other …
And teach us to honor ourselves as we honor you.
Though your light goes out in the apparent world, it remains lit
within our hearts and hearth. I thank you with a kiss.

Blow out the candle. Silently or vocally thank the other gods and spirits: "Hear my call, Ancient Ones, and blessed be your names."
The rite is ended.

March 21—The New Year

The Spring Equinox is our religious New Year. Although the equinox no longer rises in the constellation Taurus but in Pisces, nonetheless there is still value in celebrating this auspicious Dionysian day for what it brings us. The Spring Equinox is a time of harmony between the ever-growing light and fading darkness, when equilibrium reaches night and day. In my understanding, this day is dedicated to remembering when the Seven Worlds were created by Dionysus: he was rent apart, and we reenact this myth to reshape the energy of ourselves moving forward. This is a day of sanctuary: celebration, purification, newness, and oneness. In old times bulls were led to be slaughtered and their heads held up as crowns. The blood would be drunk and the flesh might in some cases be eaten raw in a ceremonial omophagia.

On this day it is important for us to look at our lives from a different perspective. All year we have worked at creating ourselves in a certain image. That image is tied to something such as our jobs, our career, our family, our sense of self-worth, our friends, our family, our lovers, our religious beliefs or secular philosophies, our successes and failures. We have looked at ourselves in overall terms of "doing" things that can be seen by others as a measure of how we are doing, and to promote an image, an ideal, about who we are and what we are to the rest of the world. But on the equinox, when harmony between what is seen and unseen is being accomplished, we take a few moments to stop and turn inward at the chaos that pervades our lives; the overwhelming sense of outer self must now be paused.

The inner self—that is, the face beneath the masks just listed above—is the true part that we must recognize. The goal is harmony. What aspects of yourself are you ignoring in favor of others? Do you care too much about how you present yourself? Is there a sense of conformity to others that you must achieve that sacrifices some of your other talents? Or perhaps you have no lacking in any area ... or so you say. For as long as we experience loneliness, sadness, anger, or pain, there is something that we may find fulfilling outwardly but not inwardly. Should you change religions?

How about jobs? How about investing in your artistic pursuits? Your health? There is so much to notice.

This is a time of rending and uniting. It is when we pick apart ourselves each year and we look to add on to our lives. Some things might be taken away, and honestly at times the energies leading up to the Spring Equinox can be volatile. They can be life-changing. Change is scary. But ultimately, rebirth is worth it.

TOOLS

blue altar cloth

small bottle of rosemary

sea salt and lavender

bowl of water

a small bowl of three dried bay leaves

one large cookie in the shape of a bull

an offering bowl (preferably wood)

two incenses (frankincense and myrrh)

a central candle representing Hestia

a bell

a vase with flowers (larkspur, tulips, or hyacinths)

red grapes

chalice of red wine/juice

a glass of water

a thyrsus

a scourge

a veiled icon of Dionysus or of a phallic image

the green cube

blade

wand

olive oil or essential pine oil

Preparing the Bômós

Clean the bômós surface with rosemary, sea salt, and lavender. Place the ingredients in the center. Leaving your hand open and flat, meditate on the Azure Flame and its purifying power. Now bring your fingers together and begin swirling the herbs on top of the bômós from the center outward in a clockwise motion, then spiral once again inward to the center moving counterclockwise. When finished, cry "Es'tô!" Place the altar cloth on top. Prepare the rest of the bômós accordingly.

Preparation

The altar with altar cloth faces east. Place the incense holders with one on the very front of the bômós and the other below it. Put the bell in the southeast corner. Place the blade and wand next to each other in front of the bell. The glass of water and the three dried bay leaves go on the side in the northwest corner. The central candle (Hestia) goes in the center, with the green cube behind the Hestia candle. The vase goes in the very back of the altar, with the bowl of grapes on left side of the vase. The icon goes on the right of the altar. The plate with the bull goes in front of the bowl. The offering bowl is placed in front of or next to the bell. The chalice of wine or juice can go anywhere, and so can the thyrsus. You may add a candle to either side of the grapes and icon. Place the scourge on the ground.

Ring the bell nine times to indicate the start of the ritual.

Light the three dried bay leaves and place them in the center of the bowl. Repeat three times as you circle the bowl clockwise:

"Hekas, Hekas, Este Bebeloi!" Anoint your forehead and say, "By the Mind of the Azure Flame I consecrate myself." Anoint your lips and say, "By the Mouth of the Sacred, I consecrate myself." Anoint your chest and say, "By the Heart of the Goddess, I consecrate myself." Fully anoint your left hand and then your right and say, "By the Touch of the Godself, I consecrate myself."

Take the bowl and place it outside somewhere and say, "Chaos has no place in Order. The Profane has no place in Holiness. Leave us in peace, and accept these offerings in appeasement. Es'tô!"

Light the incense. Meditate for a moment. Focus above you an Azure Flame that burns just above the crown of your head. The more you focus, the more alive and bright it becomes. When you are ready, perform the Fourfold Breath and begin the next part.

PRESENTATION OF THE ICON

Starting from the east, walk clockwise in a circle and throw some petals from the flowers in the vase down before you. When completed, take the veiled icon of Dionysus and walk clockwise over the flowers, presenting them to the four directions. Begin in the east. At the end make a final salute to the east by raising the image for a moment longer, and then place the icon on the bômós. Unveil the icon. Cry, "Euphêmeíte!" Wait a few moments and then ring the bell nine times.

ANOINTING

With the olive oil or pine essential oil, anoint yourself on your forehead and state your intention: "In soundness and peace I celebrate our New Year."

Incenses

Light the incense located underneath the bômós (the chthonic incense) and say, "Spirits from below, I honor you and observe these sacred rites in your praise. Es'tô!" Light the incense upon the bômós (the ouranic incense) and say, "Spirits from above, I honor you and observe these sacred rites in your praise. Es'tô!" Spend some quiet time meditating about the deities and spirits, as well as the ritual at hand to be done.

Hearth Lamp

Light the candle to Hestia. You may say anything you wish to her to welcome her. An example of welcoming her is below:

> "Hail Mother!"
> (Take a breath) "The welcoming heat of your embrace ..."
> (Take a breath) "The gentle touch upon my head ..."
> (Take a breath) "The nurturing spirit that surrounds me ..."
> "Let your holy flame light within our hearts. Let our souls be made purified even as you are. Khai'rete Hestia!"

Let the candle flame burn and for a moment focus on the dance and the spirit of she who dwells in all living fire.

Ritual

Face the bômós and raise your arms to either side. Say, "In this hallowed time that dances between Light and Shadow, I come before the Ancient Ones to remember the sacrifice of renewal that made our world possible."

Read the myth of Dionysus in the deity chapter (Chapter 6).

After reading the tale, take the thyrsus and pass it over the bômós clockwise seven times. Each time state an epithet of

Dionysus: "Antheus ... Melanaigis ... Bakkhos ... Sôtêr ... Eleu-thereus ... Dimêtôr ... Zagreus!"

Bang the foot of the thyrsus on the floor or the bômós seven times. Ring the bell seven times.

"To give life, death must occur. And for death to occur, life must be. With mine own hands I have forged the bull; consecrated it now must be."

Take the wine and use some of it to draw an equilateral cross on the bull.

Take the oil and use some of it to draw an equilateral cross on the bull.

Take the water and use some of it to draw an equilateral cross on the bull.

Now say, "In destruction comes creation. Hail the Bull Roarer!"

Take up the scourge and say, "In his name, I purify myself as I renew myself for the coming year." GENTLY scourge your back seven times, alternating between your right side and your left side.

Sacrifice and Offering

Break the bull into seven pieces, being sure to separate especially the head, and each leg. Place six pieces in the offering bowl, and set aside one piece (the one that is probably closest to where the heart would be). Eat some grapes. Pour some of the wine/juice into the offering bowl and say, "From the soil, to the vine, from the vine to the grape, from the grape to the wine. Blood of our god, return unto thee in thanksgiving and praise. Let it be acceptable in your sight. Es'tô!" Now take the glass of water and say, "In return may we receive your divine illumination! Let us hear your voice, O sacred ones! Come unto us, even as the rain fertilizes and blesses the earth. Es'tô!"

CLOSING

Thank Hestia from your own words. But you may use the ones below as an example:

> *Lady Hestia,*
> *Goddess of the Flame,*
> *Teach us to be hospitable to one another . . . .*
> *Teach us to be right in our behavior toward each other . . .*
> *Teach us to be of humble minds toward each other . . .*
> *And teach us to honor ourselves as we honor you.*
> *Though your light goes out in the apparent world, it remains lit*
> *within our hearts and hearth. I thank you with a kiss.*

Blow out the candle. Silently or vocally thank the other gods and spirits: "Hear my call, Ancient Ones, and blessed be your names."

The rite is ended.

May 1st—The Sacred Marriage of Zeus and Demeter

The Sacred Marriage of Sky and Earth is an especially potent time. Demeter is the goddess who is in sacred union with Zeus. Demeter is the third and final incarnation of the Earth Mother. The previous two are Gaia and Rhea. Each is assigned a color: Gaia is the green mother, Rhea the black mother, and Demeter the yellow mother. The corn (or wheat) is why she is assigned the color yellow. The goddess who taught us agriculture and the mysteries is also the law giver of the people.

Zeus is the storm god whose might fertilizes the land. Explaining the myths allegorically, it is the reason he impregnates many women; as a fertility god, he is the force of nature that is responsible for this phenomenon. The rain cycle is necessary for us to live, as it fertilizes and brings nourishment to the Earth Mother. However, with the fertility aspects come the ecstatic ones.

The festival is fertility- and ecstatic-based, celebrating the union of Sky Father and Earth Mother; the Storm and the Land; the Rain and the Soil; Wind and Moisture. These stimulating potencies measure the very breath and body of our biosphere: when renewal from the pneuma is respired by erotic means and sensual beginnings. The feeding of our mother begins with succulent honey, wine, milk, and cream. These are the sweet delights of the garden grove our mother revels in. Her nymphs and satyrs cavort in play and frolic about awaiting and even dancing beneath the initial ejaculate of the god: the early summer rains. Thunder is the voice of the dominant one, lightning his phallic strike. Earth-to-air strikes are the mother's intoxicating orgasms reaching up and hungering for the charge of our gods. It is finally with the fresh winds and rains that Eros has arrived in full: making love has heightened, and will now slowly diminish ... or perhaps continue unabated for some time ... love ignited!

As a polarity ritual, this festival does have heteronormative traits with regards to fertility. However, because we are dealing with gods and not humans, it is also an ecstatic rite wherein the symbol of the storm and the earth can easily be translated into symbols that touch our deepest core: remember that the sacred twins Eros and Thanatos embrace each other sexually, whether as male/female, female/female, male/male, or both androgynous at once within themselves. In other words, fertility is NOT the only thing that draws the storm to the land. It is the pull of Eros—primal desire—that causes the land and the storm to circle one another continuously and produce ecstatic wonders.

While this is a sexual-filled rite, it is also, as said, an ecstatic one. One can recognize the sexual energies in the mythic tale without needing to express it sexually if they have no desire to, Merely the celebration of the ritual itself is enough to connect one to the land, sea, and sky.

Tools

blue altar cloth

small bottle of rosemary, sea salt, and lavender

bowl of water

a small bowl of three dried bay leaves

a small cookie on a plate

an offering bowl (preferably wood)

two incenses (frankincense and myrrh)

central candle representing Hestia

bell

vase with flowers (iris, orchards, or roses)

chalice of white wine/juice

glass of water

veiled icons of Zeus and Demeter and candles

the green cube

blade

wand

olive oil or essential frankincense/cedar oil

Preparing the Bômós

Clean the bômós surface with rosemary, sea salt, and lavender. Place the ingredients in the center. Leaving your hand open and flat, meditate on the Azure Flame and its purifying power. Now bring your fingers together and begin swirling the herbs on top of the bômós from the center outward in a clockwise motion, then spiral once again inward to the center counterclockwise. When finished, cry "Es'tô!" Place the altar cloth on top. Prepare the rest of the bômós accordingly.

PREPARATION

The altar with altar cloth faces east. Place the incense holders with one on the very front of the bômós and the other below it. Put the bell in the southeast corner. Place the blade and wand next to each other in front of the bell. The bowl of water and the three dried bay leaves go on the side in the northwest corner. The central candle (Hestia) goes in the center, with the green cube behind the Hestia candle. The vase goes in the very back of the altar. The icons go on either side of the vase (Demeter on the left and Zeus on the right), with a candle next to each icon. The plate with the cookie goes in front of the bowl. The offering bowl is placed in front of the bell. The chalice of wine or juice can go anywhere, and so can the glass of water. Ring the bell nine times to indicate the start of the ritual.

Light the three dried bay leaves and place them in the center of the bowl. Repeat three times as you circle the bowl clockwise: "Hekas, Hekas, Este Bebeloi!" Anoint your forehead and say, "By the Mind of the Azure Flame I consecrate myself." Anoint your lips and say, "By the Mouth of the Sacred, I consecrate myself." Anoint your chest and say, "By the Heart of the Goddess, I consecrate myself." Fully anoint your left hand and then your right and say, "By the Touch of the Godself, I consecrate myself."

Take the bowl and place it outside somewhere and say, "Chaos has no place in Order. The Profane has no place in Holiness. Leave us in peace, and accept these offerings in appeasement. Es'tô!"

Light the incense. Meditate for a moment. Focus above you an Azure Flame that burns just above the crown of your head. The more you focus, the more alive and bright it becomes. When you are ready, perform the Fourfold Breath and begin the next part.

PRESENTATION OF THE ICON

Starting from the east, walk clockwise in a circle and throw some petals from the flowers in the vase down before you. When completed, take the veiled icon of Demeter and walk clockwise over the flowers, presenting it to the four directions. Begin with the east. At the end, make a final salute to the east by raising the image for a moment longer, and then place the icon on the bômós. Unveil the icon. Cry, "Euphêmeíte!" Repeat the same directions with the icon of Zeus. Wait a few moments and then ring the bell nine times.

ANOINTING

With the olive oil or essential frankincense or cedar oil anoint yourself on your forehead and state your intention: "In soundness and peace I celebrate this sacred union."

INCENSES

Light the incense located underneath the bômós (the chthonic incense) and say, "Spirits from below, I honor you and observe these sacred rites in your praise. Es'tô!" Light the incense upon the bômós (the ouranic incense) and say, "Spirits from above, I honor you and observe these sacred rites in your praise. Es'tô!" Spend some quiet time meditating about the deities and spirits, as well as the ritual at hand to be done.

HEARTH LAMP

Light the candle to Hestia. You may say anything you wish to her to welcome her. An example of welcoming her is below:

> *"Hail Mother!"*
> (Take a breath) *"The welcoming heat of your embrace ..."*
> (Take a breath) *"The gentle touch upon my head ..."*
> (Take a breath) *"The nurturing spirit that surrounds me ..."*
> *"Let your holy flame light within our hearts. Let our souls be made purified even as you are. Khai'rete Hestia!"*

Let the candle flame burn and for a moment focus on the dance and the spirit of she who dwells in all living fire.

RITUAL

Are you the storm or the earth? The phallus or the vagina? Are you male or female? Are you both simultaneously? Think on this. Focus your blue flame on your sexual organs, and allow images to come to you. Lie down on the ground if you must. Sense the sexual embrace of the earth, of Demeter as the wild mare. She prepares herself for the stallion Zeus. Which one calls to you? Which one shall you aspect? Or perhaps it is none. Perhaps it is the female Zeus: Dione. Perhaps it is not green Demeter, but the wild, lascivious Pan, the "All." Feel the rhythms within you. Dance. Growl. At once you are both Pan and Zeus, Demeter and Dione ... and at once none. The holy dance of the cosmos reaches down into your very being. Raise your hands and declare:

> *Zeus!*
> *Hero of Olympus!*
> *Wild Stallion and Serpent Father!*
> *God of Gods, King of Kings!*

Come forth,
Mighty Phallic One,
Embrace the Earth,
For she is ripe and ready
For thy sacred union!

Now kneel and declare:

Demeter!
Lady of the Corn!
Wild Mare and Serpent Mother!
Queen of Heaven, Queen of Earth!
Come forth,
Mighty One,
Embrace the Sky,
For he is ready and mighty
For thy sacred union!
Es'tô!

Continue to dance until you feel exhausted and the worship is over.

Ring the bell nine times.

Sacrifice and Offering

Break the cookie into two pieces. Eat one piece and leave the other in the offering bowl. Pour some of the wine / juice into the offering bowl and say, "From the soil, to the vine, from the vine to the grape, from the grape to the wine. Blood of our god, return unto thee in thanksgiving and praise. Let it be acceptable in your sight. Es'tô!" Now take the glass of water and say, "In return may we receive your divine illumination! Let us hear your voice, O sacred ones! Come unto us, even as the rain fertilizes and blesses the earth. Es'tô!"

CLOSING

Thank Hestia from your own words. But you may use the ones below as an example:

> *Lady Hestia,*
> *Goddess of the Flame,*
> *Teach us to be hospitable to one another ...*
> *Teach us to be right in our behavior toward each other ...*
> *Teach us to be of humble minds toward each other ...*
> *And teach us to honor ourselves as we honor you.*
> *Though your light goes out in the apparent world, it remains lit*
> *within our hearts and hearth. I thank you with a kiss.*

Blow out the candle. Silently or vocally thank the other gods and spirits: "Hear my call, Ancient Ones, and blessed be your names."

The rite is ended.

The Summer Solstice—The Triumph of Apollo

The height of summer comes to us in a moment of triumph. After this time, the days will begin to grow darker, and the Time of the Wolf is upon us. From the winter solstice until the Summer Solstice is the Time of the Bull, when Dionysus reigns over the tradition proper in our year. It is exemplified by the springtime and the sacred value of the Spring Equinox itself: our religious New Year.

However, we join with Apollo Helios in prayer, invocation, and dance. We speak four barbarous words of power, or words that carry great power but are activated through the sound rather than making sense intelligibly. The last of these words is the sacred name belonging to him as Apollo Helios. He strums his seven-string lyre, pushing Eros to whirl the cosmos about him. For a moment, we are both external and internal, as he is external and internal to us. For he is the ruler of what we call our solar body, or energetic body.

TOOLS

rosemary, sea salt, and lavender

scarlet or gold altar cloth

a bowl of water

a bowl of twelve dried bay leaves

a cookie for an offering

an offering bowl (preferably wood)

incenses (frankincense and sandalwood)

a central candle representing Hestia

a bell

a vase with flowers (fire bush or orchids)

music

glass of white wine / juice

icon of Apollo (veil him before the ritual begins)

a laurel crown or any light crown of golden leaves

a blade

a wand

the green cube

olive oil or essential frankincense oil

PREPARING THE BÔMÓS

Clean the bômós surface with rosemary, sea salt, and lavender. Place the ingredients in the center. Leaving your hand open and flat, meditate on the Azure Flame and its purifying power. Now bring your fingers together and begin swirling the herbs on top of the bômós from the center outward in a clockwise motion, then spiral once again inward to the center moving counterclockwise. When finished, cry "Es'tô!" Place the altar cloth on top. Prepare the rest of the bômós accordingly.

Preparation

The altar with altar cloth faces east. Incense holders: one on the very front of the bômós and the other below it. The bell is placed in the southeast corner. The blade and wand are side by side in front of the bell. The bowl of water and three of the dried bay leaves go on the side in the northwest corner. The central candle (Hestia) is placed in the center. The green cube is placed behind the Hestia candle. The vase is placed in the very back of the altar. The icon of Apollo goes in front of the vase. A candle can be placed on either side of him. The plate with the cookie goes in front of the bowl. The offering bowl is placed in front of the bell. The plate or bowl with the remaining nine dried bay leaves goes in front of the offering bowl. The glass of wine or juice can go anywhere.

Ring the bell nine times to indicate the start of the ritual.

Light the three bay leaves and place them in the center of the bowl. Repeat three times as you circle the bowl clockwise: "Hekas, Hekas, Este Bebeloi!" Anoint your forehead and say, "By the Mind of the Azure Flame I consecrate myself." Anoint your lips and say, "By the Mouth of the Sacred, I consecrate myself." Anoint your chest and say, "By the Heart of the Goddess, I consecrate myself." Fully anoint your left hand and then your right and say, "By the Touch of the Godself, I consecrate myself."

Take the bowl and place it outside somewhere and say, "Chaos has no place in Order. The Profane has no place in Holiness. Leave us in peace, and accept these offerings in appeasement. Es'tô!"

Light the incense. Meditate for a moment. Focus above you an Azure Flame that burns just above the crown of your head. The more you focus, the more alive and bright it becomes. When you are ready, take a breath four times and begin the next part.

PRESENTATION OF THE ICON

Starting from the east walk clockwise in a circle and throw some petals from the flowers in the vase down before you. When completed, take the veiled icon of Apollo and walk clockwise over the flowers, presenting it to the four directions. Begin in the east. At the end make a final salute to the east by raising the image for a moment longer, and then place the icon on the bômós. Unveil the icon. Cry, "Euphêmeíte!" Wait a few moments and then ring the bell nine times.

ANOINTING

With the olive oil or essential frankincense oil anoint yourself on your forehead and state your intention: "In soundness and peace I celebrate this rite to Apollo."

INCENSES

Light the incense located underneath the bômós (the chthonic incense) and say, "Spirits from below, I honor you and observe these sacred rites in your praise. Es'tô!" Light the incense upon the bômós (the ouranic incense) and say, "Spirits from above, I honor you and observe these sacred rites in your praise. Es'tô!" Spend some quiet time meditating about the deities and spirits, as well as the ritual at hand to be done.

HEARTH LAMP

Light the candle to Hestia. You may say anything you wish to her to welcome her. An example of welcoming her is below:

"Hail Mother!"
(Take a breath) *"The welcoming heat of your embrace ..."*
(Take a breath) *"The gentle touch upon my head ..."*
(Take a breath) *"The nurturing spirit that surrounds me"*
"Let your holy flame light within our hearts. Let our souls be made purified even as you are. Khai'rete Hestia!"

Let the candle flame burn and for a moment focus on the dance and the spirit of she who dwells in all living fire.

RITUAL

At the Summer Solstice, the sun reaches its zenith in the sky. With this ascent, day overpowers night. This was the time of Apollo Helios. He is the solar light and it was his flame that inspired the Pythia to oracle. He strums his seven-stringed lyre and the cosmos whirls about him in a dance. In this festival, Apollo himself is equated with the sun as Helios. Wear a golden veil or a laurel wreath. As outer, so inner: Apollo rules the solar body and is the bright spark within.

For this, recite this hymn as you point your blade toward the sun:

Gracious Lord,
Illuminator of Gnosis,
Golden Star of the Heavens:
Whirl me into Your Heavenly Dance.
Sacred Spirals join:
I weave myself into Your music.
I am the Bee,

You are the Flower.
I am the Bee,
You are the Nectar.
I cry the Sacred Words:
*"Phoneos Phoebos Helios Achebukrom." (*say nine times*)*

Burn a bay leaf after each time you say these words of power.

After you have said this prayer, put your blade away. Focus on the red fire within located at the heart center. Meditate as it burns. What images come up? What thoughts? What emotions to heal? Memories? Meditate for ten minutes.

Remember the Breath

Finally, at the end play some music and begin to dance in a circle. Start off very slow, and then pick up the pace. Dance as if you had a spider on you that has bitten you, and you are going mad with the venom within you. Dance for as little or as long as you like. Be sure to always go clockwise, mimicking the movement of Apollo Helios. He is the center and we are one with him. When you are finished, take a moment and center. Then close the rite.

Sacrifice and Offering

Break the cookie into two pieces. Eat one piece and leave the other in the offering bowl. Pour some of the wine/juice into the offering bowl and say, "From the soil, to the vine, from the vine to the grape, from the grape to the wine. Blood of our god, return unto thee in thanksgiving and praise. Let it be acceptable in your sight. Es'tô!" Drink some. Now ring the bell seven times.

CLOSING

Thank Hestia from your own words. But you may use the ones below as an example:

Lady Hestia,
Goddess of the Flame,
Teach us to be hospitable to one another ...
Teach us to be right in our behavior toward each other ...
Teach us to be of humble minds toward each other ...
And teach us to honor ourselves as we honor you.
Though your light goes out in the apparent world, it remains lit
within our hearts and hearth. I thank you with a kiss.

Blow out the candle. Silently or vocally thank the other gods and spirits: "Hear my call, Ancient Ones, and blessed be your names."

The rite is ended.

August 1st—Aphrodisia

The Aphrodisia is in honor of Aphrodite Pandemos, the goddess of the people. She is the fierce one who destroyed the giants who killed the infant Dionysus. She is the great harmonizer, the other half of Ares; together they create and destroy the elemental cosmos and the four elements. Aphrodite Pandemos is symbolized by water, and enjoys the finer things.

By worshiping her, we are bringing her sacred sexuality and affirmations of harmony within us to the fore. She is materialistic, not just spiritual. She blesses us with the good things in nature, surrounding us with creation. Whereas Ares separates the four elements so that they return to their pure state and bring dissolution, Aphrodite Pandemos draws them together to create.

She is the alchemical ideal, and together we draw on our sexual alchemy to manifest our desires. We also become comfortable with our bodies.

TOOLS

rosemary, sea salt, and lavender

pink, blue, red, or white altar cloth

a bowl of water

a bowl of dried bay leaves

an apple

a knife

an offering bowl (preferably wood)

incenses (frankincense and jasmine preferred)

central candle representing Hestia

bell

vase with flowers (preferably roses)

a plate of cookies

mirror

music

glass of red wine or juice

an icon of Aphrodite, whether a picture or a statue (veil her before the ritual begins)

green cube

wand

blade

massage oil

olive oil or essential jasmine/rose oil

Preparing the Bômós

Clean the bômós surface with rosemary, sea salt, and lavender. Place the ingredients in the center. Leaving your hand open and flat, meditate on the Azure Flame and its purifying power. Now bring your fingers together and begin swirling the herbs on top of the bômós from the center outward in a clockwise motion, then spiral once again inward to the center moving counterclockwise. When finished, cry "Es'tô!" Place the altar cloth on top. Prepare the rest of the bômós accordingly.

Preparation

The altar with altar cloth faces east. Incense holders: one on the very front of the bômós and the other below it. The bell is placed in the southeast corner. The blade and wand are side by side in front of the bell. The bowl of water and three of the dried bay leaves go on the side in the northwest corner. The central candle (Hestia) is placed in the center. The green cube is placed behind the Hestia candle. The vase is placed in the very back of the altar. The plate of cookies goes in front of the bowl. The offering bowl is placed in front of the bell. The glass of wine or juice can go anywhere. The apple on a plate with a knife next to it. The mirror (not the Eye of Nyx) may go anywhere. Ring the bell nine times to indicate the start of the ritual.

Light three bay leaves and place them in the center of the bowl. Repeat three times as you circle the bowl clockwise: "Hekas, Hekas, Este Bebeloi!" Anoint your forehead and say, "By the Mind of the Azure Flame I consecrate myself." Anoint your lips and say, "By the Mouth of the Sacred, I consecrate myself." Anoint your chest and say, "By the Heart of the Goddess, I consecrate myself."

Fully anoint your left hand and then your right and say, "By the Touch of the Godself, I consecrate myself."

Take the bowl and place it outside somewhere and say, "Chaos has no place in Order. The Profane has no place in Holiness. Leave us in peace, and accept these offerings in appeasement. Es'tô!"

Light the incense. Meditate for a moment. Focus above you an Azure Flame that burns just above the crown of your head. The more you focus, the more alive and bright it becomes. When you are ready, take a breath four times and begin the next part.

PRESENTATION OF THE ICON

Starting from the east, walk clockwise in a circle and throw some petals from the flowers in the vase down before you. When completed, take the veiled icon of Aphrodite and walk clockwise over the flowers, presenting it to the four directions. Begin in the east. At the end make a final salute to the east by raising the image for a moment longer, and then place the icon on the bômós. Unveil the icon. Cry, "Euphêmeíte!" Wait a few moments and then ring the bell nine times.

ANOINTING

With the olive oil or essential jasmine or rose oil anoint yourself on your forehead and state your intention: "In soundness and peace I celebrate this rite to Aphrodite."

INCENSES

Light the incense located underneath the bômós (the chthonic incense) and say, "Spirits from below, I honor you and observe these sacred rites in your praise. Es'tô!" Light the incense upon the bômós (the ouranic incense) and say, "Spirits from above, I honor you and observe these sacred rites in your praise. Es'tô!" Spend some quiet time meditating about the deities and spirits, as well as the ritual at hand to be done.

Hearth Lamp

Light the candle to Hestia. You may say anything you wish to her to welcome her. An example of welcoming her is below:

> "Hail Mother!"
> (Take a breath) "The welcoming heat of your embrace ..."
> (Take a breath) "The gentle touch upon my head ..."
> (Take a breath) "The nurturing spirit that surrounds me ..."
> "Let your holy flame light within our hearts. Let our souls be made purified even as you are. Khai'rete Hestia!"

Let the candle flame burn and for a moment focus on the dance and the spirit of she who dwells in all living fire.

Extend your power hand and, above the altar, make an Invoking Pentagram of Fire and cry, "Hugieia!" Then place your hand in the "center" of the pentagram, meditating on Aphrodite and the element of change, ecstasy, and sex.

Ritual

Recite the Orphic Hymn to Aphrodite:

> O heavenly, much hymned Aphrodite,
> loving laughter, born from the sea, goddess
> of birth, lover of all-night festivals,
> holy nocturnal and wily goddess
> who binds, and mother of Necessity:
> For everything exists because of you,
> who yoked together the whole universe
> and govern three shares; you gave birth to all,

what's in the sky, upon the fruitful earth,
in the depths of the sea. Revered companion
of Bakchos, taking joy in abundance,
mother of the Erotes, preparing
weddings, Persuasion of the marriage bed,
you give joy in secret, decked with love-locks,
visible and invisible, daughter
of a great father. You join the bridal
feasts of the gods, with a scepter, she-wolf,
giver of birth, lover of men, longed for
giver of life, who yoked mortals with spells
to unbridled needs, and the many kinds
of beasts to an erotic madness. Come,
goddess born in Cyprus, whether you are
on Olympos, divine queen, with gladness
on your lovely face, or in Syria
with fine frankincense, seated on your throne,
or even if, on the plains with golden
chariots, you occupy the fruitful
baths of sacred Egypt, or coming in
swanlike carriages on the ocean waves,
you rejoice, dancing in circles with beasts
of the sea, or if you are delighted
with the dark-eyed nymphs in their holy land
upon the shores of the sandy beaches,
with the nimble salt sea; or in Cyprus,
lady, land of your nursing, where lovely
virgins and the unwed brides all year sing
hymns to you and to immortal, holy
Adonis. Come, blessed goddess, who has

a very beautiful form, for I call you
with a pious soul and these holy words.[94]

Begin by performing the Fourfold Breath: Inhale to the count of four … hold to the count of four … exhale to the count of four … hold to the count of four. Repeat three more times for a total of four. Each time, think of your blue fire. Watch it rise from the crown of your head. See it burn brightly as you take time to focus on your magic.

Look in the mirror. Stare at yourself. Now lie back comfortably naked and take some massage lotion. Rub it on your body. Massage different parts of your body: your neck, your arms, your thighs, your feet. As you do so slowly, breathe slowly with each body part. Again, this is for your body and mind. It is to relax you and cause you to be comfortable touching your own body. Perform this massage for ten minutes.

Chant, "KYYYYPPRRRIIAAAA … PAAANNDEEMOOSSSS …"

When you have finished, ground yourself. Take your apple, and slice it horizontally, revealing the mystery of the pentagram. Eat half, leaving the other half as an offering for her.

Sacrifice and Offering

Break the cookie into two pieces. Eat one piece and leave the other in the offering bowl. Pour some of the wine/juice into the offering bowl and say, "From the soil, to the vine, from the vine to the grape, from the grape to the wine. Blood of our god, return unto thee in thanksgiving and praise. Let it be acceptable in your sight. Es'tô!" Drink some. Now ring the bell nine times.

---

94. Dunn.

CLOSING

Thank Hestia from your own words. But you may use the ones below as an example:

> *Lady Hestia,*
> *Goddess of the Flame,*
> *Teach us to be hospitable to one another…*
> *Teach us to be right in our behavior toward each other…*
> *Teach us to be of humble minds toward each other…*
> *And teach us to honor ourselves as we honor you.*
> *Though your light goes out in the apparent world, it remains lit*
> *within our hearts and hearth. I thank you with a kiss.*

Blow out the candle. Silently or vocally thank the other gods and spirits: "Hear my call, Ancient Ones, and blessed be your names."

The rite is ended.

Autumn Equinox—The Sacred Marriage of Hades and Persephone

It is autumn, and we are at equal length between Light and Shadow, with the latter overcoming Light until it, too, is conquered at the winter solstice. During this time, the ground beneath our feet is already humming as we approach winter. The trees are already losing their leaves. If you live in the tropics, you won't notice much of a change. However, the seasons still turn with migrations of birds and other seasonal plant life. Even in some places on the planet, the cycles of nature continue to shift and change as the wheel turns. In this vein I encourage you to ask yourself these questions: What do I have to surrender? Where in the darkness is wisdom? Have I been challenged with my personal power? How can I reclaim it? How can I maintain it? What parts of my hidden self can I find to love? What part of me will hurt when I separate myself from the attachments that keep me imprisoned in the light? Think on these things as you prepare to celebrate the Autumn Equinox.

Tools

rosemary, sea salt, and lavender

purple altar cloth

bowl of water

three dried bay leaves

an offering bowl (preferably wood)

incenses (jasmine and myrrh)

central candle representing Hestia

bell

vase with flowers (preferably roses or crocuses)

glass of red wine or pomegranate juice

green cube

blade

wand

pomegranate seeds

icons of Hades and Persephone (veil them before the ritual begins)

a candle

cake or cookies

Eye of Nyx

essential jasmine oil

PREPARING THE BÔMÓS

Clean the bômós surface with rosemary, sea salt, and lavender. Place the ingredients in the center. Leaving your hand open and flat, meditate on the Azure Flame and its purifying power. Now bring your fingers together and begin swirling the herbs on top of the bômós from the center outward in a clockwise motion, then spiral once again inward to the center moving counterclockwise. When finished, cry "Es'tô!" Place the altar cloth on top. Prepare the rest of the bômós accordingly.

PREPARATION

The altar with altar cloth faces east. The incense holders go in the very front. The bell goes in the southeast corner. The blade and wand are side by side in front of the bell. The bowl of water with three dried bay leaves is placed on the side in the northwest corner. The central candle (Hestia) is placed in the center of the altar. The green cube goes behind the Hestia candle. The vase is placed in the very back of the altar. The bowl of pomegranate seeds goes in front. The offering bowl can go anywhere. The glass of wine or pomegranate juice can go anywhere. The icons are placed on either side of the vase. A candle is placed next to the icons. The Eye of Nyx is placed on the ground and veiled until you are ready to use it. You should also have cake or cookies to help you ground yourself after the ritual (not to be given to the deities as an offering).

Ring the bell nine times to indicate the start of the ritual.

Light the three bay leaves and place them in the center of the offering bowl. Repeat three times as you circle the bowl clockwise: "Hekas, Hekas, Este Bebeloi!" Anoint your forehead and say, "By the Mind of the Azure Flame I consecrate myself." Anoint your lips and say, "By the Mouth of the Sacred, I consecrate myself."

Anoint your chest and say, "By the Heart of the Goddess, I consecrate myself." Fully anoint your left hand and then your right and say, "By the Touch of the Godself, I consecrate myself."

Take the bowl and place it outside somewhere and say, "Chaos has no place in Order. The Profane has no place in Holiness. Leave us in peace, and accept these offerings in appeasement. Es'tô!"

Light the incense. Meditate for a moment. Focus above you an Azure Flame that burns just above the crown of your head. The more you focus, the more alive and bright it becomes. When you are ready, perform the Fourfold Breath and begin the next part.

PRESENTATION OF THE ICON

Starting from the east, walk clockwise in a circle and throw some petals from the flowers in the vase down before you. When this is completed, take the veiled icon of Persephone and walk clockwise over the flowers, presenting it to the four directions. Begin in the east. At the end make a final salute to the east by raising the image for a moment longer, and then place the icon on the bômós. Unveil the icon of Persephone. Cry, "Euphêmeíte!" and repeat the steps with Hades. Wait a few moments and then ring the bell nine times.

ANOINTING

With essential jasmine oil anoint yourself on your forehead and state your intention: "In soundness and peace I celebrate this sacred union of Hades and Persephone."

INCENSES

Light the incense located underneath the bômós (the chthonic incense) and say, "Spirits from below, I honor you and observe these sacred rites in your praise. Es'tô!" Light the incense upon the bômós (the ouranic incense) and say, "Spirits from above, I honor you and observe these sacred rites in your praise. Es'tô!" Spend some quiet time meditating about the deities and spirits, as well as the ritual at hand to be done.

Hearth Lamp

Light the candle to Hestia. You may say anything you wish to her to welcome her. An example of welcoming her is below:

> *"Hail Mother!"*
> (Take a breath) *"The welcoming heat of your embrace ..."*
> (Take a breath) *"The gentle touch upon my head ..."*
> (Take a breath) *"The nurturing spirit that surrounds me ..."*
> *"Let your holy flame light within our hearts. Let our souls be made purified even as you are. Khai'rete Hestia!"*

Let the candle flame burn and for a moment focus on the dance and the spirit of she who dwells in all living fire.

Ritual

Recite the Orphic Hymn to Persephone:

> *Come, Persephone, daughter of great Zeus,*
> *blessed one, only begotten goddess.*
> *Accept these gracious offerings to you.*
> *Many-honored wife of Plouton, you give*
> *life diligently, and control the gates*
> *of Hades, beneath the depths of the Earth.*
> *Praxidíke, with lovely locks of hair:*
> *Holy child of Deo, and the mother*
> *of the Furies, queen of the underworld,*
> *maiden whom Zeus sired with ineffable*

seed—you are the mother of loud-roaring
and many-formed Eubouleus. The shining
and luminous playmate of the seasons,
honored and mighty, maid bursting with fruit.
Mortals long for you alone, bright, horned,
springtime goddess, who is delighted with
meadow breezes, revealing your holy
body in the green and yellow new shoots.
In autumn, you were seized and forced to wed.
Now you, Persephone, alone are life
and death to toiling mortals, for you feed
us always, and also kill everything.
Hear, blessed goddess, and send up the fruits
from the earth, blossoming in peace and with
the soothing hand of health, and a rich life
that leads old age, sleek and shining, downward,
queen, to your kingdom, to mighty Plouton.

Recite the Orphic Hymn to Hades:

Mighty spirit, you have your home under
the earth, a grassy mead in Tartaros,
deep shadowed and sunless, Chthonian Zeus
holding a scepter, kindness in your heart.
Accept these holy offerings, Plouton,
you who hold fast the bars that bind the whole
earth, and give yearly fruit to mortal kind.
You who won the third share: earth, queen of all,
foundation of the deathless gods, and strong
support to mortal kind. You established
your throne beneath a shadowy, distant
realm; never tiring and never breathing,

indiscriminate Hades, and blue-black
Acheron, who holds the roots of the Earth.
You who governs the grace of mortal death,
O host of many, Euboulos, who once
tore the daughter of holy Demeter
from her meadow as a bride; with your four
yoked steeds, you dragged her through the ocean, down
to an attic cavern in the region
of Eleusis, that very place where lie
the gates to Hades. You alone came forth
to be the judge of deeds, obscure and known.
The inspired ruler of all,
most holy, most highly honored, rejoicing in rites
majestic, revered, and pious, I call
you, come with kind joy to the worshipers.

Now unveil the Eye of Nyx, and be sure to relight any incense you may need. Take the two icon candles and place them on either side of the Eye. Focus your mind on the Azure Flame, and breathe the Fourfold Breath. Now look into the Eye of Nyx, and allow the gates of the underworld to be opened to you as you travel.

You may come upon the Guardian, and hear whistling like wheels or flutes in the background. This is good. These are the chariots of the underworld guiding you before the giant gates of Persephone.

Your guides are the Daughters of the Sun; look to them to help you as you make your way to and fro. When you know you are ready to leave, simply turn to them and let them know. Your guides will help you travel backward, and you will awaken in your body. Perform the Fourfold Breath, and ground yourself by eating something.

Ring the bell nine times.

In the offering bowl, pour some wine or pomegranate juice and say, "I give unto you this libation, that you may be honored and worshiped. Thank you for your guidance in the underworld, O sacred ones. May you be praised evermore. Es'tô!"

The rite is ended.

November 1st—The Feast of the Dead

The Feast of the Dead is a time in which we communicate with the underworld spirits—in particular the Makárioi. In this ritual, we dig a ritual pit and open a portal between us and the otherworld. The Feast of the Dead is also just that—a feast. Specific food is to be separated between that for the living and that for the dead. Food for the dead is never eaten; it is a sacrifice prepared for them and them only. As in Chapter 11, we will be creating a pit to the underworld. Ideally, you would perform this ritual in a cemetery. However, cemeteries are generally off-limits at night and you will be arrested for trespassing. Also, you can be charged with desecration if you dig in a cemetery, especially if you are caught with a giant pit in the ground surrounded by candles and offerings while muttering strange words. Therefore, as a viable substitute, I encourage you to use whatever space you have available. The Eye of Nyx and the pit will help you transform your ordinary space into something extraordinary.

The feast is also a celebratory time. It doesn't have to be solemn. If you have been speaking with your ancestors and venerating them, you'll find this ritual is enhanced and the results very rewarding. I've always said that if I am family and only invited to be with you once annually, and expected to help each time, I will quickly withdraw. How do you think your ancestors are going to feel? Alternatively, if you use this to throw the dead a party and continue to develop your relationship with them afterward, you will also find it rewarding.

The Feast of the Dead has no mythos attached to it; it simply is for the dead. The entire focus is on summoning and veneration. The ritual is to take place after sunset, when the etheric energies of the dead are able to manifest easier. When the sun rises, the etheric energies will dissipate and the dead will return to where they are from. However, before this happens, there is a part in the rite in which the portal is completely closed so that the dead return to where they are from.

Deities that are a part of this rite include Hekate, Hades, and Persephone. Hekate is the psychopomp between the worlds. She leads the dead and also takes them back. Persephone, as queen, keeps the gates open or closed. Hades, as king, also functions with Persephone as the keeper. Invoking these deities also brings their attending spirits, who keep the dead under control. They tend to get overexcited and can get out of control. You may end up with a lingering spirit or spirits who don't want to go back, who might want to attach themselves to someone, or you may have hitchhiking spirits that attach themselves to the dead and invade the space of the living. It happens, and so keeping the deities happy and petitioning them for protection and overseeing the rite will help keep things under control.

TOOLS
rosemary, sea salt, and lavender

purple altar cloth

bowl of water

three dried bay leaves

an offering bowl (preferably wood)

incenses (jasmine and myrrh)

central candle representing Hestia

bell

vase with flowers (preferably roses or crocuses)

glass of red wine or pomegranate juice

pomegranate seeds

green cube

blade

wand

scourge

icons of Hades, Persephone, Hekate, or all three, although
   Hekate is preferred (veil them before the ritual begins)

a candle and three black taper candles

Eye of Nyx

cake or cookies (puppy-shaped)

essential jasmine oil

a muslin bag filled with lavender, hyssop, roses, and / or rosemary

Preparing the Bômós

Clean the bômós surface with rosemary, sea salt, and lavender.
Place the ingredients in the center. Leaving your hand open and
flat, meditate on the Azure Flame and its purifying power. Now
bring your fingers together and begin swirling the herbs on top of
the bômós from the center outward in a clockwise motion, then
spiral once again inward to the center moving counterclockwise.
When finished, cry "Es'tô!" Place the altar cloth on top. Prepare
the rest of the bômós accordingly.

Preparation

The altar with the altar cloth faces east. The incense holders are placed in the very front. The bell goes in the southeast corner. The blade and wand are placed side by side in front of the bell. The bowl of water with three dried bay leaves goes on the side in the northwest corner. The central candle (Hestia) is placed in the center of the altar. The green cube goes behind the Hestia candle. The vase is placed in the very back of the altar. The bowl of pomegranate seeds goes in front of the bowl of water. The offering bowl can go anywhere. The glass of wine or pomegranate juice can also go anywhere. The icons are placed on either side of the vase (or in front of the vase if it is just one). A candle is placed next to the icons. The Eye of Nyx is placed on the ground and veiled until you are ready to use it. You should also have cake or cookies nearby to help you ground yourself after the ritual (not to be given to the deities as an offering). The scourge can go anywhere.

Ring the bell nine times to indicate the start of the ritual.

Light the three dried bay leaves and place them in the center of the offering bowl. Repeat three times as you circle the bowl clockwise: "Hekas, Hekas, Este Bebeloi!" Anoint your forehead and say, "By the Mind of the Azure Flame I consecrate myself." Anoint your lips and say, "By the Mouth of the Sacred, I consecrate myself." Anoint your chest and say, "By the Heart of the Goddess, I consecrate myself." Fully anoint your left hand and then your right and say, "By the Touch of the Godself, I consecrate myself."

Take the bowl and place it outside somewhere and say, "Chaos has no place in Order. The Profane has no place in Holiness. Leave us in peace, and accept these offerings in appeasement. Es'tô!"

Light the incense. Meditate for a moment. Focus above you an Azure Flame that burns just above the crown of your head. The more you focus, the more alive and bright it becomes. When you are ready, perform the Fourfold Breath and begin the next part.

Presentation of the Icon

Starting from the east, walk clockwise in a circle and throw some petals from the flowers in the vase down before you. When this is completed, take the veiled icon of the gods or deity and walk clockwise over the flowers, presenting them to the four directions. Begin in the east. At the end make a final salute to the east by raising the image for a moment longer, and then place the icon(s) on the bômós. Unveil the icon. Cry, "Euphêmeíte!" Wait a few moments and then ring the bell nine times.

Anointing

With jasmine essential oil, anoint yourself on your forehead and state your intention: "In soundness and peace I celebrate this Feast of the Dead."

Incenses

Light the incense located underneath the bômós (the chthonic incense) and say, "Spirits from below, I honor you and observe these sacred rites in your praise. Es'tô!" Light the incense upon the bômós (the ouranic incense) and say, "Spirits from above, I honor you and observe these sacred rites in your praise. Es'tô!" Spend some quiet time meditating about the deities and spirits, as well as the ritual at hand to be done.

Hearth Lamp

Light the candle to Hestia. You may say anything you wish to her to welcome her. An example of welcoming her is below:

"Hail Mother!"

(Take a breath) *"The welcoming heat of your embrace ..."*

(Take a breath) *"The gentle touch upon my head ..."*

(Take a breath) *"The nurturing spirit that surrounds me ..."*

"Let your holy flame light within our hearts. Let our souls be made purified even as you are. Khai'rete Hestia!"

Let the candle flame burn and for a moment focus on the dance and the spirit of she who dwells in all living fire.

RITUAL

For the pit, you will need your wand, your dagger, and the Eye of Nyx. Dig a hole about three feet deep in your yard, or a foot or so deep in a large pot. Be sure it is deep enough to hold three black taper candles. The shape of the hole should be as triangular as possible.

Place a black candle at each corner of the triangle. For the ditch, offerings should be puppy-shaped cookies (in the place of black puppies) covered in pomegranate and wine. Burn some incense that has the following:

1 part dittany of Crete

1 part vervain

½ part myrrh

½ part black copal

This incense will help give form to the one being called. When you are ready, place the Eye of Nyx behind the triangle and the incense in front. Take your wand in your dominant hand (right if you are ambidextrous) and point the wand at the pit. While waving it in a figure eight motion toward the pit, recite the following nine times:

Taifes kato
Kalesma mou
Prokyptoun!
Prokyptoun!
Prokyptoun!

(Translation):

Wisps of below,
Heed my call:
Arise!
Arise!
Arise!

The loved one or whomever you are contacting will appear. Listen carefully. Watch slowly as the incense creates a figure—the wisp of a face, the shady figure of a person—or perhaps triggers a familiar smell. Be very careful, as the dead tend to rush in to eat the offerings in the pit. In order to control them, have your dagger out and ready. But this is a feast, and so I encourage you to allow the spirits to be fed while you dine on your own food until dawn approaches.

To close the ceremony, bid them depart and blow the candles out. Then cover the candles with the dirt by putting it all back into the hole. Say the following: "The gates have closed. All have departed. The feast is ended. So be it!" Knock three times on the ground. Dispose of all of the soil and what is in it to the garbage. When this operation is finished, take a purification bath by adding a muslin bag filled with lavender, hyssop, roses, and/or rosemary to your bathwater. Be sure to cover the mirror.

SUMMARY

We have explored the festivals and the ways in which we can celebrate them. Some have an appropriate mythos. Others do not. Strix Craft, while rooted in magic, is also polytheistic and so our focus is also always deity-centered. Worship and devotions are what fuel our craft, and empower us to explore the inner spaces of our being in order to further enhance our own magical workings.

CONCLUSION

Exploring the magics of Strix Craft has been quite the adventure. With the foundation established, this can be a starting point for many who desire to explore ancient Greek magics for the modern witch. Strix Craft is a beautiful tradition, and an ancient way that melds both old and new.

While there are plenty of things to be thankful for, I am encouraged that we all will find our own ways to be seasonally blessed. The gods live on, and they exist in a dimension next to us. In us. All around us. The Divine is beautiful.

As you begin your own exploration into the shadows of the underworld, one thing that I hope you have gained is an appreciation for our spiritual and physical ancestors. They worked diligently and we are thankful that so much of what they practiced has been recorded. But, as always, we must be mindful of the elements that we need to adapt to in our own era.

For example, we no longer need to sacrifice black dogs to Hekate, or commit one hundred bulls for a festival, or unite city and state in order to sponsor a festival for the people. All we need are the tools given to us and the energy within our bodies. Our imagination does the rest.

Magic was an important component of the ancient Greeks' daily life. It wasn't something set apart for only certain times of the year. The living and the dead dwelled in tandem, in a way that was almost symbiotic. I hope I was able to help get some of that across.

Despite my attempts to ensure that the information presented herein is applicable and perhaps even simple to do, I confess that practicing these magics and festivals as I do can be impeded by not having the "correct stuff." I hope that I was able to help you, the reader, find out that some magics aren't so scary, but they do come with warnings. Magic, after all, is a dangerous business. If everyone could do it, they would.

This book is only a small road map, and while we all long to worship the gods and practice magic, in the end we are all unique, and so we will have unique revelations on how to implement these practices into our daily lives. I hope that by asking and defining what Greek magic is, it has helped to unveil this controversial topic in Hellenic circles. Magic, while a taboo subject for some, is real and does exist. It is real. It is palpable. And the gods desire for us to have this gift and do with it what we can. Yes, magic can be used for malefic purposes. But by keeping our ethics in mind, practicing our virtues, practicing piety and devotion, and keeping our aim true, I have confidence we'll be okay. Magic is to be used by us, by humans. But it is always a gift. Treat it as such.

In the first chapter we looked at what Greek magic was; we defined it, and looked at the various practitioners involved. In the second chapter we explored the mythical land of Thessaly, the home of the Strix, our motherland and root of our powers in ancient times. In the third chapter we explored our ethics and virtues.

In the fourth chapter we looked at tools and how Strix use them. In Chapter 5 we looked at certain herbs. Most of them are toxic; where appropriate, substitutions were given. Remember that plant spirits are our allies. In Chapter 6 the various deities and spirits of our craft are described. We have our own unique mythos and understanding of how we approach certain deities. Finally, in Chapter 7 we learned about altars and shrines.

In the eighth chapter we began to look at magics such as healing. We began with healing because it is powerful and effective. Using kolossoi and other tools of the trade manifest healing. But we must always remember that medicine is a gift for the modern Western world. In the ninth chapter we delved into erotic magic with Aphrodite and Pan. I hope I presented some unique methods that will ignite your passions.

In Chapter 10 we delved into the shadow world of binding and hexing. Looking at sympathetic roles and the use of certain sigils brings forward techniques that will help you overcome obstacles so you can find success. In Chapter 11 we learned how to commune with the dead, a skill as ancient and revered as it has been for thousands of years. In Chapter 12 we aligned ourselves with the seasonal celebrations.

Whatever you get from this, I hope you will find a new passion for the Greek gods. I hope that you have found your way into Thessaly—that, at last, you have come home. Hekate welcomes you, O traveler.

GLOSSARY

LIST OF GREEK NAMES AND TERMS

Introduction

Strix (Strix): "Screecher."

Pamphilë (PAHM-feelie): The name of a Strix in Apuleius's novel *The Golden Ass.*

Gnosis (NAH-sis): Knowledge.

Hekate (Hek-AH-tay): "Far off," though this is debatable.

Brimo (Breem-oh): "Angry, terrifying."

Orpheus (OR-fee-us): "The darkness of night."

Magna Graecia (MAG-na Greesha): "Greater Greece."

Apollo (Uh-PAA-low): "Destroyer."

Asklepios (Ah-skleep-ee-uhs): Meaning currently unknown.

Eirene kai Hugieia (eye-REEN-ee ky He-JEE-uh): "Peace and health."

Chapter 1

Magice (MAJ-i-kee): "Of the magicians."

Magike (MAJ-i-kee): "Of the magicians."

Magoi (MAJ-oy): "Magicians."

Kathartai (KAUTH-ar-tay): "Purifiers."

Pharmakeia (Farr-ma-kay-uh): "A medicine."

Manteis (MAN-tees): "Seer."

Nekromanteia (NEK-ro-MAHN-tay-uh): "Place of the necromancer."

Iatromanteia (I-AH-trroh-MAHN-tay-uh): "Place of seership."

Goēs (GAH-ees): "Summoner."

Thaumauturgy (thaow-mah-TURJ-ee): "Wonder working."

Theurgy (THEE-ur-jee): "God working."

Thiasoi (thee-AH-soy): An ecstatic retinue of the god Dionysus.

Dionysus (dee-oh-NYE-sus): "God of Nysa."

Cybele (ki-BELLE): "Mother of the gods."

Aphrodite (Affro-DEE-te): "Born from the sea foam."

Hermes (HERM-ees): "Boundary marker; cairn."

Odysseus (oh-DIS-ee-uhs): "Son of pain."

Circe (KIR-kee): "Hawk."

Aelian (ee-LEE-an): "Of the wind."

Medea (meh-DEE-uh): "Cunning."

Pharmakis (farm-ahkis): "Poisoner, sorceror."

Gaia (gai-ya): "Earth."

Zeus (zoos): "Sky."

Prometheus (pro-MEE-thee-uhs): "Forethought."

Olympus (uh-LIMP-uhs): "Mountain."

Charis (KAH-rees): "Grace, kindness."

Theoi (thee-OY): "Disposers, dispensers."

Athanatoi Theoi (AH-than-ah-toy thee-OY): "Deathless dispensers."

Miasma (me-AHZ-muh): "Defilement."

Khernips (KIR-nips): "Lustral water," possibly.

Xenia (ZEE-nee-uh): "Guest-friendship."

Theoxenia (THEE-oh-ZEE-nee-uh): "God-friendship."

Xenios (ZEE-nee-ohs): "Guest-friendship."

Chapter 2

Thessaly (THEHS-uh-lee): A region in Greece.

Achilles (AH-kill-ees): Possibly "pain."

Jason (JAY-sun): "Healer."

Chiron (KYE-ron): "Hand."

Erictho (Erik-tho): Meaning currently unknown.

Sesklo (Ses-kloh): Meaning currently unknown.

Lucan (LOO-can): "From the Lucania."

Lucius (loo-KEE-uh): "Light."

Plato (PLAY-toe): Meaning currently unknown.

Homer (HOE-mir): "Hostage" or "pledge."

Pindar (PIN-dar): Meaning currently unknown.

Aeolia (ee-OHL-ee-uh): "Of Aeolus."

Othrys (OHTH-ris): Meaning currently unknown.

Hesiod (HESS-ee-ed): "Song," "to speak."

Artemis (AR-tem-is): Meaning currently unknown.

Akraia (ahk-RYE-uh): "Of the heights."

Phosphoros (fahs-FO-rahs): "Light bringer."

Throsia (THROW-see-uh): "Support, protection."

Polis (POH-lis): "City-state."

Athens (ATH-ens): "Of Athena."

Poleis (POH-lees): "City-states."

Theophrastus (THEO-frast-uhs): "Divine expression."

Aristotle (AR-is-thot-el): "The best purpose."

Ossa (AH-sah): "Of bones."

Pelion (PEH-lee-on): "Gray." Possibly also "dark."

Axis Mundi (AX-is MOON-dye): "Line that connects with the world."

Iatromantis (EYE-aht-trroh-man-tis): "Physician-seer."

Ŝamān (SHAY-muh-n): "One who knows."

Ekstasis (ek-STAY-sis): "To stand outside of oneself."

Sosiphanes (so-SIF'a-nees): Meaning currently unknown.

Plutarch (ploo-TARCK): "Master of wealth."

Pliny the Elder (plye-nee): "Abundant."

Aristophánes (arr-istoh-FAHN-ees): "Best appearing."

Strepsiades (strep-see-AHD-ees): "Deceptive."

Socrates (SAH-kraht-ees): "Master of the unwounded."

Apuleius (apoo-LEE-oos): Meaning currently unknown.

Hippocrates (hi-PAHK-ruh-teez): "Horse power."

Oulios (OOL-ee-uhs): "Healer."

Asclepions (ASK-leep-ee-uhns): Meaning currently unknown.

Epidaurus (epee-DOW-ruhs): Meaning currently unknown.

Pergamum (per-GAH-mum): "Citadel of Priam."

Cos (Kohs): "Crab."

Chapter 3

Nyx (nix): "Night."

Nymphs (nimfs): "Bride."

Daimones (DAY-mohn-ees): "Divine power."

Hubris (hyoo-bris): "Excessive pride," "outrage."

Arete (are-EET-ee): "Excellence."

Eusebia (EU-seeb-ee-uh): "Good reverence."

Sophia (SOHF-ee-uh): "Wisdom."

Chapter 4

Bômós (BUM-ohs): "Altar."

Chthonic (kuh-THON-ik): "Of the underworld."

Bômói (BUM-oy): "Altars."

Temenos (the-MEN-ohs): "Cut off for the sacred."

Eros (EE-rruhs): "To love," "desire."

Abaris (AHB-ar-uhs): Meaning currently unknown.

Pythagoras (PIE-thag-or-uhs): "Pertaining to the market."

Pythagorean theorem (PIE-thag-or-ee-an THEE-or-em): "Formula pertaining to the market."

Crotona (KRO-tone-uh): Meaning currently unknown.

Metempsychosis (metem-psyk-OH-sis): "Change to put a soul in."

Orphic (OR-fik): "Of Orpheus."

Orpheus (OR-fee-us): "The darkness of night."

Salacaceae (SAHLIK-kay-see-eye): Meaning unknown; possibly related to Salix trees, e.g., willow.

Populus (pop-oo-loos): "People."

Xanthorrhoea (ZANTH-or-ria): "Yellow flow."

Kylix (KYE-lix): "Cup."

Caduceus (kuh-DOO-see-uhs): "Herald's wand."

Thyrsus (THUR-sus): "Plant stalk."

Hermes (HERM-ees): "Declaration."

Poseidon (pohs-EYE-dun): Meaning currently unknown.

Aeaea (ee-EE-yah): Meaning currently unknown.

Helios (HEE-lee-ohs): "Sun."

Perse (PER-see): "To destroy."

Aegean (uh-JEE-uhn): "Waves."

Maenads (MAY-nuhdz): "To rave."

Pasiphaë (PAHS-i-fay): "Wide-shining."

Aether (Ether): "Upper air."

Hestia (HES-t-uh): "Hearth."

Hearth (haarth): "Burning."

Ekas (EH-kahs): "Far, outside, removed."

Este Bebeloi (EH-stee BEB-eh-loy): "Be far from here."

Nemesis (NEM-eh-sis): "Retribution."

Artemis Orthia (AR-tem-is OR-thee-uh): Orthia means "Straight."

Kakodaimones (KAH-koh-day-MOHN-ees): "Evil spirit."

Chapter 5

Herakles (HAIR-ik-kuhls): "Glory of Hera."

Cerberus (KKER-bur-uhs): "Spotted one."

Eleusinian (EL-yoo-sin-ee-uhn): "Of Eleusis."

Argonautika Orphica (ar-goh-NAUT-ika OR-fik-uh): "Of Orpheus and the voyage of the Argo."

Argemone (ar-JEH-men): "Of cataracts."

Areian (AAR-ee-an): "Of Ares."

Hypnos (IP-aws): "Sleep."

Morpheus (MOR-fee-uhs): "Fashioner."

Melissae (mel-ISS-ay): "Bee."

Daphni (DOF-nee): "Laurel."

Peneus (pen-EE-uhs): Meaning currently unknown.

Pythia (PITH-ee-uh): "Of Pythos."

Orsilokhia (orsi-LAHK-ya): "Helper of childbirth."

Eileithyia (el-ih-THEE-ya): "The bringer, the deliverer."

Kolossos (kol-os-SEE-yah): "Gigantic statue."

Persephone (PER-sef-oh-nee): "Bringer of destruction."

Chelidon (khel-ee-DON): "Swallow."

Atropa (AH-trop-ah): "Without a way forward."

Strigum (strrig-om): "Screecher."

Deipnon (DAYP-nun): "Supper."

Hyoskyamos (hi-ya-SKY-ahm-us): "Pig bean."

Aspergillum (asper-JIL-ee-om): "Sprinkle."

Minthe (MIN-thee): "Mint."

Cocytus (koh-KY-tus): "Lamentation."

Hades (HADE-ees): "Unseen."

Kore (KOR-ay): "Maiden."

Chloris (KHLOR-is): "Pale green."

Zephyrus (ZEF-uh-rus): "West Wind."

Chapter 6

Lokri (LOH-kree): Meaning currently unknown.

Adonis (AHD-don-is): "Beautiful young man."

Kypria (KYE-pree-uh): "Of Cyprus."

Ouranic (OR-ahn-ik): "Of the heavens."

Erebos (eh-RREE-bus): "Nether darkness."

Thespiae (thes-PI-ay): "Inspired by the gods [of Thespia]."

Ourania (oorr-ah-NEE-uh): "Of the heavens."

Ananke (ahn-NAHN-kee): "Necessity."

Agathosdaimon (AH-gath-ohs-day-mon): "Good spirit."

Graiai (GRAY-ay): "Gray ones."

Pamphredo (PAHM-free-doh): "Wasp."

Enyo (EEN-yo): "Warlike."

Deino (DAY-no): "Dreadful."

Gorgons (GOR-gohns): "Terrible."

Gorgoneion (gor-GOHN-ay-on): "Of the Gorgons."

Ericapaios (EE-rik-ah-PIE-yos): Meaning currently unknown.

Metis (MEE-tis): "Wisdom, skill."

Kronos (KRO-naus): "He who cuts."

Metieta (met-AY-tah): "Of wisdom."

Ouranos (our-RAHN-ahs): "Sky."

Delphyne (del-FEEN-ee): "Woman from Delphi."

Thalassa (THA-lah-sa): "Sea."

Horai (KHOR-eye): "Seasons."

Pontos (POHN-tos): "Sea."

Themis (THEE-mis): "Divine law."

Aphrodite Pandemos (Affro-DEE-te PAHN-dee-mohs): "Aphrodite common to all the people."

Daktyloi Idaioi (DAHK-til-oy EYE-dye-oy): "Fingers of Ida."

Amalthea (ahm-AHL-tha-ya): "To soothe."

Aigaion (eye-GIE-yon): "Stormy one."

Korybantes (kori-BAHN-tiz): Meaning currently unknown.

Selene (SEL-ee-nee): "Brightness."

Auxo (AUSK-show): "Spring growth."

Thallo (THAL-lo): "Blooming."

Karpos (KAR-pahs): "Fruit."

Pangenitor (pan-JEN-it-or): "All birth."

Panphage (pan-FAYJ): "All devourer."

Philyra (fil-EE-ra): "Lover of music."

Pholus (FOH-loos): "Of the cave."

Mnemosyne (nem-oh-SEE-NEE): "Memory."

Maia (MIE-yah): "She who brings increase."

Arcadia (are-KAY-dee-ya): "Region of peace."

Mount Cyllene (MOUNT KYE-leen-ee): "Sweetheart Mountain."

Arcas (ARK-us): "Born by a bear."

Eurynome (YUR-ee-nohm-ee): "She of broad pastures."

Nerites (nair-EET-ees): "Son of Nereus."

Himeros (HIM-er-aws): "Burning love, unleased desire."

Pothos (PAH-thos): "Yearning, longing."

Cyprus (KY-prus): "Land of cypress trees."

Theogonía (thee-OH-gahn-ya): "Birth of the gods."

Hekatoncheires (hek-AHT-on-khair-rees): "Hundred handed."

Cyclops (KYE-klops): "Round eyed."

Onkios (AHN-kee-ohs): Meaning currently unknown.

Arion (air-EE-on): "Enchanted."

Despoine (DES-poy-nee): "The mistress."

Demeter Erinyes (DEM-eh-ter EE-rin-yees): "Demeter of the Furies."

Adraste (AHD-rrahs-tee): "Inescapable."

Telchines (TEL-kheen-ees): "Maligners."

Kapheira (KAPH-ay-rra): "Storm breather."

Halia (HAHL-ya): "Briny."

Rhodes (ROHD-ees): Meaning currently unknown.

Amphitrite (AAM-fit-rite-ee): "Encircling third."

Ariadne (ARR-ee-ahd-nee): "Most holy."

Zeus Katachthonios (ZOOS KAHTA-kuh-thone-ee-oos): "Zeus of the underworld."

Danaus (DAN-ee-uhs): Meaning currently unknown.

Aeschylus (ee-SKUH-lus): "Shame."

Oceanids (ohk-EE-AHN-eeds): "Of the ocean."

Kyane (kee-YAHN-ee): "Azure-blue."

Leto (LEE-toe): "Wife."

Asteria (Aah-STEIR-ee-ya): "Star."

Delos (DEE-luhs): "Brought to light."

Python (PEE-thon): "Serpent."

Omphalos (AHM-fah-los): "Navel."

Harmonia (HAR-mohn-ya): "Harmony."

Hephaestus (hef-EYE-stoos): Meaning currently unknown.

Alcippe (AHL-seep-ee): "Mighty mare."

Halirrohtius (hal-eerr-OH-tee-uhs): "Sea foam."

Xiphos (ZEE-fohs): "Sword."

Kourotrophos (kow-roh-TRO-fahs): "Rearing boys."

Paniskoi (PAHN-is-koy): "Little Pans."

Príapus (PREE-ah-puhs): "Phallus."

Hermaphroditus (herm-AH-fro-dee-toos): "Effeminate."

Semele (sem-EL-ee): "Earth."

Heraclitus (HAIR-ahk-lee-tuhs): "Glorious one of Hera."

Parmenides (PAR-men-ee-dees): "To stand one's ground."

Empedocles (em-PED-oh-klees): "Glory to our lands."

Bacchio (BAHK-i-yo): "Of Bacchus."

Chapter 7

Temnein (TEEM-neen): "To cut."

Hieron (HI-ron): "Consecrated temple."

Perirrhanterion (pairee-RRHAHN-ter-ee-yon): Meaning uncertain.

Khairete (KHAI-ree-tee): "Hail."

Oikos (eek-AHS): "Household."

Chapter 8

Thamauturgeia (thow-MAH-ter-jay-uh): "Wonder workers."

Machaon (mah-KAY-on): "Son of Asklepios."

Podalirius (poh-da-LI-ree-uhs): Meaning currently unknown.

Pausanias (PAU-sahn-ee-ahs): "Pause the sorrow."

Epidauros (epee-DAU-ruhs): Meaning currently unknown.

Koronis (KOR-ohn-is): "Curved object."

Glaukos (GLAU-kohs): "To shine."

Nosoi (NOH-soy): "Sad dwelling."

Chapter 9

Epistrophia (epee-STRO-fya): "Deviser."

Sappho (SAF-oh): "Lapis Lazuli" or "Sapphire."

Philtron (FIL-tron): "Love incantation."

Stergēma (stir-GEE-ma): "Love charm."

Charitēsion (khari-TEES-ee-yon): "Beauty charm."

Saturion (sat-UR-ee-yon): "Having to do with satyrs."

Agōgimon (ah-GOHG-ee-mahn): "Spell that leads."

Philtrokatadesmos (FILTRO-kahta-DES-mohs): "Love binding tablet."

Phusikleidion (foos-ik-lay-DEE-on): "Genital key spell."

Anacreon (ANAK-ree-on): Meaning currently unknown.

Iunx (EE-yunks): "Wryneck bird."

Cyprogeneia (KI-pro-GEN-ay-uh): "Cyprus-born."

Peitho (PEE-tho): "Persuasion."

Chapter 10

Argonautika (argo-NAUT-ik-uh): "Of the Argonauts."

Apollonius Rhodios (AHP-ohl-lohn-ee-us ROE-dee-ohs): "Of Apollo of Rhodes."

Colchis (KOHL-kis): Meaning currently unknown.

Argos (arr-GAUS): "Of Argo."

Aeetes (A-YEET-ees): "Eagle."

Euripides (E-yor-ip-idees): "Of Euripos."

Aradia (ah-RAHD-ee-uh): Meaning currently unknown.

Praxidíke (PRAX-id-ee-kee): "Action of justice."

Lycophron (leek-oh-fron): Meaning currently unknown.

Cassandra (KAHS-sahnd-drah): "Unheeded prophetess."

Hecuba (Hek-yoo-buh): Meaning currently unknown.

Eubouleus (eyoo-bowl-EE-YUS): "Good counselor."

Plouton (PLOW-tuhn): "Wealth."

Eumenides (yoo-MEN-id-ees): "Kindly ones."

Alêktô (Al-ek-tuh): "Unceasing anger."

Megaira (meg-AIR-uh): "The jealous one."

Tisiphonê (tis-IF-oh-nee): "Avenging murder."

Katadesmoi (KAHTA-des-moy): "Binding tablet."

Matiasma (MAH-tee-ahs-mah): "Evil Eye."

Pherecrates (FAIR-eh-kraht-ees): Meaning currently unknown.

Phthonos (fthohn-ohs): "Jealousy."

Chapter 11

Makárioi (mak-KAR-ee-oy): "Blessed."

Psyche (SU-kee): "Breath."

Próthesis (pro-THEES-is): "Setting forth."

Ekphora (ek-PHOR-uh): "Carrying out."

Taifes kato (TOUGH-ees KAH-toh): "Wisps from below."

Kalesma mou (KAHL-es-mah Mow): "Heed my call."

Prokyptou (pro-KEEP-tow): "Come forth."

Baia (BAI-yah): "Of Baius."

Nekromanteion (nekro-MAHN-tay-on): "Oracle of the dead."

Chapter 12

Miletos (mil-EE-tohs): "Red land."

Danaós (dan-OWS): Meaning currently unknown.

Lukeios (lu-KAY-us): "Of Luca."

Pyrrhus (PEERR-oos): "Flame-colored."

Minos (MEE-nohs): "King."

Theseus (THEE-see-oos): "To place."

Es'tô (EHS-toe): "So be it!"

Euphêmeíte (yoof-EM-a-tee): "Speak no evil!"

Boulaia (bow-LAY-uh): "Council!"

Pyrtaneia (per-THAN-ay-uh): "Public flame."

Hilathi (hil-AH-thee): "Be propitious!"

Antheus (AHN-thee-uhs): "To bloom!"

Melanaigis (mel-AHN-ai-gis): "Of the black goatskin."

Bakkhos (BAH-kkus): "Riotous one."

Sôtêr (SO-tir): "Savior."

Eleuthereus (el-yoo-THER-ee-us): "Liberator."

Dimêtôr (DIM-ee-tor): "Of two mothers."

Zagreus (ZAH-gree-us): "Hunter who catches animals."

Bakchos (BAHK-ohs): "Of bacchic frenzy."

Erotes (EE-rroh-tees): "The desired ones."

Tartaros (TAR-tar-ohs): Meaning currently unknown.

Acheron (AHK-eer-on): "The river of woe."

BIBLIOGRAPHY

Adrados, Francisco Rodriguez. *A History of the Greek Language: From Its Origins to the Present*. Boston, MA: Brill Academic Publishers, 2005.

Aelianus, Claudius. *On the Nature of Animals*. Translated by Gregory McNamee. San Antonio, TX: Trinity University Press, 2011.

Aeschylus. *Classics in Translation*. Edited by Paul MacKendrick and Herbert M Howe. Translated by Louis MacNiece. Madison, WI: University of Wisconsin Press, 1952.

———. *The Complete Works of Aeschylus*. Translated by H. W. Smith. Delphi Classics, 2013.

———. *The Suppliants*. Translated by H. W. Weir. Delphi Classics, 2013.

Anonymous. *The Suda*. Translated by David Whitehead. "Stoa: Welcome to the Suda On Line (SOL)." *Stoa*. www.cs.uky.edu /~raphael/sol/sol-html/, 2003.

Apuleius. *The Golden Ass, or the Metamorphoses*. Translated by W. Adlington. New York, NY: Barnes and Noble Publishing, 2004.

Aristophánes. *The Comedies of Aristophánes.* Translated by William James Hickie. http://www.dominiopublico.gov.br/download /texto/gu002562.pdf (Accessed Jan. 23, 2019).

Aristotle. *Nicomachean Ethics.* Translated by W. D. Ross. Arcadia ebook, 2016.

Atha, Anthony. *The Ultimate Herb Book.* New York, NY: Sterling Publishing Co.

Bailey, James E. "Asklepios: Ancient Hero of Medical Caring." *Annals of Internal Medicine* 124, no. 2 (1996): 257–263.

Beyerl, Paul. *The Master Book of Herbalism.* Blaine, WA: Phoenix Publishing, Inc.

Blundell, Sue. *Women in Ancient Greece.* Cambridge, MA: Harvard University Press.

Bremmer, Jan. "Divinities in the Orphic Gold Leaves: Eukles, Eubouleus, Brimo, Kybele, Kore, and Persephone." *Zeitschrift fuer Papyrologie und Epigraphik (ZPE)* (2013) 187: 35–48.

Burkert, Walter. *Greek Religion.* Cambridge, MA: Harvard University Press.

Callimachus, Lycophron, and Aratus. *Callimachus: Hymns and Epigrams; Lycophron: Alexandra; Aratus.* Translated by A. W. Mair and G. R. Mair. Vol. 129. London: William Heinemann, 1921.

Castleman, Michael. *The New Healing Herbs: The Classic Guide to Nature's Best Medicine.* 2nd ed. Emmaus, PA: Rodale, Inc.

Clark, Brian. "The Witches of Thessaly." https://dinitrandu.com /wp-content/uploads/2019/02/116814796-The-Witches -of-Thessaly.pdf, 2019.

Collins, Derek. *Magic in the Ancient Greek World.* Malden, MA: Blackwell Publishing.

Das, Moumita. *Chamomile: Medicinal, Biochemical, and Agricultural Aspects.* Boca Raton, FL: Taylor and Francis Group.

d'Este, S., and D. Rankine. *Wicca: Magickal Beginnings.* London: Avalonia.

Dickie, Matthew W. "What is a Kolossos and How Were Kolossoi Made During the Hellenistic Period?" *Greek, Roman, and Byzantine Studies* 37 1996 (3): 237–57.

Dunn, Patrick. *The Orphic Hymns: A New Translation for the Occult Practitioner.* Woodbury, MN: Llewellyn Publications.

Elliot, John H. *Beware the Evil Eye: The Evil Eye in the Bible and Ancient World.* Vol. 2. Eugene, OR: Wipf and Stock Publishers.

Elworthy, Frederick Thomas. *The Evil Eye: The Classic Account of an Ancient Superstition.* Mineola, NY: Dover Publications, Inc.

Euripides. *The Bacchae.* Translated by Gilbert Murray. Digireads. com Publishing. Overland Park, KS, 2011.

——. *Medea.* Translated by E. P. Coleridge. Vol. 1. London: Chiswick Press: Charles Whittingham and Co., 1910.

Faas, Patrick. *Around the Roman Table: Food and Feasting in Ancient Rome.* Chicago, IL: The University of Chicago Press.

Farnell, Lewis R. *The Cults of the Greek States.* Vol. IV. Oxford: Clarendon Press.

Faroane, C.A. *Ancient Greek Love Magic.* Cambridge, MA: Harvard University Press, 1999.

Friedlander, Walter J. *The Golden Wand of Medicine: A History of the Caduceus Symbol in Medicine.* Westport, CT: Greenwood Publishing Group, Inc.

Gaifman, Milette. *The Art of Libation in Classical Athens.* New Haven, CT: Yale University Press.

Gardner, Gerald B. *High Magick's Aid.* 1949.

Gimbutas, Marija. *The Living Goddesses*. Edited by Miriam Robbins Dexter. Los Angeles, CA: University of California Press.

Graves, Frank P. *The Burial Customs of the Ancient Greeks*. Goodpress Publishing.

Harrison, Jane Ellen. *Prolegomena to the Study of Greek Religion*. Cambridge: Cambridge University Press.

Hatsis, Thomas. *The Witches' Ointment: The Secret History of Psychedelic Magic*. Rochester, VT: Inner Traditions/Bear & Company.

Heraclitus. *The Fragments of Heraclitus*. Translated by G.T.W. Patrick. Digireads.com Publishing, 2013.

Hesiod. *The Poems of Hesiod: Theogony, Works and Days, and the Shield of Heracles*. Translated by Barry B Powell. Los Angeles, CA: University of California Press, 2017.

Hippo, Augustine of. *The City of God Against the Pagans*. Translated by R.W. Dyson. 13 vols. Cambridge: Cambridge University Press, 1998.

Homer. *The Homeric Hymns: A Translation, with Introduction and Notes*. Translated by Diane J. Rayor. Los Angeles, CA: University of California Press, 2014.

———. *The Iliad*. Translated by R. Lattimore. Chicago, IL: The University of Chicago Press, 2011.

———. *The Odyssey*. Translated by Anthony Verity. New York, NY: Oxford University Press, 2016.

———. *The Odyssey: A Modern Translation of Homer's Classic Tale*. Translated by R. L. Eickhoff. New York, NY: Tom Doherty Associates, 2004.

Johnston, Sarah Iles. *Restless Dead: Encounters Between the Living and the Dead in Ancient Greece*. Los Angeles, CA: University of California Press.

Kelly, Nigel, Bob Rees, and Paul Shuter. *Medicine Through Time.* Oxford: Heinemann Educational Publishers.

Kerenyi, C. *The Gods of the Greeks.* London: Thames & Hudson.

Kingsley, P. *Ancient Philosophy, Mystery, and Magic: Empedocles and the Pythagorean Tradition.* London: Oxford University Press.

Kingsley, Peter. *In the Dark Places of Wisdom.* Point Reyes, CA: Golden Sufi Press, 1999.

———. *A Story Waiting to Pierce You: Mongolia, Tibet, and the Destiny of the Western World.* Point Reyes, CA: The Golden Sufi Center.

Kravaritou, Sophia. "Cults and Rites of Passage in Ancient Thessaly," 2017.

Leland, Charles G. *Aradia, or the Gospel of the Witches of Italy.* Ballantyne, Hanson and Co.

Lemon, George William. *English Etymology: Or a Derivative Dictionary of the English Language.* University of California.

Lewis, Archibald, ed. *Aspects of the Renaissance: A Symposium.* Austin, TX: University of Texas Press, 1967.

Liberman, Anatoly. *An Analytic Dictionary of the English Etymology: An Introduction.* Minneapolis, MN: University of Minnesota Press.

Littlewood, R. Joy. *A Commentary on Ovid: Fasti Book VI.* Oxford: Oxford University Press.

Luck, Georg. *Arcana Mundi.* Baltimore, MD: The John Hopkins University Press.

———. *Witchcraft and Magic in Europe, Vol. 2: Ancient Greece and Rome.* Edited by Stuart Clark and Bengt Ankarloo. Vol. ii. London: The Athlone Press.

Marston, John M. *Language of Ritual Cursing in the Binding of Prometheus.* January 2007.

Mierzwicki, Tony. *Hellenismos: Practicing Greek Polytheism Today.* Woodbury, MN: Llewellyn Publications.

Mikalson, John D. *Ancient Greek Religion.* 2nd ed. Malden, MA: Blackwell Publishing, Ltd.

Nilson, M.P. *Greek Folk Religion.* Philadelphia, PA: University of Pennsylvania Press, 1972.

Ogden, Daniel. *Greek and Roman Necromancy.* Princeton, NJ: Princeton University Press.

Parker, Robert. *On Greek Religion.* London: Cornell University Press, Pausanias. *Description of Greece.* Translated by W. H. S. and Omerod, H.A. Jones. Cambridge, MA: Harvard University Press, 1918.

Pettis, Jeffrey B. "Earth, Dream, and Healing: The Integration of Materia and Psyche in the Ancient World." *Journal of Religion and Health* 45 2006 (1): 113-129.

Plutarch. *Plutarch's Lives.* Translated by John Langhorne and W. Langhorne. New York, NY: Harper and Brothers Publishers, 1855.

Rhodius, Apollonius. *Argonautica.* Edited by Richard Hunter. Cambridge: Cambridge University Press, 2015.

Rose, H.J. *A Handbook of Greek Mythology.* New York, NY: Routledge Taylor and Francis Group, 1964.

Rosen, Edward. "In Defense of Kepler." *Aspects of the Renaissance: A Symposium.* Edited by Archibald R. Lewis. University of Texas Press, 1967.

Salem, S. *The Near East: The Cradle of Western Civilization.* Writers Club Press.

Schmitt, Charles B. *The Cambridge History of Renaissance Philosophy*. Edited by Charles B. Schmitt and Quentin Skinner. Cambridge: Cambridge University Press.

Valiente, Doreen. *Witchcraft for Tomorrow*. London: Robert Hale Limited, *WebMD*. https://www.webmd.com/vitamins/ai/ingredientmono-604/agrimony.

Webster's English Dictionary with Pronunciation Guides, 2015.

Weekley, Ernest. *An Etymological Dictionary of Modern English*. Vol. 2. New York, NY: Dover Publications, Inc.

Westlake, H. D. *Thessaly in the Fourth Century BC*. Ann Arbor, MI: University of Michigan.

Williams, Cheryll J. *Medicinal Plants in Australia: Volume I: Bush Pharmacy*. Vol. I. Dural, New South Wales: Rosenberg Publishing Pty Ltd.

Wilson, Debra Rose. "Is Aconite Actually Dangerous?" *Healthline*. July 5, 2016.

Zhmud, Leonid. "Orphism and Graffiti from Olbia." *Hermes* 120 1992 (2): 159-168.

To Write to the Author

If you wish to contact the author or would like more information about this book, please write to the author in care of Llewellyn Worldwide Ltd. and we will forward your request. Both the author and publisher appreciate hearing from you and learning of your enjoyment of this book and how it has helped you. Llewellyn Worldwide Ltd. cannot guarantee that every letter written to the author can be answered, but all will be forwarded. Please write to:

Oracle Hekataios
℅ Llewellyn Worldwide
2143 Wooddale Drive
Woodbury, MN 55125-2989

Please enclose a self-addressed stamped envelope for reply,
or $1.00 to cover costs. If outside the U.S.A., enclose
an international postal reply coupon.

Many of Llewellyn's authors have websites with additional information and resources. For more information, please visit our website at http://www.llewellyn.com.